'Given the tremendous confusion about the purpose of marriage and sex in both contemporary society and the church, it is vital that evangelical Christians and church leaders have a firm grasp of the Bible's teaching regarding the place of marriage in the plan of God. Rick Shenk's stimulating new book combines detailed exegesis of the central biblical texts with historical, systematic and biblical theological synthesis, to show that human marriage is intended to testify to and manifest the Trinitarian nature of God, and his love and covenant faithfulness to his people. Not everyone will agree with his claim that the church should reclaim marriage as a sacrament, but every reader will be challenged to value marriage more highly, and to live more faithfully in obedience to God's word. He is especially helpful in showing how chastity, properly understood, is essential both within and without marriage, in explaining how single Christians honour God's purpose for marriage by their sexual purity, and in teasing out the relationship between Christian marriage as recognized by the church and civil marriage as regulated by the state.'

John Stevens, National Director,
Fellowship of Independent Evangelical Churches

'Rick Shenk's work is always rigorous and provocative. This latest book may have pinpointed the source of the current crisis in our understanding and valuation of marriage – the denial that marriage is a sacrament by the Protestant Reformers.'

Simon Oliver,
Durham University

T0313663

The Genesis of Marriage

God's Declaration, Drama, and Purpose

Richard A. Shenk

Paternoster:
thinking faith

Copyright © 2018 Richard A. Shenk

24 23 22 21 20 19 18   7 6 5 4 3 2 1

First published 2018 by Paternoster
Paternoster is an imprint of Authentic Media Ltd
PO Box 6326, Bletchley, Milton Keynes MK1 9GG.
authenticmedia.co.uk

British Library Cataloguing in Publication Data

A catalogue record for this book is available from the British Library

ISBN 978-1-78078-994-1
978-1-78078-995-8 (e-book)

Cover design by David Smart
Printed and bound by CPI Group (UK) Ltd, Croydon, CR0 4YY

Contents

Tables

To Lynne

my wife of forty years,
my best friend,
and my partner in the Drama
of redeemed sinners
who seek to display God's nature and character
through the sanctifying sacrament of marriage

Acknowledgments

I am deeply grateful to Bethlehem College & Seminary for the privilege of teaching Systematic Theology in our MDiv program to young men who are in training for leadership roles in the church. These men are hungry for the Word, delight in the glory of God, and do so with a rare humility. Without their insights and questions I could not have written this book. I am also deeply grateful to God for Lynne, my wife of forty years: Lynne, you listened to my ideas (over and over!) and helped me clarify my thinking; God teaches me constantly through your wisdom and persevering love. And I am also grateful to the many friends who have been willing to read, comment, and proof this manuscript through its development: Ruth Shenk (my mom who taught me to love God and ideas), Rob Boyd (my friend of forty years), Mike Littel, Mark Dickson, Dave Garwick, Pat Stejskal, Nancy Cassell, and Joel Schmidt. Also, I am grateful to my friend Janice Van Arnam, who laboured over this manuscript to make me understandable – she did her best! And I am grateful to Brian Verrett who laboured to rid my manuscript of typos and conform it to house style – a labour of love while also serving as a new church planter. Finally, I am grateful to the team at Paternoster, including Donna Harris, Mollie Barker and Becky Fawcett, and especially to Reuben Sneller, whose help, enduring patience, and risk tolerance (!) has been a gift to me.

Preface

'I've moved out!' Alexi looked both relieved and heartbroken; his two-decade long marriage was ending. With the leaves beginning to turn in autumn, I sat with Alexi, my friend of ten years, at Einstein Brothers Bagels. We had not spent time together for months. It turned out that his challenge of finding an apartment, moving, the logistics of moving alone, and all the uncertain family responsibilities, had left him overwhelmed.

I leaned into the table, and my coffee cup wafted steam on to my glasses. 'Why didn't you call me to help?'

A deep breath and a pause followed. Alexi struggled with his answer. 'Well, you know, it felt rather juvenile, like in college, "Would you help me move my boxes?" I wasn't going to do that.'

His marriage cold, and perhaps dead, Alexi felt alone. This was not good.

My friend is not a Christian, nor has he read the Bible much. We share a love of ideas, not a love of Christ. Today Alexi's pain directed our discussion to a question shared by many people in western society: what does marriage mean? Alexi showed deep insight – normal for him. He reflected on what his break-up with Charlotte meant: 'My parents are totally amazing. They've always acted as if they were one person. If I call them and my father answers, he puts my mother on by speaker phone. "Dad, I'm just calling to tell you I'll be there this weekend." But I get them both. That drives me crazy! They're like one. That is also a picture of what my marriage isn't. Never has been. She does her thing; I do mine. But my parents' marriage – as maddening as they are – is how it should be.' He understood: marriage should be two people who live together like one.

Alexi continued, 'Most of my friends don't even know what I mean. First, they don't have parents like mine. Who does, now? And so my friends also tell me, "Look, it's over. Get past it. Move on. Make yourself happy." They don't understand. But they are right; there really is nothing for us to fix. I do need to move on. This has been coming for years – many years. We've been to therapy. If there was anything left alive in our marriage, the therapist would have helped us find it and fix it. But there is nothing left. If there was ever something there, it's broken completely. Nothing. Yes, but all my friends treat marriage just like a contract that failed. "So, get out and be done with it." No, there is nothing to fix, but there should be.' He understood: marriage, even a failed marriage, is more than a contract.

Alexi and I share a deep passion: words and story. He is a playwright, actor, director, producer, and even a professor – the whole kit. He has the soul of an artist. And he is in demand in theatre – though never quite in demand enough so that theatre pays all of the bills. I am an author and pastor of a small church – and never in demand at all! But we both love our work and we love drama; we delight in words which move people. We understand that words, presented by a person, are an opportunity not only to entertain, but to persuade. We live in different worlds with very different perspectives – a good basis for a friendship. Alexi often tells me about the play he's working on, plays which display the stories, beliefs, and passions of many different kinds of people – murderers, swindlers, sexual boundary-pushers, and everything in-between. Alexi doesn't share the values of all of his characters, but the craft of the theatre artist is to validate and advocate for those beliefs from the point of view of the character. Over the years, I have learned much from Alexi and his plays – ones I have attended and ones he has told me about. Likewise, Alexi, who does not agree with me, has listened to and critiqued my sermons and even coached my delivery. We enjoy learning from each other.

'Alexi, you've just outlined the book I'm working on!' While Alexi had heard of the book of Genesis, God's work of creation, and Adam and Eve, he did not know many of the details of the Genesis story. So I told him the story – both stories of creation. In the first story, God created the heavens and the earth in six days, making Man and Woman on the sixth; he rested on the seventh. Then Moses tells the story again, a second time from a different perspective. This retelling is more personal, more up-close. Adam and Eve are named. This second telling focuses on the Garden where God will meet with his people. Finally, Moses concludes these two stories with the marriage – a climax and conclusion to both stories: 'they shall be one'. The introduction of this marriage begins with a confusing statement, 'It is not good that man should be alone.' This raises the question for us: if God is only One, then how does he know – and why is it even the case – that it is not good to be alone? Alexi, a storyteller, understood right away: this disturbing and disjunctive statement needs to be understood in the context of the story itself! I had to admit that quite a few Christians have missed just this point. Still, many ancient readers of the Bible (and not a few modern ones) actually did see in Genesis 1 and 2 clear indications that the author knew God to be not only One, but also Many. This needed explanation: 'You see, Alexi, when God said, "they [the two] shall become one flesh", this was the announcement, not only of the marriage, but that Adam and Eve together represented the final imaging of God, who is One-and-Many. God did this in people who are now one, but also still two.' This is just what Alexi saw in his parents and intuitively knew should be a normal part of marriage.

I told Alexi about the Fall, which damaged the relationship not only between God and his people, but also between the first couple. Immediately, Adam threw Eve 'under the bus' when God asked him what happened: 'the woman *you* gave me . . .!' Then Eve told God about the serpent: 'It deceived me!' Was she complaining that Adam (or perhaps God?) had not done his job of keeping such dangerous creatures out of the Garden? Then God declared that their relationship was indeed ruined: 'Your desire shall be for your husband, but he shall rule over you.' That is, they are going to fight a lot over who controls things . . . This 'curse' is not good news for the couple.

'Alexi, their curse is your curse. This is like what you experienced; there is nothing left alive to fix in your relationship.'

There is more. Throughout the rest of the Bible, God uses marriage (or more precisely, the pervasive human failures of marriage) as the key metaphor for our treason against God: we are an adulterous wife to him. We are not one with him as we were designed to be and there is nothing left to fix. I showed Alexi the shocking story of Hosea: his marriage to Gomer and her prostitution (or her prostitution and then their marriage – either way, a serious problem!) and (their) children who were named in keeping with their conception: 'Not My People' and 'Not Loved', and also one named 'in honour' of the expected outcome, 'I Will Punish', as God did in Jezreel. Then everything fell apart. What other outcome could be anticipated from Hosea's messy marriage or our marriage-like relationship to God? Gomer left Hosea. So also God's people, his bride, left him. And when there was nothing left to repair, God spoke: 'Therefore . . .' What judgment will he declare in response to this? Certainly divorce! Shockingly, God said: 'Therefore . . . I will take her into the desert and there I will allure her!'[1] To complete the drama that was Hosea's life, Hosea sought his wife (his ex-wife, or were they still 'married'?) and found her for sale at the slave auction. He bought her back and he brought her home. Rather than live with her as man and wife, immediately, he gave her space. Alluring her back to his bed would follow. If the end of this story is untold, still the meaning is clear: this covenant of marriage runs much deeper than a mere contract. When there is nothing left, God is willing to create something new.

Then I told my friend about the real end of this story. 'Look! When we come to the book of Revelation, God makes us into a *virgin* bride! Virgin! That is not possible, except by the amazing effect of the work of Jesus on the cross. This is how God sees marriage – a metaphor for his faithfulness to his covenant with his people that makes of us something new.' Human marriage is the Bible's key metaphor to reveal his relationship with us and to reveal to us who he is.

'Alexi, when you assess what marriage is, you have written my book! God shows us his nature in marriage: in marriage the two become one, while remaining two. That is just like God who is Trinity, Three-in-One. God chose marriage to reveal his character: he is faithful to his covenant; he is faithful to his rebellious wife. Marriage is the metaphor for both.' But there was more I wanted to risk telling Alexi. 'You see, in your grief, God is pursuing you, Alexi. In your pain, you see something few are willing to see. Yes, marriage is too significant to bury with the simple words, "Move on. It's over." This is because marriage points to something. It points to God, the author of marriage, and the one who is seeking us. I wonder if you see this truth *because* God is hunting you? He desires to restore what is broken between you and him.'

Our coffee was cold. The hard bench-seats in the booth were getting uncomfortable. We were out of time. But God is not. Marriage is God's declaration of who he is and what he is doing. He is pursuing Alexi in his pain. And he is pursuing you, you who read these words.

Luther Seminary Library, Minneapolis
October 2016

Introduction

Quite a few people are confused and disillusioned by the irrelevant power of marriage. Katie and Jeff grew up in church surrounded by the Minnesota culture of secular Christian religion. By God's grace they rejected the pretence of religion, and also by God's grace, they rejected God and marriage. Strange grace, God's. As a result, they chose to live together – not ready for marriage. For six years their 'marriage' succeeded. Then they did it; they got married. It is only a piece of paper! Yet, within three years their marriage collapsed. Katie, feeling disillusioned with the reality of marriage, found another man. Looking back, Jeff wondered, 'How could living together work so well, and marriage fail so thoroughly? It's only a piece of paper!' How could something which is assumed to be irrelevant, 'just a piece of paper', have such power? How, indeed, could such a paperweight crush a relationship?

Quite a few people are confused and disillusioned by the irrelevant power of marriage. While this confusion and disillusionment is not new, nevertheless, we feel it acutely today, perhaps more acutely than prior generations. Many among the heterosexual majority in western culture reject marriage and choose instead to 'live together'. Some abstain from marriage while arguing that marriage is 'just a piece of paper'. Others abstain, protesting that marriage is a commitment that 'I am just not ready for'. Is it too weak or too strong? These may seem in tension: one person weighs marriage and discovers it to be of too little weight to bother with, as if it had no substance at all, while the other finds it too massive for them to bear. Yet at a deeper level, both express a unity of disillusionment with marriage. Marriage failed them in some deep way in their past: their own, or that of their parents or friends. None of this is new. It is not new to witness the failure of marriage. It is not new to observe that our demands of marriage may be quite high ('I want fulfilment and satisfaction!'), while our expectations are low ('But it will never work!'). What is new is this: the deepening disillusionment with marriage among the heterosexual culture occurs just as the LGBTQ (lesbian, gay, bisexual, transsexual, and queer) community is celebrating marriage. Having been excluded from marriage by law and custom in the past, many in this community eagerly desire to have access to marriage. This desire for marriage is distinct from access to other constructs such as civil unions or legal protections. While such structures might provide all the privileges of a marriage, and laws could provide for the extension of employment benefits even to significant-other relationships, it is marriage which is desired. There is a desire for 'marriage' as marriage, not merely for the cultural and legal benefits of marriage. What is new, then, is that one group is moving away from marriage while another is moving toward it, even demanding it. Perhaps this movement is not hard to understand. All of us desire control over our own lives and opportunities, not mere crumbs from the table of those who hold the power and resources. So in our day it seems that marriage offers self-determination and respectability for some, but quite the opposite for others. This confusion, this irrelevant power of marriage, results in movement both toward and away from marriage.

Interestingly, for both those who are confused and disillusioned by the irrelevant power of marriage, and those who want to engage marriage for new purposes, there is a shared sense of religious disillusion and disaffiliation.[1] There is something right about this disillusionment! Those who become disaffiliated with the church because of failed marriage(s) are identifying the deep connection between, not merely God and the church, but God and marriage. In this they have reversed the flow, rejecting God because of marriage as they have experienced it. But in this response, perhaps more than they may realize, they honour the deep importance of marriage, even in their rejection of both God and marriage.

But is marriage something under our authority such that we can weigh it and find it wanting – and then reject it? Is marriage something we are able to redefine and adapt for our own purposes, even for the good purposes of encouraging a disenfranchised and injured group? There are analogies in God's creation that might help. Could it be that marriage, like the mass of an electron or the structure of a galaxy, is not something we can change by our disapproval or modify by our will? Physicists can measure the mass of any particle of matter, and astronomers may observe galaxy formation and classify their types. But so far, we cannot explain why they are as they are from basic principles, *a priori*, predicting the mass of a particle we measure or the location or nature of a galaxy as observed. We can only observe and model *a posteriori*, from what exists. And while we can destroy an electron with an anti-electron, we cannot create one with a different mass or different properties. However, our disillusionment with marriage may be meaningless, a self-assessment rather than a deep understanding of marriage. Our disappointment may be from distorted expectations rather than an objective assessment of marriage. In fact, God may have expectations for marriage which are distinct from our own and wholly unaffected (and unaffectable) by our feelings or debates. Our disillusionment with marriage may say nothing about marriage or the God who created it. Marriage remains, like the electron, as something we can study, but not change. It is. Yet, like the electron, while we cannot change marriage, we might be able to destroy it.

If God is the author and definer of marriage, a thing that humans cannot change but might be able to destroy if we do not understand it, then we must look to the Author to discern its meaning. To do so, I intend to discern and display a biblical theology of marriage – a theology based on God's own communication to us in regard to marriage. Specifically, this project is grounded in the Marriage Text of Genesis 2:18–25, 'It is not good that the man should be alone . . . they shall become one flesh.' While this text is known to most readers of the Bible, fewer have investigated how it fits in its own context of Genesis 1–3 and the whole of Scripture. Distinct from our disappointments, experience, expectations, and failures, God did (and does!) not see marriage as a frustration, but as a solution to a 'frustration'. In the Garden, during the sixth day, God observed that Adam was 'alone' and that this was 'not good' (Gen. 2:18). His response to this was quite curious: God commanded Adam to investigate and name all the other creatures. Moses pronounced this activity, which proposed to resolve the 'not good' assessment, a failure: 'But for Adam there was not found a helper fit for him' (Gen. 2:20b). Or, if not a 'failure', it did not achieve the stated goal, but this was not a wasted day in the life of Adam. Not at all! For in this day, God accomplished his purposes: he led Adam into a 'holy frustration'. That is to say, God helped Adam see how 'not good' his situation was. Now what would God do to make his 'not good' situation 'good'? Even after the naming of the animals, it is likely he did not have a real concept of what God was about to do. What groom could say he has significantly advanced over Adam in this regard?! Yet, God understood marriage. That is not a minor point. God, the author and definer of marriage, introduced marriage against the pronouncement 'not good', God's resolution.

Marriage is not only 'good' for Adam. Marriage, as we will see, is God's climax and conclusion to creation. When God announces, 'they shall be one', two realities are created by this declaration. First, God's word causes the curious and mysterious reality of two who are now also one. Second, it creates the faithful and binding covenant. It is just these two realities, which the marriage pronouncement established, that I will explore in this book.

To unpack this, I will first examine the Marriage Text exegetically and historically, and show it as the climax and conclusion of the two creation accounts. This will take us deep into the image of the Trinity perfected in God's human wilful-creatures[2] by marriage, revealing God's nature. Also, it will draw us into God's character as we perceive this same text in its position between creation and un-creation, the Fall. Second, moving from exegesis to theology, I will consider the Marriage Text in the larger context of biblical theology, testing these two exegetical observations in the Torah, the Prophets, and the Writings of the Old Covenant. I will examine the same text, and the same two realities, as the key to understanding marriage in the gospels, the epistles, and the Revelation of John. Flowing out of the exegesis and theology, I will consider whether marriage should be considered a sacrament – which will first require us to understand 'sacraments' – a concept lost to some evangelicals after the Reformation. Finally, I will explore the doctrinal implications of the Marriage Text – how the Holy Spirit intends the church to enact this drama before the Throne and the world. This includes: What are the ethics of marriage? How do we approach the real-world concerns of separation, divorce, remarriage? What is the deep connection between marriage and forgiveness? And how do we understand marriage and the tangle of LGBTQ demands? And also, how might thinking about marriage as a sacrament allow us to show the world the glory of our trinitarian God and his faithfulness to his people?

A brief word about method. As I explained above, this book divides into three parts: exegesis, theology, and doctrine. Here I am indebted to Kevin Vanhoozer who understands God's speech-acts as the model for his work in us by the Word.[3] Simply put: to speak is to do something. To speak is to say, to intend, and to accomplish by saying. I will not make Vanhoozer's case here, but I will apply his model as a pattern of the work of the Word to exegesis, theology, and doctrine in the context of marriage.[4] I understand the work of exegesis as our attempt to understand God's 'speech', his word (called in speech-act theory his *locutio*n).[5] If we do our exegesis well, we will understand what God has said. Also, I understand theology as the study of God's intent in speaking (called in speech-act theory his *illocution*). If we do our theology well, we can know what God intends and means by his speaking. Finally, I understand doctrine as the drama enacted by the Holy Spirit through us, the people of God (called in speech-act theory his *perlocution*). This is the effect of God's word in the life of the church. When properly performed, when God's drama is enacted by his people, doctrine is the effect his word has in us by his Spirit. The use of 'doctrine' in this context may be confusing to some. Doctrine is usually a synonym for theology, and what I am calling 'doctrine', others refer to as application or practical theology.

While not in keeping with tradition, calling this work our 'doctrine' is neither without semantic warrant nor without symmetric beauty. Our English word 'doctrine' derives from the Greek *didasko* (*didaskolia*) or teaching, which always is to work itself out by obedience. Obedience is the fitting outcome of the Great Commission, 'teaching them to obey' (Matt. 28:20, NIV).[6] In fact, we have learned from God only if we are doing his work (see Jesus' own argument in John 6). So, *doctrine is theology rightly played in God's drama.* For this reason, I will begin with exegesis, in order to discern the words with clarity, then move to theology (biblical and historical theology) in order to discern the meaning of this word from God, and finally to doctrine, the dramatic action intended by God and accomplished by his Spirit, in order that we may obey him.[7]

Now I begin a study to discover God's own intent in marriage. By this work, perhaps I can begin to dispel our disillusionment with marriage – or at least our ideas and beliefs about marriage which may be at odds with God's.

Part One

Exegesis: What God Says about Marriage

When God speaks, God acts. Our first introduction to YHWH at the beginning of history is as God who speaks: 'And God said' (Gen. 1:3). At the end of history Jesus will destroy those who stand against him 'with the breath of his mouth' (2 Thess. 2:8). God is a god who acts by speaking.

It is for this reason that our first move in this investigation of a biblical theology of marriage is exegesis, a careful examination of what God is saying to us. In awe of this reality, and before we dare to try to discern the meaning and intent of God's words or our active response to them, we must first hear him and his words with clarity and in their context.

What is God doing in speaking to us about marriage? Why is the Marriage Text, Genesis 2:18–25, located at the end of two creation accounts? Why is it balanced like a great rock on the precipice of Genesis 3, about to fall? The very situation of the Marriage Text within the canon, and within Genesis, may be the first hint at an explanation of the place of marriage in God's speaking. Does it fit with creation, or is it a transition and preparation for the Fall narrative of Genesis 3? It is probably both. It is also more. In this first section, the exegesis, I intend to display what God says to us.

1

Genesis 2:18–25: Imaging the Trinity

The Marriage Text (Gen. 2:18–25)

Then the LORD God said, 'It is not good that the man should be alone; I will make him a helper fit for him.' [19]Now out of the ground the LORD God had formed every beast of the field and every bird of the heavens and brought them to the man to see what he would call them. And whatever the man called every living creature, that was its name. [20]The man gave names to all livestock and to the birds of the heavens and to every beast of the field. But for Adam there was not found a helper fit for him. [21]So the LORD God caused a deep sleep to fall upon the man, and while he slept took one of his ribs and closed up its place with flesh. [22]And the rib that the LORD God had taken from the man he made into a woman and brought her to the man. [23]Then the man said, 'This at last is bone of my bones and flesh of my flesh; she shall be called Woman, because she was taken out of Man.' [24]Therefore a man shall leave his father and his mother and hold fast to his wife, and they shall become one flesh. [25]And the man and his wife were both naked and were not ashamed.

Rarely have readers of Genesis focused exegetically on the Marriage Text so as to understand its broader relationship to Genesis 1–3. In the last hundred years, many books and commentaries have focused on the length of days and the age of the earth, the connection (or radical disconnection) between the Bible and science, and the 'how' of God's work in creation. We are in danger of allowing the important issues to eclipse the intention of this text and its author(s). Karl Barth helps us here:

> But we must return to the story of the creation of man and woman in Genesis 2:18–25, and note that it is not merely in its obvious sense that it forms the climax to the second saga and the biblical account of creation generally. It does, of course, point to the divine basis of love and marriage as the due fulfillment of the male-female relationship.[1]

Barth casually mentions what few have noticed: *marriage is the climax and conclusion* of Moses' twin creation accounts, *even if* he also sees the text as the 'basis of love' and explanation of marriage itself.[2] This is an unexpected turn, at least for those of us who were raised on the seven-day controversies and questions of cosmology. In this light, the Marriage Text may seem to be a mere coda which follows the really interesting stuff of creation. Marriage is necessary in order to create families in which children would be born, but it hardly seems to be as significant as the glorious days of creation. Barth suggests that the Marriage Text, and marriage, is much more to the author of Genesis – and should be to us. Only too rarely do we receive it in its 'obvious sense that it forms the climax' to both accounts of creation. What if this Marriage Text, a full tithe of Moses' words in the twin accounts, redirects our attention from God's decisive speech-acts of forming and filling the heavens and the earth, *to* God's intended conclusion and climax, marriage?

What is this marvel toward which Moses drives?[3] If it is a conclusion to Genesis 1&2, then marriage may be the means by which God expresses the fullness of the image of God in his human wilful-creatures. The God who is One-and-Many declares, 'they [the *two*] shall become *one* flesh' (Gen. 2:24). This is not only a declaration about the exclusive bond of marriage, nor does it merely reflect the bond of intimacy between a husband and wife. It is also a declaration of a new reality, a reality not yet seen in God's creation. It is the culmination of God's work of imaging himself in his creatures; he does this by a marriage covenant.

Consider this marvel of Moses as he turns toward his climax and conclusion with the radically disjunctive 'not good'. These words impose a break in the previous rhythm of 'and God saw that it was good' and his crescendo at the close of the creative week, 'it was very good!' So here, in the second 'saga', in the introduction to the Marriage Text, 'not good' jars us to attention. Something in God's perfect work is 'not good' – or perhaps 'not fitting' – for his human wilful-creatures. But what is not fitting? What is not good? It is not good for Adam to be alone. If we imagine this to be merely a personal statement about Adam's feelings, it effectively blunts the jarring force of God's abrupt declaration. While many hear the words this way, I suspect we are too eager to affirm our own experience of loneliness with a collective 'of course!' We know this instinctively: it is not good for anyone to be absolutely alone, cut off from all human intercourse. Such a reading may serve like earplugs which attenuate the screeching 'fingers on the chalkboard' of the words 'not good'. But notice it is not Adam who judges his situation as 'not good', but God. Quite the opposite, Adam stands alone in confused contentment. After all, he has God and is therefore not alone. But Adam has something to learn; and so do we.

Now we are in for a second surprise: already afflicted by the 'not good' loneliness, now God 'frustrates' Adam! This may seem strange in a perfect Garden, but now God mercifully leads Adam to agree with him: his situation is not fitting; his situation is decisively not good. God does this with holy frustration; he creates a holy hunger for what God intends. In this, God succeeds in his intent. After a time – how long? – Adam names 'every living creature'. In so doing, he discerns that 'man's best friend' is not to be found among God's non-human creatures. Now, at the end of verse 20, Adam is ready for God's solution – one could say that God has awakened a holy desire through holy frustration. Now, creation waits for its completion. So Adam, and the reader, is ready to witness the Marriage Text.

But I have gone ahead of myself here. Let me begin an ordered exegesis of this Marriage Text and discover it as the climax and conclusion to the twin accounts of creation and that it is the heart of God.

The Relationship of Genesis 2:18–25 to Genesis 1&2

Given the location and strange prominence of the Marriage Text, I consider it perplexing that it is not assumed to be the 'climax and conclusion' to the twin creation accounts of Genesis 1&2. This text offers us many prominent firsts: the first time Adam speaks, the first time God teaches, the first time a negative adverb is used of God's created order, the first time the man exercises his role of dominion (by naming), and more firsts. While such prominence may not make the case, it offers warrant for supposition and investigation along such lines. So, I will first survey the lack of engagement historically with this idea that Barth later considered so obvious: the Marriage Text is the climax and conclusion of the twin creation accounts. Surveying such a lack may seem strange, yet I think a preliminary survey is helpful to display the nuances of an almost univocal opinion.

In *Against Heresies*, Irenaeus (130–202, Bishop of Gaul) had much to say about Genesis 1–3 to his Gnostic challengers. But in all he wrote, and he wrote quite a bit, Irenaeus did not investigate a specific theological role for the Marriage Text. Later, Chrysostom (349–407, Archbishop of Constantinople) took no little care to link his individual homiletical texts with the context of prior texts. Yet in his *Homilies on Genesis* he made no move to explain the place of Genesis 2:18–25 (referenced in Homilies 14, 15, and 16) to Moses' overall argument in Genesis 1&2. In Homily 14, he only noted (and rightly so!) that in this text the Lord God is 'adding kindness to kindness'.[4] For Chrysostom we might say this Marriage Text fitted into Genesis 1&2 as a cumulative blessing, rather than a conclusion and fitting climax.[5]

Jerome (347–420) understood this text as a pointer to the creation of the church. In 'Homily 66' he wrote, 'The concept of building, as we have said before, is wont to denote the construction of a great house; consequently, Adam's rib fashioned into a woman signifies, by apostolic authority, Christ and the Church, and that is why Scripture said He formed a woman from the rib.'[6] This is typological reading – that is, a reading in which the historical significance of an event is overshadowed by the greater events and persons it points to. In so doing, Jerome ignored the historical and contextual significance of this event. Continuing the pattern of most of his predecessors, Jerome does not give intense exegetical attention to the Marriage Text, even in his work, *Hebrew Questions on Genesis*. He certainly did not dwell in the place of climax or conclusion to creation.

Augustine (354–430) wrote extensively on Genesis, making three editions of his 'literal' commentary. He understood the second creation account, Genesis 2:4–25, to be a recapitulation of the sixth day in which 2:18–24 is a continuation of that day and so an expansion of Genesis 1:27–28.[7] In this context, marriage was given as a safe haven for procreation. Later, Augustine returned to this text and suggested that it offers more: it prepares the reader and advances the narrative toward the Fall (Gen. 3).[8] These are not trivial or misplaced observations in regard to this text. Still, this is a rather meagre return on Moses' investment of so many words – 10 per cent (a tithe!) of his total words in the two creation accounts. Yet, for all of Moses' words, and all of Augustine's words, Augustine did not read this text as a climax to either creation account.

As massive and significant as are their works, neither Anselm (1033–1109, Archbishop of Canterbury) nor Thomas Aquinas (1225–74) added significantly to the discussion on this text in its context. So I move us forward a millennium to Martin Luther (1483–1536). He moves us into the deeper waters of this text, but even so he did not understand the Marriage Text as a climax. Luther seemed quite content with Jerome's use of this text, specifically in regard to the naming of the animals (v. 19). This Jerome typologically applied to Christ's work of building the church, though Luther insisted on seeking the exegetical meaning first and foremost.[9] For Luther, Moses' use of the language of edification and building ('he built a woman', in regard to Eve) refers not to the church (as for Jerome), but distinctly to the building of the household, and so the production and bringing up of children. All in all, this Marriage Text, while important, merely fits into an exposition which clarifies God's work of the sixth day with greater detail.

John Calvin (1509–64) can hardly be distinguished from Augustine in regard to his exegesis of this text. He also focused on procreation. Specifically, explaining the transition from 2:17 to 2:18, Calvin wrote, 'Moses now explains the design of God in creating the woman, namely that there should be human beings on the earth who might cultivate mutual society between themselves.'[10] So on Calvin, the Marriage Text provides for human procreation, an expansion of the first account's simple phrase, 'be fruitful and multiply' (Gen. 1:28). There is a bit more; I will return to this when I consider the Trinity.

Moving to the twentieth century, Gerhard von Rad (1901–71) spoke from the perspective of the documentary hypothesis (JEDP theory). In brief, this is the idea that the five books of Moses (the Torah or Pentateuch) are a sewn-together patchwork of different sources and competing perspectives. From within this framework, knowing the source for any text in the Torah might be viewed as an end in itself.[11] And given the patchwork nature of his perceived text of Genesis, it is no surprise that von Rad pursues no essential thematic connection(s) between the first creation account (which is from the Priestly tradition, the 'P' of JEDP, 1:1–2:4a) and the second account (which is Yahwist material, the 'J' in JEDP, 2:4b–12:3).[12] Given this, it would seem unlikely for him to perceive the Marriage Text as the conclusion to both accounts. Of this text he noted that in 'God's kindliness we see that it would do man good if a helping creature were given to him "as his opposite," "a helper fit for him" . . . Solitude is therefore defined here very realistically as helplessness (cf. Eccl 4:9–11). From this point of view, the wife receives quite an unromantic valuation that the OT never forsakes.'[13] Later I will address how wide of the mark he falls here, when he speaks of Adam's loneliness and brings the misogynistic charge (Eve's 'unromantic valuation') against the author of Genesis.[14] Perhaps he could have still suggested a connection between the Marriage Text and the creation accounts as an intention of a later redactor, but he does not. What he does propose, as he reflects on Genesis 2:24, is an explanation that is merely aetiological, that is, an explanation of modern practice in the light of historical doings:

> 'Therefore' . . . is not, of course, a continuation of the first man's speech, but rather a concluding, summarizing word of the narrator, a short epilogue, as it were, after the curtain has fallen. One must say, in fact, that in this statement the entire narrative so far arrives at the primary purpose toward which it was oriented from the beginning. This shows what is actually intended. The story is entirely etiological, i.e., it was told to answer a definite question. A fact needs explanation, namely, the extremely powerful drive of the sexes to each other.[15]

On his proposal, the 'therefore' in verse 24 introduces an intention of the author, even a 'primary purpose'. This is hopeful, but he acknowledges only a connection to the second account. Rather than being deeply connected to what went before, the material provided merely the background which permits the narrator to make his point for which no clear ground has been laid outside verses 18–25.[16] So it seems that the Marriage Text stands in a rather odd isolation, an explanation for *marriage as it is now experienced*, asymmetrically: benefiting men by creating a woman as an 'unromantic valuation'. On this account, and by his perspective, one might ask: who helps her?

Similarly, Claus Westermann (1909–2000) proposed that this text is intended to help us understand the community of a man and a woman in relationship, and is neither an explanation of the institution of marriage nor of human sexuality:

> There is a change of speaker between vv. 23 and 24. It is not the man who is speaking now but the narrator . . . It is clear that verse 24 is but an addition to the narrative which is complete without it, ending with verse 23; it is a 'short epilogue, as it were, after the curtain has fallen.' (G. von Rad). However one cannot say that 'in this statement the entire narrative so far arrives at the primary purpose toward which it was oriented from the beginning' . . . The significance of the verse [24]

lies in this that in contrast to the established institutions and partly in opposition to them, it points to the basic power of love between man and woman.[17]

Westermann perceived in this Marriage Text no culmination to either creation account, but rather finds it to be merely an explanation of marriage – aetiological. He did not follow von Rad here into marriage as we find it today, but instead into the community of love between a man and a woman. In the end, while distinct, both theologians rejected any significant theological or necessary connection between this text and the accounts which precede it.

Derek Kidner (1913–2008) expanded on the position held by Calvin (and others) which link the marriage account to 1:28 and the first creation account. He writes of 2:18–25 as the 'crowning paragraph of the chapter, which is the dynamic, or dramatic, counterpart of 1:27,28.'[18] Even so, Kidner stopped short of exploring this material as the author's conclusion of the twin creation accounts. The Marriage Text is significant, but in some sense out of place, and not a theological climax to the twin accounts.

If these few examples are representative, they reveal a limited role which Bible scholars, teachers, and pastors allow to this Marriage Text. This is not to argue that this text is unimportant to these scholars – not at all. Yet none engage with what Barth has called the 'obvious sense' that the marriage account is the climax of the twin creation accounts. They neither deny this idea (presumably its obviousness antedates Barth himself!) nor investigate the connections which seemed so obvious to Barth. Yet to Barth, it was as if everyone understood that Genesis 2:18–25 forms the climax and so the conclusion to the twin accounts of creation. And it does.

What grounds might prove sufficient for such a claim? John Sailhamer is helpful, giving us reasons for including 2:18–25 as a conclusion to both creation accounts. First, Sailhamer exposes a literary pattern in Genesis in which poetry serves as a conclusion to the narrative which came before. He writes, 'The technique of using a poetic speech and a short epilogue to conclude a narrative is well known in biblical literature and occurs frequently within recognizable segments of the Pentateuch itself.'[19] He goes on to note that this is precisely the case for Genesis 1&2 which 'concludes with the short poetic discourse of Adam (2:23) and an epilogue (2:24).'[20] In so doing Sailhamer has put the Marriage Text in a place of prominence for both accounts, a conclusion to the twin accounts of creation. Second, Sailhamer discovers another way that the author reveals his ideas to us through literary structure. It is grammatical rather than narrative. Sailhamer observes a significant break, a disjunction, which sets boundaries at 1:2 and 3:1, framing the material between them as one unit.[21] Looking at the text, we find this disjunctive pattern in 1:1, 1:2 and 3:1, but not elsewhere in Genesis 1&2.[22] If he is correct, then Sailhamer has displayed strong support that 2:18–25 belongs with the twin creation accounts and so the Marriage Text forms some kind of epilogue, perhaps even a climax to the twin accounts.[23]

Now, finally, I turn to Karl Barth (1886–1968), seeking his reasons for this strong claim about the Marriage Text. Genesis 2:18–25 is cast as the decisive turn which draws together both accounts into a climax. First, Barth considers semantics as a key connection between the two accounts. Both the first account and the Marriage Text refer to the creation of the 'living creatures' (1:24 and 2:19). So also Barth observes the blessing of 2:25 as parallel to 1:31.[24] Twice in the Marriage Text we see Adam's role as one who has the right to name, an outworking of 'dominion' established in 1:26–28. Also, in each of these three examples, the Marriage Text amplifies and concludes what had begun earlier in the account. Then, most significantly, Barth observes *God's significant pause*, which directs our attention to the climax.[25] He perceives this signal in 1:26 ('Let us make man in our image') and 2:18 ('it is not good that the man should be alone') as divine pauses prior to decisive acts. He writes:

> At this point, and at this point alone, immediately prior to the climax of the creative act, we have in both sagas a kind of *divine pause, a Word directed by God Himself to Himself.* The effect is the same in both cases, for the hearer or reader will observe that the climax has now been reached, and that the reference is now to the decisive moment in the whole creative act.[26]

This observation of such a distinctive turn by the author of the text to a deliberative communication *of God and to God* happens only once in each creation account. In both cases he suggests that it prepares the reader for a climactic turn toward marriage. The first account gives us a glimpse of the intention, but sets the stage for the second and decisive turn. For Barth, Genesis 2:18–25 concludes the themes of creation, man and woman, dominion, and blessing, and comes to us after the pregnant pause of God. It is the climax of these twin creation accounts.

Barth and Sailhamer stand mostly alone in asserting such a deep and climactic connection between the Marriage Text and the twin creation accounts.[27] Both go further than mere aetiological accounts of marriage (the use of history to 'explain' our current practice of marriage), sexuality, or even the love between a man and a woman (though the former is important to Barth as well). Both go beyond a deep connection, and assert that the Marriage Text brings the reader to the theological climax to which these accounts pointed. I stand with them. If they are correct, then a closer exegetical exploration of the text should reveal the substance of this climax.

How Does God 'Know' that It Is 'Not Good' to Be Alone? (v. 18)

So far, I have given my reasons for accepting the Marriage Text as the conclusion. Now I want to discover how and in what ways it declares the climax of the twin accounts of creation. Paul Evdokimov writes, 'There is but one suffering: to be alone. A one-personal God would not be love. God is Trinity, one and at the same time three.'[28] This truth, not merely the interior, and derivative, experience of loneliness, is the key.

Verse 18, which introduces this Marriage Text, has a most interesting beginning as I noted in the introduction to this chapter: 'Then the LORD God said, "It is not good that the man should be alone."' Henri Blocher writes, 'The remark amazes us. It is the only negative assessment in the creation narrative, and it is emphatically negative. By this divine reason of the creation of woman, Scripture could not underline better the degree to which solitude contradicts the calling of humanity . . . human life attains its full realization only in community.'[29] With Blocher, most exegetes are fully alert to the radical shift which is in this text: 'It is not good'. So, it hardly needs to be mentioned that these words, 'not good',[30] capture our attention like fingers on a chalkboard. We are jolted awake – or should be. As we know, all that has occurred in the first account has been affirmed as 'good' and even very good.[31] How radically distracting verse 18 is to us! The state of affairs is not simply without affirmation, rather goodness is denied. This is a radical departure from day six in the conclusion of Genesis 1, 'very good'. This 'not good' which introduces the Marriage Text is different. It is not an assessment of something which was made, but a declaration that something essential is yet missing from what was made. The effect is dissonant. Now readers are on alert, as intended.

But why are we put on the alert? Why is it not good to be alone? More importantly, since God is the subject of the narrative, how does God *know* that it is 'not good' to be alone? No doubt my question may cause readers to wonder at my lack of perception in regard to the obvious! First, God knows all things; this knowing is no 'reach' for our omniscient God. And even we, as the readers, intuitively know and discover the existential reality – loneliness is a crisis. No one need tell us. Our libraries are filled with this same assessment: Odysseus' longing for home (Homer, 800 BC), the isolation of Robinson Crusoe (Defoe, 1719), and even the lonely misery of Frankenstein's creation (or as we have learned to think, Frankenstein's monster) longing to be loved by his father/creator (Shelley, 1818). We know this terror: alone is not good! And given the context here in Genesis, one might consider the literary genre of 'romance' as an example of our intuitive conception that alone is not good. And again, what we know, surely God knows! The real question I am asking is not 'What does God know?' but 'Why would God think that 'alone' is a problem, if he is One and only One and Adam images him?' The Shema declares: 'The LORD our God, the LORD is one' (Deut. 6:4). If so, what is so terribly 'not Good' (that is, 'not God') about being alone? To God who is only one, and therefore eternally alone, alone should be rather good! While it might be good for God to be alone, and 'not good' for a man (or humankind), we should consider the point of this text, to make humankind in God's image. If God is alone, we might expect then that his image-bearer would also be alone – and it would be good.

But perhaps God discerns and declares this assessment for us, having nothing to do with himself, who is One and happy about being only One. That is, perhaps 'not good' is God's observation on our behalf, a condescension of God to our distinct experience of aloneness as loneliness. After all, Genesis was written by and to God's human wilful-creatures, who in our fallen state have entered into loneliness. Did not sin, the Fall, isolate us from God and each other? Perhaps a reader could argue that this account was written by a fallen human for fallen readers, even inerrantly by God's inspiration and by God's authority. Such readers would intuitively identify with the problem of loneliness (alone-ness). But this cannot be. There are no 'fallen actors' in this text, only Adam, still in his God-given goodness. The breaking of the covenant is yet to happen. The proposal has no context in the story. Moreover, such a proposal also fails in its intent to tell us about God, for neither the grammar nor the story can be perceived *only* in human terms. It is God who makes this observation. And while this text is about God's first human, God is the subject and the one revealed so far in this story. This text is revealing God to the reader, and so aloneness is best understood in relationship to God as he has displayed himself to this point in the story. This, the character of God, is what the author wants us to discern. When we do, and rightly, we will begin to perceive the climax anticipated in the words 'not good' which introduce the conclusion, the Marriage Text. It is God who makes this judgment through the human narrator, and from his own character. God is One-and-Many, and he has never been alone. In his aloneness, Adam does not image God.

Let me not rush to this conclusion. There are two other means we should consider for God to know that this state of affairs is 'not good' for Adam. First, God has already shown us that the animals 'should not be alone'. God has provided to each of his plants and creatures an ability to 'multiply' after their kind. This is a blessing of God and his means to sustain creation. Indeed, this blessing is textually antecedent to the creation of humankind and perhaps is a warrant for the realization of the words 'not good' in regard to his creatures, though aloneness is good for God. But this argument only regresses the question back one step. God, who creates all things good, created the higher-order animals to be progressively *less* alone: the plants produce seeds and fruit, and the animals have mates. While lower forms of life procreate by pollination, others by hermaphrodite or asexual procreation, the more complex forms of life reproduce with increasing intimacy. This is evident even in the language of creation in which the higher forms of life are 'blessed' by multiplication, while the lower forms are merely granted multiplication, implicitly. However, for humankind, this 'blessing' is not merely a phrase. Instead, it takes on an even greater importance and intimacy in just this text. Interestingly, that particular intent, multiplication, is missing here. Henri Blocher writes, 'Procreation is not the purpose of marriage as such. For his institution the Lord give only one reason: "It is not good that the man should be alone." The Song of Songs, which sings of the love of husband and wife as the flame of the LORD (Song 8:6), preserves a similar silence.'[32] This text is not about procreation. Indeed procreation is not mentioned or even alluded to in this text. Something much deeper is happening in regard to the pinnacle of God's creation. We must ask: why is it the case that the good creation includes pairing within kinds? What is it about God's image in his human wilful-creatures, and the completion of God's creation in humankind, that would be 'not good' if God did not complete his work *in just this way*? This is not merely provision for multiplication, if multiplication is even in the author's immediate focus! No, the answer cannot be mere procreation; it is the connection of those who are other in a kind of oneness.[33] And this is derived from the nature of God himself. For if God himself is alone (not One-and-Many) in himself prior to creation, then the textual progression from lower (implicit grant) to higher (explicit blessing) simply regresses the problem of aloneness. Now, the reader is faced with a discontinuity between man who will be soon paired, and God who is alone. This discontinuity does not fit with the goal of imaging himself in human-kind. However, this discontinuity disappears if God himself is not alone in himself.

This touches on a second means by which God could know that it is 'not good' for a human to be alone: God's omniscience. God certainly knows all truth, even truth that is beyond his direct experience – human temptation and sinning, for example. So, by invoking omniscience, God *could* know that Adam is alone and he *could* know that aloneness does not feel good to Adam. But this declaration of 'not good', just here in the story, does not seem to fit. For example, in the case of the animals, when they were created, their mates were created with them. And then God joyfully declared, 'be fruitful and multiply'. There was no intermediate pause of concern. Why is this story different? Moreover, even after Eve is created to resolve the tension of the Marriage Text, there is not even a whisper of 'multiplying' – not in this climax and conclusion. Something else is happening that calls us to push deeper into the story and ask: why is this state of aloneness 'not good' for Adam? So, the question is not how *would* God discern that Adam is alone or that Adam needs a wife. His omniscience clearly supports this, but such is thin soup for this story as it unfolds. Rather the question is: how does the story support Moses' strange and startling disjunction?

If God's omniscience is sufficient logically, still this does not support the storyline. What then might the words 'not good' reveal to the reader? By inference, these words declare that God himself is not alone. On the one hand, if God existed alone and he saw Adam in his fitting, image-bearing aloneness, God might well declare, 'Good!' over Adam's solidarity. But he did not. On the other hand, if God were only singular, God might have observed Adam and exulted over him: 'Now, I am no longer alone!' But God did not hover over his new creation, expressing such relief. YHWH is uncreated and eternally content in himself. It follows then that God did not create out of need.[34] For this reason, it has become normal for theologies to refute such conceptual-izations of God, with the dis-affirmation: God was not lonely![35] God has always enjoyed his own society, the Trinity. This declaration, 'not alone', is telling us about God himself even as he declares this of Adam through Moses: God is not, and never was, alone, yet distinct from God, the image-bearer is. This state is not good.

In this declaration God is alerting us to his deep and marvellous intent in this story – to create an image-bearer. In his omniscience, God knows that man's aloneness, something that is not in God's One-and-Many nature, is not fitting for his image-bearer. Creation is incomplete, as long as Adam is 'discovered' by God in such a state. Bruce Waltke writes of this verse, 'Relationship is modeled after God who does not exist in isolation but is a triunity, surrounded by a heavenly court.'[36] As this story unfolds, and if God is Trinity, and if Adam is his image-bearer, then God *should* declare such a state as 'not good'. And he does. This is not merely an observation that Adam feels bad when alone and needs a wife. Indeed, omniscience permits these observations, but they do not fit the story. Rather, by God's trinitarian nature and his goal of imaging himself in his people, the One who is never alone, will image himself in just this way: the two shall be one.

What of the Shema? Does Deuteronomy 6:4, the anchor text of the Torah, refute my assertion that Moses is already teaching that God is One-and-Many? The reading given by the ESV is, 'Hear, O Israel: The LORD our God, the LORD is one'. This text testifies to the monotheism of Judeo-Christianity, over against polytheism. Does this also imply not only that God is one but also that God is not many? While this is not the place to tease out the full implications and limits of the Shema, I will state that it is not an argument against God's trinitarian nature.[37] It is a statement that God alone is to be worshipped.

Others might wonder if this text is simply a 'modern' explanation for the ancient practice of marriage – an aetiology of marriage. That might be possible if this text focused on childbearing, but as noted above, that is not the case. It is grander, more beautiful, bears greater weight, and most importantly, offers us insight into God himself. While this Marriage Text certainly introduces us to God's image-bearers, it is a text that is first and foremost about God. God is not alone; the problem is this: Adam is. This text introduces God to us, YHWH Elohim, who made the heavens and the earth. He now explains our existence in relationship to himself. God, and the author, perceives Adam's loneliness as a problem. The 'fingers on a chalkboard' alert the readers to something significant. Indeed, as we shall see, God has already been revealing himself as more than one; He is One-and-Many. Adam, alone, must be brought into image-bearing likeness to his Creator.

Excursus from Verse 18: The One-and-Many Problem in the Context of Genesis 1&2

It is worth saying a word here about the One-and-Many 'problem'. This is a most ancient discussion in philosophy: is the world composed of many fundamentally distinct parts, which are experienced as a whole (such as atomic elements which we experience as 'things'), or is it one-thing, which we engage with in various parts (such as 'energy' which we experience as distinct material objects in everyday life)? Van Til expresses it this way, 'Man's problem is to find unity in the midst of the plurality of things. He sometimes calls this the one-and-many problem.'[38] Is the universe that we engage composed of parts which seem like a whole, or a whole which is experienced as parts? Or both?[39] It turns out that *both* is quite a good option. In regard to God, he himself is the unique answer to the confusion that arises in people as we reflect on the reality of plurality and our perception of unity: God reveals that both oneness and plurality are equally ultimate. God is the reality who is One in his nature (he alone is the One God) and Many in regard to the persons of the Trinity (Father, Son, and Spirit) in their distinct relations. We cannot perceive his existence as primarily One, or primarily Many, but One-and-Many. In the reality of such a God, we discern this universe more clearly. Van Til rightly observes that the Christian God is the only answer: 'As

Christians we hold that there is no answer to these problems from a non-Christian point of view . . . [It is in] the Christian doctrine of the triune God, as we are bound to believe, that we really have a concrete universal.'[40] And so, we believe that our temporal existence, in which we experience the tension of the one and the many, has its unique origin in the One who is himself, One-and-Many.

However, in regard to these first two chapters of Genesis, an initial objection must be faced. While I have shown above that it is difficult to understand how God, who is often perceived as (and declared to be) only One, could know that it is 'not good' for man to be alone, I have not established any reasons from this text to think God is other than One – that God is also, Many. But in fact, the text does give us reason to think that God is Many and (not merely) One. And though evidence from this text alone is not a conclusive witness to the Trinity, yet evidence that he is One-and-Many is plainly here in this early text. To begin, it is also worth demonstrating that such a reading is not a new reading.

In the second century, Justin Martyr (100–65), read this text as trinitarian. In 'Dialogues with Trypho', he asserted to his Jewish disputant (regarding the agreement of Genesis with Proverbs):

> In saying, therefore, 'as one of us,' [Moses] has declared that [there is a certain] number of persons associated with one another, and that they are at least two. For I would not say that the dogma of that heresy which is said to be among you is true, or that the teachers of it can prove that [God] spoke to angels, or that the human frame was the workmanship of angels. But this Offspring, which was truly brought forth from the Father, was with the Father before all the creatures, and the Father communed with Him; even as the Scripture by Solomon has made clear.[41]

Later, Augustine was among the early commentators who perceived the triunity of God in these Genesis creation accounts. He wrote, 'We understand the Father in the word "God" and the Son in the word "beginning" . . . and the Spirit of God was being borne over the water (Genesis 1:2), we recognize the complete indication of the Trinity'.[42] He also observed a trinitarian declaration in Genesis 1:26.

When God says, 'Let us make man', he notes a distinct change from the established pattern: 'God said: let it be made'. Augustine attributes this change as a way 'to insinuate, that is, a plurality of persons, if I may so put it, on account of Father and Son and Holy Spirit.'[43] Augustine adds: 'He immediately advises us, however, of the unity to be understood in the godhead by saying, and God made man to the image of God; not as though the Father made to the image of the Son, or the Son to the image of the Father – otherwise it would not be true to say "in our image."'[44] The Marriage Text reflects just this observation, as Augustine perceives it. In the making of the woman, who is like man ('from his side') but not identical, not actually Adam, God has made two with similarity and distinction. Yet this is not what God finally intends. God is not yet finished. Then, bringing them together in marriage, God does something new: these two, who yet remain two, also become one. In this God is imaging not merely the One God, but his own One-and-Many trinitarian nature. Augustine was wholly convinced that Genesis 1&2 spoke from a trinitarian perspective. It is worth adding the confirming reflections of Peter Lombard (1100–60), the first author of a 'systematic theology': 'In Genesis, the Lord shows at once the plurality of persons and the unity of nature by saying: "Let us make" and "our image and likeness". By saying "Let us make" and "our", he shows the plurality of persons, but by saying "image", he shows us the unity of essence.'[45] In this we hear his dependence on Augustine.

Luther saw the Trinity even in Genesis 1:22. Where the text says, 'and [he] brought her to the man', Luther writes, 'Who? No doubt . . . the entire Divinity – Father, Son, and Holy Spirit.' Calvin, as he often does, is in agreement with Augustine in regard to the Trinity in Genesis 1. He notes the distinctive turn in the narration in verse 26, when God deliberates with himself, as a unique change. He rejects the idea that God is deliberating with the earth or the angels, for Adam was made specifically in God's image, not any other image. He also rejects the possibility of the royal 'we' ('Let us') as barbarous. He concludes simply, 'Christians, therefore, properly contend, from this testimony, that there exists a plurality of persons in the Godhead.'[46] Going a bit beyond

Augustine, Calvin does come very close to understanding the Marriage Text to be a climax of both accounts, or at least lays the groundwork for that idea. He says that it completes and defines the image of God in man when he writes: For this form of speaking,

> 'God created man, male and female created he them,' is of the same force as if he had said, that the man himself was incomplete. Under these circumstances, the woman was added to him as a companion that they both might be one, as he more clearly expresses it in the second chapter.[47]

His idea of 'incomplete' is to the point. God's image is not complete in his wilful human-creature until woman is made and they are joined in marriage.

From Justin Martyr to Calvin, many found the Trinity, or at least the One-and-Many (the number unspecified), revealed in these twin accounts. Barth summaries and affirms this historical position in this way: 'The fathers were right when they saw glimpses of the whole mystery of the Trinity in the *way-yōmer Elohim* [the Hebrew for 'and God(s) said'] of Genesis 1:3ff'.[48] Let me highlight five specific texts which may be hints, even God's own claims, to his nature as the God who is One-and-Many. I will evaluate each briefly, and in sequence.

Elohim (Gen. 1:1ff.)

Elohim is a plural form for the name of God: literally, the exalted ones or gods. In fact, this is the specific form to which Barth was referring above, though he referenced verse 3 and God's created act of speaking. Still, it must be asked if Elohim is fairly read as an indication of plurality in God. As shown above, Augustine finds in favour of understanding in Elohim a hint of trinitarian plurality. Calvin, however, finds it tantalizing, an inference, but rejects it as an insufficient 'proof of so great a matter'.[49] His judgment is fair and his candour is appreciated. Nor is Calvin alone; most rightly reject this as significant evidence of God's

One-and-Many nature. For example, the (so-called) 'plural of majesty' is not unknown in the biblical text. Elijah commands Obadiah, 'Go and tell your *lords*', referring to Obadiah's singular master, King Ahab (1 Kgs 18:8, literal translation). Here seems to be an example of the 'plural of majesty'. Brian Murphy argues that Elohim, in its customary plural form, could be a regular use of the 'plural of majesty' in reference to God.[50] Yet Calvin, even in his hesitation to see it as trinitarian, still rejects the possibility of a royal 'we', as does Millard Erickson.[51] On the other hand, John Frame, who rejects the plural of majesty, still suggests a 'plural of abstraction' in which the plural form is used to indicate the abstract idea. Going further, Frame asserts that even if this form represented a true and intentional plural, God is plural in some way, yet this does not demonstrate that God is triune.[52] In the chaos of ideas in regard to the singularity or plural intent in the use of Elohim, it must be rejected as a significant indication of Trinity, at least in itself. At best it is an ambiguous hint.

Still there is one more possibility worthy of consideration. The 'plural of majesty', and the idea that a king refers to himself with a royal 'we', originates somewhere. Could it be here? Could it be in the One-and-Many nature of our King who introduces himself in the plural in the first words of his communication to us? Could the human invention of the 'plural of majesty' be a way to confer a hint of trinitarian greatness on an earthly, but otherwise quite singular, lord? I have no case to make, but only a question.

Spirit of God (Gen. 1:2)

What of the movement of the Spirit who hovers over the face of the waters in Genesis 1:2? Certainly this could be understood as a wind or, alternatively, as a way to speak of the One God who is spiritual. However, rather than either of these, Augustine takes this as an indication of God's plurality. Calvin takes it just as certainly as the person of the Spirit of God who creatively broods over the chaotic mass created in verse 1, citing Psalm 104.[53] Modern commentators are divided, of course. While this case may not be proven, it is also not easily dismissed.

'Let us make man' (Gen. 1:26–27)

This text is fascinating in its mixing of the singular and plural: 'Let us make man [*adam* with no article; singular] in our [plural] image, after our [plural] likeness. And let them [plural] have dominion . . . So God [the singular but plural-form name of God, 'Elohim'] created man [singular] in his own [singular] image, in the image of God he [singular] created him [singular]; male and female [two] he [singular] created them [plural].' On this text, Augustine and Calvin are in agreement, perceiving it as representing the One-and-Many nature of God. Yet this position is not monolithic; options are manifold. Victor Hamilton rehearses most of them. I will note only one of the most prominent, a mythological counsel of other gods. Such a biblical adaption of a kind of pantheon, a heavenly court, or perhaps God addressing all of creation and 'consulting' with creation is possible, at least logically and culturally.[54] Cassuto notes that the rabbis supported the explanation that it connotes that God took counsel with someone or something.[55] Yet, Calvin rightly dismisses such options as impossible given creation is in the image of those who constitute 'us'. Hamilton, after 500 years of further discussion, also rejects such possibilities. He notes the possibility that in agreement with 'Elohim' (understood as the plural of majesty), this might be some kind of plural of internal and magisterial self-deliberation. However, he rejects this as well. But citing Hasel (plural of fullness) and Clines (God consulting his Spirit), Hamilton rightly sees in this a trinitarian plural.[56] His summary statement is worth repeating in full: 'What we often so blithely dismissed as "foreign to the thought of the OT" may be nothing of the sort. True; the concept may not be etched on every page of Scripture, but hints and clues are dropped enticingly here and there, and such hints await their full understanding "at the correct time" (Gal. 4:4).'[57] Do our presuppositions determine what is 'foreign', or the text itself?

The reader does not have to attribute to the author of Genesis a fully developed trinitarian theology in order to see that in this momentous pause before the high point of creation, the author intends to communicate the complexity of God who is not only One, but also Many.

This trinitarian understanding of Genesis is neither new nor novel. Peter Lombard (1100–60), citing Hilary (300–68) in his *Sentences*, wrote, 'God said: "Let us make man in our image and likeness." The solitude of a solitary does not allow for "Let us make", and one would not say "our" to someone alien from oneself.'[58] More recently, Michael Horton brings the evidence together in this way: 'While monotheism (belief in one God) lay at the heart of biblical religion, the triunity of God was maintained from the very beginning. To be sure, it becomes clearer with successive chapters of redemptive history; nevertheless, even in the opening acts of the drama we see God acting in the triune Godhead.'[59]

'It is not good that the man should be alone; I will make him a helper fit for him' (Gen. 2:18)

Finally we come to the text which led us here. As I have shown above, this declaration, 'not good', makes no sense from within the story itself – unless the story prepares us with plurality in God. My friend Alexi saw this – the playwright whose observations I shared in the Preface. To him I can add two biblical scholars. First, Henri Blocher writes, 'Might there be more here than analogy? Would the being-with of mankind be necessary for him to be able to respond to God as quasi-son to his Father? This we have the right to suppose.'[60] He is saying that something in the created plurality of man and woman is essential for us to respond to God. That is, God is fundamentally a society, neither one nor many, but many in essential communion. We can only know him if we are in that image. An observation from Barth makes a similar point: there is a certain necessity that first-readers perceived something of the One-and-Many reality of God in order to understand this text: 'It is worth noting that in the divine statement: "I will make him an help meet . . ." the LXX uses "ποιήσωμεν" [*poiasomen,* we make] and the Vulgate *faciamus* [we make]. So strongly was the parallel to Genesis 1:26 felt that even at this early time it was thought necessary to introduce here too that mysterious plural.'[61] While this does not prove my point, it does decisively show how significant is the plural in 1:26 and how it may affect the reading of 2:18, 'not good to be alone'. It may even indicate that a plural is required for comprehension.

So, Adam's aloneness is 'not good' because he does not sufficiently image God in his aloneness. What will God do? For this, we move deeper into the Text.

Woman: A Fitting Helper for the One Man (vv. 19–23)

Now on alert, let us move into God's response. God's goal in verses 19–20 is to prepare the man for God's intended work: creating a fitting helper, a helper that Adam would recognize and cherish as 'very good' – solving the problem of 'not good'. But implicit in this account of the search for a fitting helper we discovered that God knew it was not good to be alone. We saw above that God discerned this because he himself was never alone; he is One-and-Many. But there is another surprise waiting here for us in this text: man was clearly not alone; man was with God. Is it the case that *God is not enough for this man*? Are we being told that this perfect communion with God was 'not good' (enough)? So offensive is this, and to some it is out of keeping with the narrative so far, that Walter Brueggemann calls this move of the author a turn toward secularization.[62] Brueggemann is reacting to the idea that Adam needs another human, the not yet created Eve; God is not enough! However, rather than a move to secularization, I believe it is just here that we begin to see more clearly the answer to both the question of 'how and why' God knew this state of affairs to be 'not good'. It is not simply that Adam had no one to speak with or commune with. He had that in God. We the readers have seen this. And we have also seen that God himself was not alone before Adam. Now we are about to learn that the aloneness of Adam is highlighted in order to display the nature of God by the creation, not merely of Eve, but of Woman for marriage to the Man. Marriage is the climactic creation flourish of God which completes the image of God in his human wilful-creatures.

Before I move forward, I should address the confusion that many have felt when reading the 'twin accounts of creation' side by side, Genesis 1 and Genesis 2. For example, there is a difference in the relationship of the order of creation in Genesis 2:19 and that of chapter 1: the animals were created before humankind in the first account and after humankind in the second. This is not unlike certain differences that are noted in the gospel accounts – indeed we could think of Genesis 1 and Genesis 2 in the same light. In the synoptic gospels, Jesus clears the temple after his entry into Jerusalem on a donkey, but in John he clears the temple at the beginning of his ministry. I pose the parallel only as an example, not to resolve.[63] In regard to Genesis 1 versus Genesis 2, there are a few possibilities. Considering the flow of the creation events, Genesis 2 might be related to Genesis 1 such that the first account was the creation of the universe (macro) and the second was of the Garden (micro). If this is the case, animals created in the Garden, Genesis 2, are distinct from those created in Genesis 1. If so, there is no tension between creating all animals and creating specific animals for the Garden. Or it might be that both accounts are Garden accounts, and this second is an expanded and personal account with a close focus on the sixth day. In this case, God is free to create more than once. That considered, observe (merely) that plausible answers exist, so questions about this particular sequence of creation need not stand in our way.[64] That is, solutions abound, even if we do not identify a particular solution as the right one. So we move on.

This is the more crucial question: how does the crisis of verse 18, and God's process and solution (v. 19), contribute to God's narrative goals of this Marriage Text? As presented in this text, God made creatures to resolve Adam's situation (aloneness), but this did not 'work'. So in verse 20 ('but for Adam there was not found a helper fit for him') the author seems to raise the question: did God, and so the man, fail in his intentions? Quite the opposite, according to this story as told by the narrator.

In the process of naming the animals, the man discovered and began to resonate with God's desire. Here we discover a holy process that causes *frustration* in Adam, even in the perfection of the Garden, before the Fall. In this act of naming, Adam did not accomplish the explicit goal which God set out. He did not find a fitting helper and so, feelings aside, he was *frustrated* in his explicit objective. And if he experienced an emotion associated with such failure of his mission, and if we could call this 'frustration', then such 'frustration' must be a holy frustration, in keeping with perfection. There is no sin in this, nor could sin be posited prior to the Fall of Genesis 3 without destroying the narrative. Instead, 'frustration' represents God's chosen means toward a fully awakened eagerness for what God desired for Adam. 'Frustration', at least in this sense, was God's intention and Adam's motivation and a driving potential, which caused the man to fully adopt God's desire for him. If this is so, we have a reversal. If this is so, then Adam has indeed accomplished God's intent for him on that day. Although this is implied by the text rather than explicitly stated, yet it is also God's goal in the act of naming: that Adam would discern that there was no helper fit for him (at least not yet to be found) in creation and so God enflamed a desire for that fitting helper. This is God's desire for Adam. Adam now saw with clarity: the dog is not man's best friend! So Man is prepared for what comes next.

Now, having 'frustrated' him, and so awakened the man's right desires, God's next move is to create Woman for Man, from the man's side (in vv. 21–22). Fully prepared by the 'frustrating' exercise of naming, the man is now eager for the fitting helper, 'a helper opposite to him'[65] and a person whose soul is 'bound up in his'.[66] She is his life.[67] Now with this new life from his side facing him, the man erupts with deep joy in verse 23: 'this at last is bone of my bones and flesh of my flesh!' Then, exercising his authority, he makes explicit what God has done, naming her after himself: 'She shall be called Woman, because she was taken out of Man.' Drawing on this text, and throughout the biblical narrative, this language of 'bone and flesh' will be used to indicate the closest of relatives and the deepest of family ties (Gen. 29:14; Judg. 9:2; 2 Sam. 5:1; 19:13). Indeed, Brueggemann goes further, asserting that Adam's declaration is a covenant formula, a pledge of loyalty.[68] It is that; it is Adam's vows, later exegeted by the apostle Paul in Ephesians 5.

So we see that God is successful in his primary and implicit goal, to prepare the man and make him ready for the fitting helper before he presented her and bound them together. And as we are about to see, he did this in order to image himself more completely in two, rather than in one.

The Meaning of 'therefore' (v. 24)

Verse 24 begins with the Hebrew particle *al-ken*, 'therefore'. This particle represents a significant shift in the text from narrative to sermon – the very first explanation of the words of the Torah by the Torah, and therefore the first of the Bible. Or not? This same particle, 'therefore', might merely introduce an aetiological explanation: displaying an *ancient* event as the sufficient reason for a *contemporary* practice. At face value, this could be. There are many examples of such aetiology in the Bible (in the following quotations I will put the English for *al-ken*, usually 'therefore', but not always, in *italics*).[69] For example, in Genesis 32:32 we read, '*Therefore* to this day the people of Israel do not eat the sinew of the thigh that is on the hip socket.'[70] An ancient story, Jacob's wrestling with an angel who defeated him by wounding his hip, explains a contemporary practice. Similarly, and quite frequently, this particle is used to indicate the reason for a place name. Exodus 15:23 reads, 'When they came to Marah, they could not drink the water of Marah because it was bitter; *therefore* it was named Marah.' (*Marah* in Hebrew is 'bitter'.) Yet, this same structure can express purpose. In Exodus 20:11 we read, 'For in six days the LORD made heaven and earth, the sea, and all that is in them, and rested on the seventh day. *Therefore* the LORD blessed the Sabbath day and made it holy.' It can also offer insight into the motives or intent of another as in Exodus 5:17, 'But he [Pharaoh] said, "You are idle, you are idle; *that is why* you say, "Let us go and sacrifice to the LORD."' Or it can also introduce instruction as in Deuteronomy 15:11, 'For there will never cease to be poor in the land. *Therefore* I command you, "You shall open wide your hand to your brother, to the needy and to the poor, in your land."' I intend no complete assessment of this Hebrew particle and its place in linguistic structure, but this is sufficient to show the breadth of its use beyond mere aetiological use, even if the use here might be aetiological. What is intended by Moses (by God!) here in verse 24?

Luther, recognizing that there were no mothers or fathers in this narrative ('therefore a man shall leave his mother and father'), understood this declaration as Adam's prophetic word.[71] But the introductory 'therefore' breaks the narrative flow,[72] and does not continue the speech of Adam. This is even more obvious in verse 25 where the narrator refers to Adam in the third person. This declaration is an interjection of the narrator's thoughts which break into the flow of his story. And what he gives to the reader is not a simple aetiology of practice (as in Gen. 32:32), for the narrator is not giving the reason for marriage, but instead explaining the effect of marriage. And certainly this effect is not in any way explained on the basis of Adam & Eve, for whom, as Luther noticed and all readers must as well, no parents are introduced except God himself. Nor can it be an aetiology of a place (as in Exod. 15:23), but no place name is explained by marriage. The very complexity of this section, distinguishing it from such uses, would seem to put the burden of proof on the one who would consider it as *only* aetiological in the above sense. Here, instead, the particle introduces a complex teaching which *reveals God's purposes*, rather than the mere historical antecedent of contemporary (in the day of any reader) marriage. As we will see, it draws us to a climax, revealing the image of God in his human wilful-creatures: the two become one. Or they are both two and one, imaging God in his One-and-Many trinitarian glory. This particle presumes to give us understanding, not of people's practice, but of God's being imaged in his human wilful-creatures. What are we to learn of God in this?

Marriage: A Fitting Image for the 'One-and-Many' (vv. 24–25)

It is here, in the concluding poetry and epilogue, that we have the climax and fitting conclusion to the twin creation accounts – an account of God's image in his human wilful-creatures. God has called attention to a problem: the human is alone. Now he repairs that problem. On the way, he has led the human (and the reader) to agree with him that the problem he identified is indeed a problem. And then, in this first use of the particle 'therefore', we were introduced to God's purposes in this section: God, who is One-and-Many, desires to have his human wilful-creatures fully reflect his image.

This is the conclusion; this is the climax: 'and they [the two] shall become one flesh'. This is the response to the challenge of verse 18, 'It is not good that the man should be alone.' Here, finally, is aetiology of a kind: all who marry are also displaying the very nature of God as One-and-Many[73] by marriage.[74] God has imaged himself most fully in his human wilful-creatures by marriage. Augustine sees the image of God in man, the trinitarian image, apart from any counting of three human persons. He writes, 'What I mean is, why does scripture make no mention besides male and female in the nature of man made to God's image? To complete the image of the trinity it ought to have mentioned a son also, even though he was still in the loins of his father like the woman in his side.'[75] It is worth noting for clarity that Augustine is writing here in regard to Genesis 1, and when God said he made Man, male and female in his image, Eve was still 'in' Adam and was only 'released' in Genesis 2, and their firstborn was still in Adam's loins. Again, Augustine rejects this speculative counting of persons that we might total three. Rather, through marriage, the image is now in human marriage. And if that image does not add up to three, yet it is trinitarian, in that the many (two in this case) have become one.

Of course, not all perceive the Trinity in the creation account(s). Let me, for balance, display some of the detractors to my argument. Elaine Pagels, who gives significant weight to the *Gospel of Thomas*,[76] explains the connection between Genesis 1:27 and 2:24 this way:

> When 'God created adam in his image,' he first created a singular being ('in the image of God he created him'). Yet immediately after that, humankind devolved into a dual species, divided into male and female ('male and female he created them,' 1:27b). Logion 11 [*Gospel of Thomas*] describes the dilemma this devolution has caused: 'On the day you were one, you became two. When you become two, what will you do?'[77]

As Pagels understands the flow of the text, the original state of people was to be man-and-woman, together in one being (Gen. 1). The Marriage Text, then, is not creating the image of God in his One-and-Many nature in Adam & Eve, but rather *restoring the unity* that he enjoyed in the primordial light, before being 'divided' into man and woman. But this cannot be the intention of the author. Such an understanding is at odds with the challenge God identified in 2:18 as I showed above. Still, Pagels' proposal does in some ways highlight the trinitarian intent – though in an entirely backwards move. Also Chrysostom (349–407, Archbishop of Constantinople) writes of Paul's commentary in Ephesians 5 of the Marriage Text, 'How is it a mystery? They come together, and the two make one . . . image, nor yet the image of anything upon earth, but of God Himself, and after his likeness.'[78] Like Pagels, he understands that Adam was first one, then divided into two (Eve drawn out from the man as if already there), and then united again into the original one through the bond of marriage. Yet, like Pagels', even this (somewhat Gnostic, and so dualistic) perspective reflects a trinitarian image of God in man.

What does it mean, then, in the flow of the biblical narrative, for the 'two' to become 'one' [flesh]? Notice that, as is the case with God who is One *and* Three, they also are yet two. Even as they are now related in the oneness of marriage, they are still persons in every sense. The very next phrase in the text of Genesis identifies them as two, 'the man and his wife' (2:25). After the Great Treason of Genesis 3, God addresses each, 'To the woman he said . . .' (3:16) and 'to Adam he said' (3:17). They are not only one, but two. Nor can we suggest that this act of sin destroyed the oneness in a fundamental way. In verse 21, God recognizes the enduring nature of the marriage: 'for Adam and for his wife'. They are both two and one. Again the observation of Pagels, (or Thomas or Chrysostom), even as I reject it, seems to emphasize the importance of this Marriage Text as a conclusion and climax to the twin creation accounts. As Solomon speaks through the voice of the bride: 'my beloved is mine, and I am his' (Song of Songs 2:16). Rather than simple oneness resulting from the first marriage, the text of Genesis emphasizes oneness which retains twoness, imaging the One-and-Many nature of God. As Cyril of Alexandria writes, 'God created co-being'.[79]

Even here, it may be worth a peek ahead into the biblical theology of this Marriage Text, with help from Malachi and Calvin:

> Did he not make them one, with a portion of the Spirit in their union? And what was the one God seeking? Godly offspring. So guard yourselves in your spirit, and let none of you be faithless to the wife of your youth. 'For the man who does not love his wife but divorces her', says the LORD, the God of Israel, 'covers his garment with violence, says the LORD of hosts'. So guard yourselves in your spirit, and do not be faithless (Malachi 2:15–16).

Calvin explains: 'Malachi also means the same thing when he relates, (ii. 15,) that one man was created by God, whilst, nevertheless, he possessed the fullness of the Spirit.'[80] Not only does he tell us that the two are one, but to the two, God adds his Spirit, so three, constituting a minor trinity. Did Malachi enhance the simple understanding of the Marriage Text as One-and-Many into something that is specifically trinitarian? Marriage is, at least for Malachi through Calvin's pen, three-in-one.

Excursus: Why Use 'One-and-Many' for God Instead of 'Trinity' or Even 'Three-in-One'?

I do not want any of you, my readers, to be distracted by the language, 'One-and-Many'. The Bible affirms and I agree: the God of the Bible is trinitarian. But what is 'Trinity'? In the fourth century, the church was forced by the new and errant teachings of Arius (256–336) to find clear language to refute Arius and assert what they had always believed. So, in 325 at Nicea, they began wrestling with the correct language for the relationship between Jesus Christ and the Father. And over the next century, the church continued to wrestle, not so much about *what* they believed, but for precise language with which they could accurately reflected the Bible's witness about the relationship of the Father, the Son, and the Spirit. This took place in the context of two cultures, reflected through their dominant languages, Latin and Greek. The Cappadocian Fathers provided the dominant voice and clarifying wisdom. Augustine, in the fifth century, wrote the major work that summed up the century-long work, *de Trinitate*. In English, the best wording they discovered was this: God is Trinity: one *nature* and three *persons*. More simply, YHWH is One-and-Three. So, why do I not simply say, God is Trinity? Or even God is Three-in-One? Why say God is One-and-Many?

My first response is that both 'Trinity' and 'Three-in-One' are correct and would serve well here. Nonetheless, for two considerations, I chose the more general 'One-and-Many'. The *first reason* is the Marriage Text, itself, which is the anchor for this biblical theology of marriage. Here Adam & Eve are represented as two-and-one. Augustine (as noted above), noticed this glaring numeric 'discrepancy' in the Marriage Text. He would add their forthcoming children to make a numerical match, grouping their children together into 'one' or counting only their first. Also, as I noted in the previous section, Malachi declared that all marriages are, in fact, three-in-one, a minor trinity. While I have no interest in dismissing Malachi, this is a development on the original theme, one which is not revealed nor explicitly expressed by Genesis 2. Christ agrees. When Christ recounts

Genesis 2 in Matthew 19, he cites Moses with no emendation or consideration of Malachi or help for Augustine, noting with precision that 'the two shall be one'. This brings me to the *second reason*. It is *the class* of 'one-and-many' which is the key that allows humans to image God, not agreement of number, two or three. In other words, some might ask, how can a two-in-one human marriage image the Three-in-One God? The reason is this: 'one-and-many' is a class or kind to which Adam & Eve enter in marriage as two-in-one, joining YHWH who is Three-in-One. This is not based on a strict counting, but rather the one-and-manyness of marriage. Humanity ('man') is not 'alone' (which is 'not good'), nor is humanity 'two' but not united, nor is humanity merged into a monolithic 'one' by marriage (recall that individual naming continues in the very next verse, 2:25). Instead, Adam & Eve image God in that they are neither one, nor many, but one-and-many. One-and-many stands distinct from all that is monolithic and all that is partitioned. The imaging of God is not in the 'counting' of the how-manyness, but rather that, like God, Adam & Eve in their two-in-oneness are like God who is Three-in-One, bearing all the distinctions and all the unity. 'One-and-many' highlights this 'class' rather than the actual 'counting'. I will continue to use this term throughout the book.

Summary: Genesis 2:18–25 as the Trinitarian Climax and Conclusion of Creation

At the end of this first of two exegetical sections, I have shown reasons to affirm Barth's observation that Genesis 2:18–25, the Marriage Text, is the climax and conclusion to the twin creation accounts. This included Sailhamer's observation of the disjunctive markers in 1:2 and 3:1, markers which frame both accounts by separation, and his narrative framing with a concluding poetic section and an epilogue. Also Barth's own argument which included the observation of the dramatic pauses of God before each of the human creation accounts. I have also shown reasons to consider that the climatic position of this text is revealed as it displays God in his One-and-Many nature in the marriage of Adam & Eve. The argument is from a constellation of indications which support the otherwise inexplicable climax, 'they shall become one' (Gen. 2:24). Genesis 2:18–25 is, for all the reasons given above, a climax and a conclusion to what came before. Marriage provides the drama (perhaps I should say, a sacrament)[81] which resolves the otherwise incomplete imaging of God in his human creatures and the ancient philosophical 'problem' of the one-and-the-many. Kevin Vanhoozer noticed this and wrote, 'In marriage there is a recognition of both sameness (one flesh) and otherness (two distinct persons). "This is a great mystery" (Eph. 5:32) – great enough, perhaps, to illustrate the triune identity?'[82] Yes. And offering a full tithe of the words from the two chapters, the author of Genesis provides us with a basis to discern what Vanhoozer calls 'first theology', the nature of the relationship between God and the Scripture. In the opening text, God has offered us a significant insight into his triune life. In so doing, it also provides us with a grounding anchor-point for a biblical theology of marriage. In the next exegetical section, I will consider the place of the same text as it anticipates the Fall and God's nature: his covenant-faithfulness.

2

Genesis 2:18–25: Anticipating God's Covenant-Faithfulness

Therefore, behold, I will allure her, and bring her into the wilderness, and speak tenderly to her.[1]

This declaration of God in Hosea 2 displays an intense intimacy – shocking to readers who are following the storyline, but not to those who know God. Indeed, this announcement follows the stark reality of Israel's adultery: 'And I will punish her for the feast days of the Baals when she burned offerings to them and adorned herself with her ring and jewellery, and went after her lovers and forgot me, declares the LORD' (Hos. 2:13). Indeed, as Raymond Ortlund frames this tragedy, 'Israel has made Yahweh a cuckold'.[2] But against and contrary to this reality, God makes a decisive and characteristic move: 'I will allure her in the wilderness'. Who could have anticipated this?! This is characteristic for God if we are paying attention to his story, and if we understand the nature of marriage in God's word. Throughout the Bible, God is explicating his very nature and character by the real analogy of marriage which culminated creation. Marriage reveals God's One-and-Many nature and his character of faithfulness to the unfaithful.

Still, it is true that, as yet, nothing in the text of Hosea has prepared us for this response. While this alluring does anticipate the story of Hosea and Gomer, that is only if we read ahead! Readers are probably shocked when YHWH addresses faithless Israel as his beloved bride and, in so doing, uses a word we rarely use, even face to face with our own spouse: 'allure'. Such honest and joyful intimacy may be far too rare in our world, even among happily married couples. And yet, uncomfortably, this intimacy is displayed by our God toward his adulteress, when he declares, 'Therefore, I will allure her'. How can this be?

Just as the Marriage Text turns on the word 'therefore' (Gen. 2:24), so also here it alerts us to a new and critical teaching. This is so disturbing to us, so counterintuitive, that perhaps it explains why the Septuagint (LXX, the Greek translation of the Hebrew Bible) translates this verse with the verb *planao* which means to lead astray or wander aimlessly.[3] It is as if the translator could not hold God's intimate gaze and decided instead on, 'Therefore, because of your idolatry, I will lead you astray in the wilderness.' *This* makes some good sense to many readers, perhaps most! With fairness, this translation is possible, given the semantic domain of the Hebrew *patah*. But it fails in context, for God continues, unambiguously, 'there I will speak *tenderly* to her', where 'tenderly' is fitting only as a partner for the concept of 'allure', not 'lead astray'. So YHWH *characteristically* displays intimacy which we do not expect, no matter how often he acts this way. In response, we are likely to turn our face away and blush, or rant against such misplaced passion. But we must not! God would allure his people and meet them in the desert and speak tenderly to them – to us. But why?

In the previous chapter I considered the Marriage Text in relation to Genesis 1&2; it is the climax and conclusion. As such, the Marriage Text proclaims the fuller imaging of God in Man and Woman who are now not (merely) two but (also) one. In their newfound oneness through marriage they image the Trinity, the God who is One-and-Many. Now I will look at the same text in its dual role as the bridge to the Fall, the breaking of the covenant in Genesis 3, finding a second role for this text in Genesis 1–3. As such, the Marriage Text displays not only God's nature, but his character: it anticipates God's covenant-faithfulness even through and against our covenant failure.

The Relationship of Genesis 2:18–25 to Genesis 3

The survey of historical commentary on the Marriage Text in the previous chapter revealed a number of Bible teachers who not only perceived this text as a climax and conclusion to the two creation accounts, but understood it as a preparation of the reader for the Fall in Genesis 3. But is 'Fall' even the right metaphor? It is not a word selected by the biblical author in regard to this event, but our 'traditional' term of choice. The author is merely descriptive: 'they ate'; 'their eyes were opened'; and 'God cursed'. What term contains these events and describes them well? It is not as if the invention of theological terms is wrong, but is 'the Fall' precise? Henri Blocher proposes that what is happening in Genesis 3 is not a 'Fall' but rather the 'breaking [of] the covenant'.[4] 'The Fall' is more apt, perhaps, for what happened to the great dragon of Revelation 12:4 when he rebelled and was 'cast down to earth'. So, with John Milton and the author of Revelation, we say, 'Satan fell'. But in what way did Adam fall? Perhaps C.S. Lewis helps us against Milton. Given Adam & Eve's treason against God, perhaps a covenant-breaking metaphor, the Great Divorce, is more accurate than a geographic metaphor, the Fall. For the purposes of this particular project, it is more apt. It draws us to God's intended heart of the matter. Indeed, when Adam & Eve sinned, they broke the covenant with God, and so also damaged the marriage covenant established in Genesis 2. Because of custom, and the convenience of short words, I will at times use 'the Fall' (so capitalized) to stand for the tragedy Adam & Eve instigated when they broke covenant with God, divorcing him, and choosing another lover, the serpent.[5]

Who reads the Marriage Text as an anticipation of the Fall? Who witnessed in this text explicit preparation of the reader (of us) for what would follow in chapter 3? How does the Marriage Text, and what precedes it, prepare us for Adam & Eve's failure to keep the covenant which God made with them? This may be ground to propose God's deep intentionality in positioning the covenant of marriage where he did, early in the text, and as he did, before the tragic introduction of evil. While I reviewed ancient and modern commentaries on Genesis 2 in the last chapter, let me highlight and extend those observations as they reflect on the Fall.

In *Against Heresies*, Irenaeus (130–202) writes as though the Marriage Text plays no significant place, other than as the context for the first couple. This might be perceived merely as an oversight, or perhaps an indication that an investigation of the Marriage Text was not germane to his goals. Irenaeus focuses on recapitulation theory: Christ, the new and victorious Head, recapitulates Adam, the vanquished head. Similarly, he writes about the triumph of the virgin, Mary, over the fallen virgin, Eve (3.22.4 and 5.19.1). But how fitting it would have been, given these themes ('recapitulation' combines the idea of 'headship' with the role of 'representative'), if Irenaeus had explored how the Marriage Text completes creation most fully and sharpens our grief and cry for recapitulation because it anticipates Christ's restoration of his bride, the church, as a recapitulation of Adam's failed care for Eve. But he did not.

In the fourth century, Chrysostom wrote in *Homilies on Genesis* (Homily 15) that he understood this text as a bridge for the reader, connecting chapter 2 with chapter 3, focusing on 'naked without shame' (see 2:25). He observed that the author of Genesis takes up 'naked' as a lexical key to the story of the Fall (Gen. 3:1,7,10,11).[6] Yet, he proclaims no greater work or significance for this text. However, I will return to this exegetical insight as quite significant.

In the fifth century, Augustine primarily understood the Marriage Text to provide a protection of marriage for procreation – a purpose I argue does not even fit the text. Yet he saw more. He also affirms that the Marriage Text anticipates the Fall. The conclusion in verse 25, 'the man and his wife were both naked and were not ashamed', prepares us to comprehend the post-Fall declaration, 'they knew that they were both naked' (Gen. 3:7). But Augustine's observations and connections between the texts are intended to highlight 'concupiscence', lust, as the core problem. He does this, as in the case of procreation, even though it is explicit in neither the Marriage Text nor the story of the Fall.[7] It is worth highlighting this point. In Genesis 1 God provided for the sexual reproduction of his creatures. In 1:22 we read, 'God blessed them [the creatures of the waters], saying, "Be fruitful and multiply and fill the waters in the seas, and let birds multiply on the earth."' And also in chapter 1, he said to the new humans, 'Be fruitful and multiply and fill the earth and subdue it'. In both cases, sexual reproduction was God's blessing. But God is doing something distinct in chapter 2. Rather than an expansion of that blessing, it is another, one which addresses the God-identified problem, 'it is not good for man to be alone'. Surprising to many, and so surprising that some readers are sure it is there somewhere, there is in this Marriage Text no hint of sexual reproduction to the end of producing progeny. Rather, the reader is being prepared for what is about to happen.[8]

While the earliest Christian readers of Genesis understood a relationship of the Marriage Text to the Fall, there were a number of exegetical errors and very little development for many hundreds of years. Later, in the thirteenth century, Thomas Aquinas understood the creation of women as an occasion for sin, so in this way, the Marriage Text anticipated the Fall. Yet he defends Woman's place in the world as part of God's goodness: 'If God had deprived the world of all those things which proved an occasion of sin, the universe would have been imperfect. Nor was it fitting for the common good to be destroyed in order that individual evil might be avoided; especially as God is so powerful that He can direct any evil to a good end.'[9] This is less than a high view of women, but in his own way, Aquinas does make it clear that this text prepares the reader for the Fall.

Hundreds of years later, Luther (1483–1536) is helpful, but not helpful enough. Introducing this text, he writes simply, 'now the household is set up'.[10] While not making as much of this as he could, he does note that the female human is not introduced like the female animals – nothing like! Quite helpfully he corrects his Latin translation. Rather than 'like unto himself', he explains from the Hebrew of Genesis 2:18 that it is better translated, 'I shall make him a help which should be *before him*'.[11] His emphasis is rightly placed on relationship, rather than mere similarity. By this Luther intends to make the point that, unlike the animals, human couples are to be inseparable.[12] This points forward to the threat of the Fall and the danger to the first marriage covenant, giving a weight to the Marriage Text which is greater than mere 'housekeeping' for procreation. It is a significant establishment for people, distinct from the animals, which sounds a warning before the Fall, suggesting a second meaning.

More recently, Gordon Wenham suggested that the text moves us to hear the story as a bridge to the Fall. Considering Genesis 2:5–3:24 as a unit, Wenham identifies seven distinct 'scenes', chiastically[13] paired (see Table 2.1).

Table 2.1 Wenham's Chiastic Structure of Genesis 2–3

Scene 1 (2:5–17), creation of the Garden
  Scene 2 (2:18–25), Marriage Text
    Scene 3 (3:1–5), temptation by the serpent
      Scene 4 (3:6–8), the Fall
    Scene 5 (3:9–13), confrontation by God
  Scene 6 (3:14–21), judgment
Scene 7 (3:22–24), ejection from the Garden

Source: Gordon John Wenham, *Genesis 1–15, WBC 1* (Waco, TX: Word, 1987), pp. 49–51

Wenham pairs scenes 1 and 7, 2 and 6, 3 and 5, leaving scene 4 (Genesis 3:6–8) as the 'centerpiece of the narrative when the couple eat the forbidden fruit'.[14] Wenham refers to the Marriage Text as scene 2 which is uniquely paired with scene 6. At first this may not seem obvious, yet in both scenes, God, the man, the woman and the animals are all displayed, and God himself is the main actor. In this perspective, scene 2 (the Marriage Text) is the ideal, while scene 6 (God's judgment) is the actual. It is 'actual' for Wenham because it displays our post-Fall reality. By this pairing of the Marriage Text with God's Garden judgment, we witness an ongoing role for marriage after the Fall including: the promise of the proto-gospel (*protoevangelium*, 3:15; 3:20), pain in procreation (3:16a), and yes, trouble in marriages (3:16b; 3:17a). But in that very trouble, even the deadly threat to marriage, this will become the point at which God's own character is displayed and revealed to us. So in this way, the Marriage Text anticipates the Fall, and so the Marriage Text prepares us for a second insight into God's character which will be revealed even through fallen marriages. However, Wenham does little to develop this point into a biblical theology of marriage.

Dietrich Bonhoeffer (1906–45) completely separates the Marriage Text from the previous material. He argues that an underlying problem is created by the proximity of the first two creation accounts with this *inexplicable change* from creation to procreation: 'It does not seem relevant that the creation of woman is mentioned just here.'[15] His statement is almost an apology for Moses' lack of literary acumen. Seeking a place for this account of marriage in the fabric of the narrative, he understands it to point *only* forward, and with a bit of incongruity, connects it uncomfortably with Genesis 3 and the account of the Fall: 'It is clear that in the writer's view the creation of woman is part of the pre-history of the Fall of man.'[16] But even this good observation seems to be with reluctance and almost irritation at Moses. Still, he is seeing this key aspect and pointing us to it.

Similarly, Derek Kidner links the second account of creation with the Fall story, dividing the text at 2:4 and continuing through 3:24. Like some others, he perceives a radical separation between the first and second 'sagas'. As such, the Marriage Text is not a 'climax and conclusion' to both accounts. Still he notes a significant and very tight textual relationship between 1:2 and 2:5, so that 2:5 is its recapitulation:

The earth was without form and void, and darkness was over the face of the deep (1:2).

When no bush of the field was yet in the land and no small plant of the field had yet sprung up – for the LORD God had not caused it to rain on the land, and there was no man to work the ground . . . (2:5).

Kidner paraphrases both with the words, 'when God made the earth it was not initially the hospitable place that we know'.[17] This is helpful. Both accounts develop the creation of man who is the 'climax' of God's creation. He also sees a similar connection between the Marriage Text and 1:27–28, as many others have pointed out. And in this text in chapter 2, he perceives 'God's true pattern, perfect ease between them'[18] – something that is indeed about to be broken in the Fall.

And while Sailhamer was instrumental in showing the strong literary ties between the Marriage Text and the prior accounts of creation, he is also helpful in showing how it foreshadows the Fall in Genesis 3. He observes that the 'shrub of the field' and the 'plant of the field' (2:5) are not vegetation, but cultivated plants, and so they anticipate the time of cultivation after the Fall when thorns and thistles will infect the food crops (3:18).[19] Similarly, the lack of rain on the 'face of the ground' anticipates the judgment by flood (6:7; 7:4; 7:23).[20] Indeed, 'in the description of that land . . . we can already see the coming of the time when human beings would become aliens and strangers in a foreign land'.[21] Sailhamer also observes that 'the break between Gen 2:24 and 2:25ff is marked by a change in the narrative "scene" from the place of Adam's "deep sleep" to that of the place of the "temptation"'.[22]

There is one more significant connection between Genesis 2 and 3 to examine here. Many have noticed the chiastic pattern of Genesis 2:4 which I show at Table 2.2 graphically:

Table 2.2 Structure of Genesis 2:4

These are the generations
    of the *heavens* and the earth
        when they were *created*,
            in the day that the LORD God *made*
    the earth and the *heavens*.

This bridge verse sits between the two accounts and specifically at the head of the second. The chiasm shows the integrity of the verse (with the reversal of the merism: 'the heavens and the earth' into 'the earth and the heavens'), so that it cannot be divided between the accounts. The 'generations' (Hebrew, *toledot*) shows the beginning of a new idea (see below). And the name of God which Moses uses here, 'LORD God', rather than show a distinction between sources, shows movement in the Text. That is, while Genesis 1 is dominated by exclusive references to God as 'Elohim' (usually translated as 'God'), here we find not a new title, but a merger of titles: LORD God (YHWH Elohim). Interestingly, this particular reference to God is made here by Moses in chapters 2–3, distinctively, giving this text a kind of coherence. In fact, this title, 'LORD God', is used by Moses only in Genesis 2–3 (five times in Gen. 2 and four times in Gen. 3) and nowhere else in the Pentateuch except once in Exodus 9:30. The result is to show a coherence between Genesis 2:4–25 and chapter 3 while retaining a connection to chapter 1.

All of these textual and structural observations do reveal significant connections between the Marriage Text (and its contextual setting in Gen. 2) and the Fall (Gen. 3). The effect, then, is that Moses also intended the Marriage Text, which is connected to the creation accounts, to anticipate the Fall. In this we receive a crushing blow to marriage and image, but as we will discover, we are anticipating hope, a move about to come on God's part.

But a good student of the Bible might ask: what about the way Genesis is (intentionally and) structurally divided by the phrase, 'these are the generations' (the Hebrew *toledot* constructions)? We find this in Genesis 2:4, dividing the first and second accounts, and not resolved until the second occurrence of *toledot* in Genesis 5:1. This seems to present a challenge. How can I suggest a structural integrity of a section from Genesis 1:2 to 4:1, if this divides the creation accounts? No longer is there a coherent section which contains the two creation accounts, the Marriage Text and the Fall which could be the foundation for a biblical theology of marriage.

Genesis is divided, systematically, by many uses of this word *toledot*, which means 'generations'.[23] Indeed the first occurrence falls in Genesis 2:4 and the second in 5:1. The *toledot* of Genesis 2:4, 'these are the *generations* of the heavens and the earth' (or as translated by some, 'the account'), divides the first creation account from the second and continues the second division through to the end of Genesis 4. We must feel the necessity and weight of the *toledot* as a marker and divider of the text of Genesis; it cannot be dismissed or even diminished. As Jason DeRouchie asserts, the *toledot* marker is the 'shaping device for [Moses'] work.'[24] Specifically, DeRouchie's goal is to discern how the *toledot* work to establish the theology of the author and makes the case that each use narrows the focus 'from progenitor to progeny' so that the missional focus can be felt by the reader: God's intent for Israel to bless the whole world.[25] In this context, he understands Genesis 1:1–2:3 as the preface and lens to all of the *toledot* sections, which successively narrow the focus of the 'called' and 'chosen'. Key to his understanding of how the *toledot* works is his observation that five of the ten phrases (*elleh toledot*, where *elleh* means 'these', so 'these generations' or 'these are the generations') are introduced by the Hebrew conjunctive character.[26] He proposes that these five divisions in Moses' text (**velleh toledot**, '**and** these are the generations') are minor divisions, whereas the five *toledot* phrases without the conjunction (called 'asyndeton', lacking the *waw* conjunction) are the major divisions. Further, what makes them 'major' is that each of these five represents an intentional focal narrowing of God's spotlight to illuminate those who are called by God. This movement is from all of creation down to the specific descendants of Israel. DeRouchie's work should stand and indeed I agree that Moses is using this structure,[27] with and without the conjunction, to convey this idea of a theological narrowing of God's elect, through whom God will bless the whole world. What then of the Marriage Text, which falls in the middle of the first *toledot* section?

In affirming the critical significance of the *toledot* pattern, am I reversing myself, if I still see a section framed from 1:2–4:1? Not at all. This *toledot* pattern does not prevent Moses from doing many things in his multidimensional text, some of which are out of phase with each other. That is, while the *toledot* study is convincing, Moses is doing more. Sailhamer's structural argument, and Barth's literary argument, demonstrate another distinct pattern in the text that places the Marriage Text as a 'climax and conclusion' to both creation accounts and anticipatory of what follows in the Fall. The former reveals God's character in the final move to imaging, the two shall be one, and the latter foreshadows God's faithful covenant in a shattered covenant. In this regard the Marriage Text is multivalent; it serves multiple purposes at once. It serves as a climax and a bridge in one section, and the *toledot* frame in a less (locally) prominent structure. But it also serves to alert the reader to a change, fitting more closely with the *toledot*. Genesis is a multi-threaded literary work.

Marriage: Anticipating the Broken Covenant

I have already stated the second role I propose, as others have, for the Marriage Text: God's covenant-faithfulness. The Fall is the first move in the drama of our breaking with God's covenant. But before this tragedy, we discover marriage which will represent God's faithfulness to his own glory, to his covenant, and even to us, covenant-breakers. This has deep exegetical grounding.

Returning to the change in the name of God between accounts which I examined above, recall that Moses shifted his address in Genesis 1 from 'God' (Elohim) to 'Lord God' (YHWH Elohim) in Genesis 2–3. John Collins notes that this shift by Moses is to call to the mind of the readers (who sit historically downstream from these events) that YHWH is the covenant-keeping God who introduced himself in Exodus 3:12–17 and 6:2–8. He is YHWH who is faithful to his promises, a 'covenant-making and covenant-keeping God, specifically as the God who made promises to the patriarchs of Israel.'[28] The very introduction of God, who saturates this text, displays this second meaning of marriage.

We also discover the Marriage Text as full of charged words which command our attention. These include such words as 'alone', 'father', 'mother', 'leave', 'one flesh', 'naked', and 'ashamed'. Interestingly, the inflection and emotional impact of some of these words is changed in the move from the Marriage Text (Gen. 2) to the Fall (Gen. 3).

In this regard, we considered 'alone' in the previous chapter. I asked how it is that the reader (or God!) could understand that 'alone' was 'not good' since many assume that God himself is alone because God is One. This question turned out to be a key for our understanding of Moses' intention in this text and so for God's intention. This word, 'alone', is a dissonance which makes us wonder immediately about Genesis 1:27 ('in the image of God . . . male and female') and challenges what we just read in 1:28 ('be fruitful and multiply'). Readers are alert to this connection, but not yet clear how Moses will develop this disconnection. The pressure point of Moses' use of 'alone' was neither in regard to isolation (for Adam had the animals, and even more, he had God), nor particularly in regard to sexual multiplication of the species. This point may be a concern of the reader, in part, but it will not be the concern of the Marriage Text which follows and concludes as an answer to the question in verse 18. Rather, I showed that the point of 'alone' was the inability of Adam, as the one-and-the-same man, to image God who is One-and-Many. For that great privilege, God created Woman from Man's side, another person to be with him. She was of the same nature, yet also distinct from Adam (in gender and in a unique person who could be before him). The breach of 'aloneness', the breach that was called 'not good' by God, was healed when God pronounced, 'They [the *two*] shall become as *one* flesh'. In this sense the significance of the challenge of 'alone' was changed for the reader from a personal and existential concern for aloneness, to God's goal of imaging.

To see the next meaning, we observe another deeply charged word which suffers a radical distortion: 'naked' implying 'no shame' is twisted into 'naked' and full of 'shame'. At the close of the Marriage Text we read, 'And the man and his wife were both naked and were not ashamed' (v. 25). This is very like the blessing spoken by a pastor (a priest, or a rabbi or a father) over the couple at the end of a marriage covenant ceremony, a wedding. It is a good word of peace announced for all to hear, a blessing spoken with the very authority of God. But these words are a blessing, spoken not over the couple but to the reader. The words, 'not ashamed', are the author's explicit direction to the reader that we are to understand this word, *naked*, not as we might hear it today, but as intended in context, a blessing. To us, now, the word 'naked' clangs awkwardly and is most often a note of shame. It plays a minor key to our ear, refusing to resolve in the last measure of this Marriage Text. It declares that what was then is not now. Indeed, this blessing is about to be broken – terribly wrecked. From now on, the word 'naked' will be displayed in the biblical text as 'shameful nakedness'. But not yet. Not here. Not then. Here Adam & Eve's nakedness is without shame, and such is God's blessing. What is about to change?

Moses has led us with decisive intentionality. He now uses a strong play on words as he moves from the Marriage Text to the Fall. The Hebrew word for Adam & Eve's nakedness, an adjective in Genesis 2:25, is *aroom*.[29] As we now move into Genesis 3:1, the serpent is also introduced as *aroom*, more *aroom* than any other beast. Is the serpent naked? If so, that is not Moses' point. Rather than 'naked', and specifically in this context, this Hebrew homonym means something like 'crafty' (esv) or 'subtle' (kjv). Moses is not casually using this adjective for the serpent. Indeed, Hebrew narrative usually expects the reader to infer character from the explicit actions of the person within the story and does not paint the actor with adjectives.[30] It is also interesting that this particular adjective, *aroom*, is sometimes laudable (Prov. 12:16; 13:16, prudent) and other times, derogatory (Exod. 21:14, Josh. 9:4, cunning); all depends upon context. Here, the *aroom* serpent should act as an alarm for the reader. But if Eve should have been alarmed, she was not. Yet, the reader is on the alert for a snake in the grass, the one who has slithered up toward Eve. Both are *aroom*. She is naked and unashamed; the serpent is crafty and very dangerous.

The character of the serpent, crafty, is the first dissonance for the reader around the word *aroom*. But not the last. The second reveals itself in the terrible corruption of the meaning of naked from blessing to curse. This Hebrew word for naked (as an adjective, noun, and verb) appears frequently in the five books of Moses and in all of those instances its use is negative, except here in 2:25.[31] Here alone is 'naked' used in a positive way. This should not expose the reader to a great surprise, for much changes with the Fall – innocence is corrupted. Those who have read ahead in the books of Moses have been exposed to Leviticus 18, a potpourri of incest. In that later text, *aroom* sounds a drumbeat, rhythmically standing in for unlawful sexual intercourse within the family. Of most interest to me in this investigation is the change which shreds hope to tatters in Genesis 3. First in Genesis 3:7, after eating the fruit, Adam & Eve discover their state: 'Then the eyes of both were opened, and they knew that they were naked. And then they sewed fig leaves together and made themselves loincloths.' It is clearly the case that previously they could see the fact of their nakedness, but then it was a blessing. Or rather, it had no meaning, indicating their innocence. In all likelihood, there was not even a sense in Adam & Eve's minds of two possible states, naked or clothed, of which they were one, naked. Rather, they were in a perfectly good state, and the only state conceivable. But when they ate the fruit, their terror-filled observation seems to be the first sign that everything has changed. The minor key is resolved, but with resolution the theme is no longer sung. Shame has exposed all. From this point forward in Moses and in the whole of the Bible, naked has a negative implication.

Still, the brokenness and shame are not complete. They must learn something more awful: their verdant loincloths are inadequate. Though they covered what they should cover, they are still shamefully naked. So, when God blew into the Garden like an east wind of judgment, Adam confessed to him, 'I heard the sound of you in the garden, and I was afraid, *because I was naked*, and I hid myself' (Gen. 3:10). Nakedness has transformed from an idyll blessing to a cursed and shameful exposure of their sinful state that no human-fabricated clothing could cover. Indeed, both the words 'naked' and its Hebrew homonym 'crafty' have sounded a warning note, anticipating the 'curse'. No human covering can hide the shame of their nakedness before God.

What comes next is a shock, a radical move on the part of God that gives a second meaning to the Marriage Text that preceded the Fall. God responds to Adam & Eve's failure, the broken relationship between them and their God, with the *protoevangelium* (Gen. 3:15) and the first covering sacrifice (3:21), healing the nakedness. God's curse upon the serpent, the *protoevangelium*, is this: 'I will put enmity between you and the woman, and between your offspring and her offspring; he shall bruise your head, and you shall bruise his heel.' This declaration of hope is followed by a drama, a specific action of God that anticipates the fulfilment of this promise: God himself clothes Adam & Eve in the skins of animals – skins that were perhaps still bloody and warm. This constitutes the first sacrifice for the covering of sins, a promise of what was to come by the Seed who will bruise the seed of the serpent. Together these texts constitute God's promise of another lasting covenant which he himself will guarantee. Indeed, without this work, God would not be able to take his bride to himself – the relentless direction in which we are about to discover God is moving. This new covenant will be more closely tied to the marriage metaphor than any other and it will be resolved only when we come to the end of God's work in time, in the book of Revelation.

But is this marriage actually broken according to the story, according to this text? Is there specific evidence that the Garden marriage is broken by the Fall? Yes, there is. As we read Genesis 3, we discover that Woman is no longer a helper and Adam does not treat Woman according to his marital pledge. First Adam. Adam pledged to care for Eve as if she was himself, 'bone of my bones and flesh of my flesh'. But he has not done so! Eve, whom God created as a helper, now hinders Adam.

Adam failed as the priest in God's Garden. Greg Beale and others have noted that Adam's commission in Genesis 2:15, which is often translated 'cultivate and keep', is actually an indication of Adam's priesthood. Indeed, this pairing of two common Hebrew words is used only as a pair elsewhere in regard to the Levitical priesthood. Together they serve as the commission to priests: 'serve and guard'.[32] We can expect that Moses, writing this text in Genesis as support and background for the new nation of God in the desert, would make the connection, as we must as well. Did Adam fail to serve his wife and guard the Garden? He is not specifically condemned for that by God. But of a kind of necessity, he did fail. On that fateful day, the snake was in the temple – later to be declared an unclean animal.[33] In this sense, Adam did not serve Eve in his role as priest (or husband, or friend!) in her time of temptation. This did not enhance their marriage.

Also, by the story, the command of God was given to Adam alone. It was his responsibility to make it known. Adam failed as a prophet. Indeed, Romans 5 makes an explicit connection between the command given to Adam by God in the Garden with commandments given to Moses in the wilderness. There Paul writes, 'Yet death reigned from Adam to Moses, even over those whose sinning was not like the transgression of Adam' (Rom. 5:14). The point for Paul is a comparison of the positive command from God to Adam: 'do not eat', with the Law that was given through Moses. The woman's interaction with the snake makes it clear that while Adam acted as a prophet, he made God's command known to her, yet the woman was not able to recite the command with precision. So when the snake distorted God's word, 'Did God actually say, "You shall not eat of any tree in the garden"?' (v. 1), the woman failed to speak God's word back to him with accuracy: 'You shall not eat of the fruit of the tree that is in the midst of the garden, neither shall you touch it, lest you die' (v. 3). We discover errors in her catechism: the addition of a prohibition against touching the fruit ('or even touch it!') and the weakening of the penalty (to 'lest you die' from 'you shall surely die'). Did Eve fail in her lessons or did Adam fail in his prophetic work of catechetical preparation? We cannot tell.

Also, Adam failed as a king, as the co-regent of the Garden under God. He ate the fruit against God's explicit command. He was not deceived as was his wife,[34] but instead he rebelled. He saw his wife with the fruit in hand, perhaps even witnessing the event of her failure: 'She also gave some to her husband who was with her, and he ate' (Gen. 3:6). In eating the fruit, Adam failed Eve as a king and leader, or perhaps as co-regent. He neither protected her nor used his resources of strength and courage for her benefit. He also failed God as appointed sub-regent, obeying his fellow human, rather than his God. He threw in with Eve against God.[35]

But worse, Adam also turned on Eve, blaming her. When God approached Adam, perhaps as the east wind of judgment,[36] Adam panicked, abdicating his regency: 'The woman whom you gave to be with me, she gave me fruit of the tree, and I ate' (Gen. 3:12). In fact, in turning against Eve, he also turned against God – again. He blames God: 'the woman *you* gave me!' And then, God declared the failure of their marriage: 'Your desire shall be for your husband, [but] he shall rule over you' (Gen. 3:16). This text is interpreted in various ways. It should be read in the light of its only parallel text, Genesis 4:6–7: 'The LORD said to Cain, "Why are you angry, and why has your face fallen? If you do well, will you not be accepted? And if you do not do well, sin is crouching at the door. Its *desire* is for you, but you must *rule* over it."' Here, the same word pair is used by our author: 'desire' and 'rule'. Both words are common in the Hebrew Old Testament and their meanings must be discerned in context. Here they provide context for themselves both by pairing and by proximity. Clearly in the second case, no idea of 'romance' is invested in the word 'desire'. And in both, the common word 'rule' has the weight of domination and control. Linguistic symmetry links 4:7 and 3:15, so we have warrant to paraphrase the curse in this way: 'Your desire will be to control your husband, but instead of leading, he will dominate you.' While this understanding is not universal,[37] even those who disagree conceive a shift from blessed egalitarianism to fallen complementarity in Adam & Eve's marital relations.[38] Either way, marriage is broken by the Fall.

We have seen the destruction. Nakedness is no longer a blessing, but a state of abject poverty, exposed to the wrath of God – and representing a terrible change in the marriage. The judgment of God is on the marriage itself. Yet, through marriage, through the Seed, we will discover healing. It is the Marriage Text which has laid the groundwork, the human antithesis of God's covenant-faithfulness.

Summary: The Broken Covenant Anticipates God's Faithfulness to Us

It seems easy for many to observe the way that the Marriage Text anticipates the Fall – easier at least than perceiving it as a 'climax and conclusion' to the twin creation accounts. Still, I have attempted to show that it functions in both directions on solid exegetical and structural grounds. In the former sense, human marriage reveals the nature of God as One-and-Many. In the latter, anticipating the Fall, it will reveal the contrasting character of God as the one who is always faithful to his covenants. Who could guess God's next moves that will take us from 'he drove out the man' (Gen. 3:24) to Adam & Eve's descendants, transformed by the battle of the Seed into his virgin bride (Rev. 21:2)? The story in Hosea makes just this point. It is a story of unreasonable hope which cannot be guessed at by the reader: 'Therefore, behold, I will allure her.' The 'behold' of the author is a sign that he knows what we will know – this is shocking and in no way anticipated in the story. Just as there is nothing left to repair after Adam & Eve have finished their reign of terror, looting the Garden, there was nothing left to repair in the relationship between Hosea and Gomer. And at this point in the story of Adam & Eve, we can see only destruction. If the proto-gospel in 3:15 justifies hope, and Adam in naming the animals gives us warrant for understanding it this way, we receive only the barest hint that marriage itself will be the very metaphor of hope.

Especially, at the end of the first *toledot*. Moving from the first exile in 3:24, the terrible destruction of marriage gets darker, even in this same text. Interestingly this progression occurs *within* the current *toledot* (generations) division of the text of Genesis (2:4–4:26), bringing it to a close. In this Sailhamer is even more helpful than I have explained. His structure, which draws 1:2–3:25 together as a single unit, reveals itself repeatedly in the deep fractal nature of the Pentateuch – the key message is framed and revealed at the smallest and largest structure of the book. The pattern of narrative, poem, and epilogue reveals structure on the smallest scale within Genesis, and also shapes the book over the whole of the Pentateuch. If we look at the largest scale, recognizing the whole of the five books as a single narrative, it closes in a great poem (Deut. 33, the blessing of Israel) and a long epilogue (Deut. 34, the death of Moses). This reveals a single structure that connects the five books *as a whole*.[39] On the smaller scale, I have already examined this pattern in Genesis 1:2–2:25 in which 2:23 (poetry) and 2:24–25 (epilogue) closes this first great section and is bounded (on Sailhamer) by the grammatical pattern in 1:2–3:1, revealing marriage as a climax and conclusion of the twin creation accounts. But there is also a deep connection between this section and the one that follows, into the close of the first *toledot*. In Genesis 4 the narrative account of the murder of Abel finds its boundary also in a poem (4:23–24, Lamech) and an epilogue (4:25–26, the birth of Seth). It is notable that while the dominant theme in Genesis 4 centres on murders – Cain of Abel (4:1–16) and then Lamech's retaliatory murder of a young man who wounded him (the poetry of vv. 23–24) – the context is marriage for both.[40] The fruit of Adam & Eve's marriage is spoiled, corrupted, or killed, and with the closing poem and epilogue of Lamech, ended. Lamech's boastful lecture to his wives, Adah and Zillah, is more important to him than the murdered men, who are not named. Here, as with Eve, Lamech tortures the very words of God to serve the evil desires of God's wilful human-creatures, in this case, himself. It is here, in his distortion, that we discover a deep connection between the poetry and epilogue of the first structure and the second. In Genesis 4, the poetry and epilogue shows a deeply twisted marriage: Lamech abuses God's word to defend his sinful actions before his two wives, rather than teaching them God's word. In fact, the covenant-keeping name of God, YHWH, so prominent in Genesis 2–3, is not named by Lamech or the narrator. The movement, around marriage, is from great expectations (Gen. 2:25), to corruption by the Fall (3:7–13,16–17), to the distorted image of marriage in Lamech (4:23–24).[41] Yet, buried in the middle of this, the chiastic centre perhaps, is the promise, the *protoevangelium*: 'I will put enmity between you and the woman and between your offspring and her offspring; he shall bruise your head and you shall bruise his heel' (Gen. 3:15). Even as Moses uses Lamech to draw a second structure to a close, within the first *toledot*, he highlights again the death of marriage – even as he prepares to recite the death of all in the next *toledot*: 'Seth lived . . . he fathered Enosh . . . Seth lived . . . *and he died.*' If anything is to breathe life back into marriage, it is not God's wilful human-creatures. What will God do now?

If marriage is the climax and conclusion to the twin creation accounts in the Marriage Text, and the Fall is the crisis which sets up the rest of the story, so also *marriage may be the climax and conclusion to the twin covenant accounts of the Old and New Testaments*. The very first climactic move of Scripture is marriage, but the Fall destroys this, and Lamech climactically displayed its ruin. Yet, marriage will be the hope of God's rescue of his world. Through marriage will come the Seed who will crush the head of Satan. Not marriage, but this Seed, is our hope. Yet, we will soon learn that, one day, the climax of history (the climax to the twin covenant accounts) will again be marriage. There is a wedding in the planning stages even now: 'And I saw the holy city, new Jerusalem, coming down out of heaven from God prepared as a bride adorned for her husband' (Rev. 21:2). Even our great failure anticipates God's faithfulness, for God will use marriage as the key metaphor to display his faithfulness. This is the investigation for Part Two, the theological section of this study.

Part Two

Theology: What God Intends by Marriage

In Part One, I examined the exegesis of God's locution, his words, in Genesis 2:18–25 and in their immediate context in Genesis 1–3. This Marriage Text reveals two truths about YHWH. First, this text displays God's One-and-Many nature as a climactic conclusion to the twin creation accounts of Genesis 1&2. Second, anticipating the Fall in Genesis 3, this text establishes an anchor point from which God will display his covenant-faithfulness – in stark contrast to the betrayal and division witnessed here: betrayal against God that divided man and woman from God and each other. Now we turn to investigate this word from God about himself in the scope of the Bible. Using the tool of biblical theology, I hope to show what God intends for us by revealing himself, so early, intensely, and dramatically, in this Marriage Text.

What is *biblical* theology? This is not the place for a full-blown pedantic assessment – although, as a pastor and professor, that sounds like fun to me. Perhaps just a brief pedantic assessment. Skip to the end of the paragraph if you are inclined. Biblical theology is often compared to systematic theology. Sometimes systematic theology fairs poorly, accused of bringing a system to the Bible and demanding answers, while biblical theology develops both questions and answers organically and inductively from the text. Of course, the former is true in some cases, but inductive studies can also suffer from the imported ideas and experiences of the one doing the biblical theology. However, in fairness, the descriptive adjectives alone, biblical and systematic, do not actually indict systematic theology as 'unbiblical' nor biblical theology as 'chaotic'. If theology is done with the best integrity that sinners can bring, then both are tools by which we can rightly discern (something of) the meaning intended by God through his word. So, systematic theology attempts to give precise theological assessments of biblical ideas: Who is God? What is revelation? What is the church? It intends to distil the whole of the biblical witness into the best answer that can be discerned from the textual witness. Biblical theology attempts to discern similar truths, generating many intermediate answers, resulting in a picture of how revelation unfolds throughout the text of the Bible. Each answer suggested by biblical theology is limited to a single context, one author, a group of authors, a specific historical frame, or even a specific genre within a frame. Each attempts to discern its answers (even the questions) inductively, from within the text. Together they form a vector or arc that shows how the ideas unfold throughout revelation. One way to think about the distinction between the two approaches to theology is that systematic theology is like reading the speed on your car's dashboard, while biblical theology is the information you would get from a GPS device. The former gives one precise answer at a glance. The latter provides a vector, speed and direction, and often many other statistics which may include way-points and details that cover only a portion of your trip. Together, this builds a picture of your route travelled and even some indication of the route ahead. The speedometer in your car tells you nothing of direction; it gives one number: how fast you are going. While a single number from your speedometer is 'simple', it is not simplistic. If you are driving your car and notice that the speed limit has been reduced (and perhaps even see a police car in the distance), you need an immediate simple answer from sensitive and precise equipment to give you a quick read on your speed at a glance. It is not something you could do trivially. Much hard work went into generating this 'simple' answer. So, when you see a police car in the distance, you do not wade through all the detail that your GPS gives you about route travelled, speed while moving, speed over the whole trip, highest speed, and current direction – and where the closest coffee shop is located near you; you want your current speed.

Systematic theology flattens historical issues (though when done well, those were considered, but do not remain in the answer), making a 'decision' on each topic of theology. For example, systematic theology tells us that creation is a trinitarian work. While Moses is consulted in Genesis, and John in his gospel, still the development of this doctrine over the scope of revelation is less important than the 'decision': creation is trinitarian. Biblical theology, by attempting to perceive the position of theology at various times and for different biblical authors, builds a picture of 'God's footprints' over time (at least and as best as we can determine them). As a result, biblical theology is like an arrow because the various 'decisions' at different times show movement, or in some cases, no movement. So, biblical theology is more like a GPS than a speedometer, showing not only the importance and the idea as revealed by all of Scripture, but how that idea has an arc, moving through God's word and the lives of his people. In that sense, biblical theology may even indicate a way into our future. But again, this is not to claim a lesser role for systematic theology. Biblical theology focuses on the unfolding path of God as he reveals himself, while systematic theology focuses on the final (and at times simplified) picture.

I have discerned two teachings from the Marriage Text in the context of Genesis 1–3. Now I will explore these, testing them in the rest of the Bible to see their development and discern their fuller meanings, an exercise in biblical theology. We will see that after the Fall, and continuing through all of the Bible, these two meanings are clearly portrayed in the text in regard to God's relationship with us – somewhat asymmetrically. The first chapter in Part Two will explore the Old Testament in the Hebrew order: the Torah, the Prophets, and the Writings of the Old Covenant. The next chapter will explore the New Testament in a similar rubric, the gospels (like the Torah, with a focus on John), the epistles (like the Prophets, with a focus on Ephesians), and the book of Revelation (like the Writings). I will see how they all use marriage as a metaphor which demonstrates God's faithfulness, and also clearly and slowly and decisively leads us to perceive his trinitarian nature within marriage. In doing this, I am following the path set out in my introduction, a model implied by speech-act theory. Having heard God's words, his locution in Part One, now in Part Two I will examine God's meaning, his illocution, using the lens of biblical theology.

But this is a brief work. Many others have displayed the detailed pattern of Israel as God's unfaithful wife in the Law and the Prophets and also God's rapturous desire to share a oneness with his people in the Writings. I will explore these, but rather than a full and thorough display of this development, this could be considered an audit. Instead of showing everything about the marriage metaphor, I am testing my thesis that the Marriage Text serves as a seed for a rightly construed biblical theology. If so, then this seed of the Marriage Text, as I have described it, will develop, and blossom, and bear fruit. Even in this brief investigation, the spouting seed should be found in developing stages along the way, and the crop harvested should both nourish us and provide us with a biblical harvest of these ideas. If so, even this short exploration may reveal that the Marriage Text grounds an ongoing drama which reveals our God as trinity and as the one who is ever faithful to his covenants.

3

Seeking God's Trinitarian Covenant-Faithfulness in the Old Testament

Things began quite well in the Garden. Ray Ortlund writes, 'If the Bible is telling us the truth about reality, then the universe we live in was created primarily with marital romance in mind. The heavens and the earth were created for the marriage of Adam and Eve. The new heavens and the new earth will be created for the marriage of Christ and his bride.'[1] Be encouraged! What began well in the Garden will end well in Revelation as we trace the movement of the biblical theology in God's revelation. But it is no 'spoiler alert' to remind the reader that almost everything in-between is quite painful. Yet, the truth never quite disappears: marriage is a drama which displays the nature and character of God, his trinitarian covenant-faithfulness. As we reflect on the metaphor of marriage in the Old Testament, we will walk through God's Old Covenant in the Hebrew order, that of the Tanakh. The word *Tanakh* is an acrostic for the Hebrew terms, *Torah*, *Nevi'im*, *Ketuvim*, which translate as the Law, the Prophets, and the Writings – the whole taxonomy of the Hebrew Scriptures.

The Torah: The Disappointment of Marriage

We begin with the Torah, the 'T' in 'TaNaKh'. In the Torah, after the Fall in Genesis 3, we are not hopeful in regard to marriage when we witness Adam & Eve's fingers pointed accusingly toward each other. Our disappointment and grief is only reinforced when we meet Lamech and his two wives in Genesis 4. As we saw previously, he catechizes them, twisting God's word to his own purpose: 'Adah and Zillah, hear my voice; you wives of Lamech, listen to what I say: I have killed a man for wounding me, a young man for striking me. If Cain's revenge is sevenfold, then Lamech's is seventy-sevenfold' (Gen. 4:23–24). This marriage displays a tragic break from God's Garden standard. The image of God is distorted: the two shall be one, for here we have the first polygamous marriage. And the character of God is trampled when marriage becomes the forum for promoting and vindicating evil, in the form of another murder.

Even so, we discover a reminder of the real and unchangeable nature of what God has created in Genesis 5:1–2: 'When God created man, he made him in the likeness of God. Male and female he created them, and he blessed them and named them Man when they were created.' Of this text, Chrysostom writes, 'While speaking of two, God speaks of one'.[2] Indeed, elsewhere Chrysostom declares, 'When the husband and wife are united in marriage, they are no longer seen as something earthly, but as the image of God himself.'[3] This is our trinitarian God reflected in his creation as seen through marriage, both before and after the Fall.

Strangely, or at least it could seem so to some, the Bible is very transparent about marriage problems – distortions of the key image of God's nature and character. Few marriages are displayed as exemplary in the Bible. Not much is said about Noah's marriage. Here is a man to whom God gives 'grace' (Hebrew, *h-n*), for his name, Noah ('n-h'), is the Hebrew word for grace spelled backwards! And indeed, his marriage seems to be grace-filled. His marriage is an ark in which God displays his covenant-faithfulness to his human wilful-creatures when they have fallen far from him. Over 100 years of Noah's preaching, no one listened; no one turned back to God. But his family did. Even so, we have few details of his married life. Noah's wife 'let' Noah build an ark in her backyard – or so I imagine. 'Tell me again, Noah, [she asked him gently, 1,200 times – once a month for 100 years] what is this for?!' And she must have been his helper both in building and in his preaching (on his lunch breaks and on the 4,800 Sabbaths while the ark was being built). Yet, by God's grace, Noah's marriage was the ark that birthed three and preserved eight, and all of God's people who came from them. God was faithful to his covenant people through this one shipwright/preacher and his family. Truly, Noah found grace and was a preacher of righteousness. Even his sons followed him – at least into the ark. Things fell apart a bit after that. Still, they may be the last godly family in Genesis – perhaps in the Bible.

We hear very little of marriage for many years, down to the birth of Abram. Men had sons and died, but nothing about their wives. Then we are told more than we want to know in some ways. Sadly, the monogamy of Adam & Eve was overthrown by Lamech; he was married to two women. From what follows, polygamy seems to be the new (and fallen) 'standard' – at least among those whose lives are in the story.[4] We could despair that God will do anything with marriage to reveal himself. But God is patient.

The focus of that story then turned to Abram, a man who often heard from God. And Sarai was his willing, if not eager, helper. What did she think when Abram wanted to leave the comfortable city of Ur? She went. What did she think in Egypt when Abram told her to 'pretend' to be his sister? What did she think when Pharaoh took her away from Abram? She was fearless in obeying him (1 Pet. 3). And what did she think when promised a son in her old age? Sarai is a bit too helpful here – she offers Abram her servant woman in order to 'fulfil' the promise. A boy is born and things get worse for the marriage. 'Tension' is too weak a word for the grief and jealousy between the two women. Abram's family has become a 'trinity' of sorts – but not as God desired for them. The short version is that when Sarah has her son, Isaac (God's promise), Hagar and her son are driven away. But then, God tells Abraham to sacrifice his son – and Sarah (silently) obeys her husband. Did Abraham tell her? If he had, perhaps someone like Kierkegaard could imagine such a conversation just as he imagined what that day must have been like for Abraham in *Fear and Trembling*. And somehow, Abraham and Sarah succeed – muddling through between radical disobedience and radical obedience. And their marriage stays intact – a seminal victory.

And their son obeys the voice of YHWH. But not much of the image of God is in their marriage, and too little of covenant-faithfulness.

Perhaps Isaac does better. Having married Rebekah by a remotely arranged contract, yet their marriage seems to be a romance. Indeed, we should not quickly believe the rumour that romance in marriage is an historically late fantasy of western culture. But, tragically, following the tradition of Father Abraham, he too attempts to give away his wife to a king. Mercifully, God might be seen to establish a precedent here, when he returns her to Isaac. Isaac's example is hardly an exemplary marriage of two-and-one. They also play favourites with their sons and deceive each other – and perhaps themselves. They are hardly exemplars of covenant-faithfulness. But like their parents, bumping along, they remain together. That is not nothing.

Jacob is the deceiver. And he is deceived in his first attempt at marriage. No matter; he 'corrects' that a week later, striking a bargain with his father-in-law for both of his daughters. They, Rachel and Leah, are at each other's throats, competing for Jacob's affection and his children. There is nothing compellingly trinitarian about this marriage. But God blesses Jacob with a great blessing, a new name: Israel. And faithful to his covenant with God, he destroys his household idols and dedicates his whole family to God. Righteous because of his faith, he believes and obeys. Yet his marriage(s) does little to complement the testimony of this great man of God; his marriage(s) does little to show off God's nature or character. Has God really established marriage for this purpose?

Soon the story unfolds the rape of Dinah – Jacob's daughter. And the seduction or rape of his concubine by his eldest son, Reuben. These do not fit well into a story of God's glory in marriage. The situation only worsens with Judah, Jacob's son; when he suffers the death of two sons, he refuses to allow his widowed daughter-in-law to marry his youngest son. Not to be denied her God-given right, she poses as a prostitute. Judah, now a widower, takes her (unknowingly) while on a business trip. But how did she know? What gave her confidence that posing as a cult prostitute would draw Judah into her? How is the drama of marriage in this family of families showing the world our God?

Later, much later, Moses escaped Egypt. He married while in the desert, away from his people. He married the daughter of a local priest; her name, Zipporah. She gave him a son, Gershom, a sojourner in a foreign land, as was his father. With the birth of their son, it seems they had a marital disagreement over religion. Moses wanted their son, Gershom, circumcised. Or most likely God did – there is no record of God and Moses on this issue. Nor does the text preserve the prior argument between Moses and Zipporah on this point. Only this: the boy was not circumcised and Moses lay dying. Zipporah understood then that her argument was with Moses' God who was about to kill her husband for failing to obey and circumcise his son. Seems he was listening to the voice of his wife, a return to Genesis 3. It was left to Zipporah to do this thing that disgusted her. She did, even while yelling at her dying and unconscious husband – or was she yelling at God? And Moses lived. But we do not know if they thrived; we do not know how their marriage fared. She is only mentioned once more when they are reunited near Sinai. Again, the few hints we have about their marriage are neutral or negative. This is of little help.

In the very next chapters (Exod. 19–20), both of them, and all of Israel, hear God himself speaking: 'Do not covet your neighbour's wife.' Interesting that this particular point made it into the few commandments of God, just ten that God gave to his people. There is something to see here, something too quickly passed by. This tenth command, do not to covet your neighbour's wife (an injunction against *adultery*), is parallel to the first, do not have other gods before me. The Godward treason of *idolatry* is parallel to the injunction against *adultery*.[5] Here is an early hint, perhaps the first in the Bible, that God draws a metaphorical connection between idolatry and adultery. This comes as he is creating a people for himself – an act in the desert, parallel to his first act in the Garden. Indeed, he has just made them an offer: 'Now therefore, if you will indeed obey my voice and keep my covenant, you shall be my treasured possession among all peoples, for all the earth is mine; and you shall be to me a kingdom of priests and a holy nation' (Exod. 19:5–6a). And indeed, they are his treasured possession, and he is jealous over them.

God's specific and detailed commands about marriage, and those governing Israel's sexual lives, are given in extended form in Leviticus 18 and 20. The basic rule is this – our marital and sexual ethic is not defined by the culture, but by God's life: 'I am the LORD your God'! In Deuteronomy 5, when Moses repeats the Ten Commandments, this relational reality is stated repeatedly in the introduction, the commands, and the concluding coda. Strong emphasis! That is, the 'rules' are more about God and his relationship to his people than they are an abstract 'ethic'. These tables of law are very personal. If they could be stripped of their covenantal reality (perhaps redacting the words 'the LORD your God'), historical context, and the personal presentation from God himself, perhaps the laws might be considered an ethic, comparable to other ethical systems of the world. This is attempted in some public places in the United States. Yet such attempts are self-exposing, for unless the commands were reduced in number, the first command strikes out and shatters all pretence of a bare ethic. These tablets of law, intrinsically personal and covenantal, cannot be successfully reduced to less than they are. They declare: 'I am I Am; I Am is your God!' On first hearing these commands, not least the extended sexual prohibitions of Leviticus, the people may have been more than a little uncomfortable for two reasons. First, these commands forced them to perceive themselves as shaped more by Egypt's gods than by YHWH. Leviticus 18 begins with just this warning, 'You shall not do as they do in the land of Egypt' (v. 3). But there was more, a second and even more painful reason: these prohibitions (especially as they were extended and amplified by Moses in the rest of the Torah) indicted the marriages of their patriarchs: Abraham, Isaac, and Jacob. Genesis, just published by Moses, told them that Abraham was married to his sister, the daughter of his father though not of his mother. Leviticus 18:9 explicitly prohibits this. Jacob was married to rival sisters. Leviticus 18:18 very explicitly prohibited this, too. Then there is Isaac. It is with relief that we read these commands and find that in marrying one woman, the daughter of his mother's brother, he has not violated the law. But he did fail God in his marriage. Following his father, he claimed 'she is my sister' to Abimelech (Gen. 26:7). But, thinking they were unseen, he treated her like a wife. This was reported to Abimelech who thundered at Isaac, 'She is your wife!' How close he had come to losing her – just as Abraham had. They sorted things out like gentlemen, but still Isaac's words echo in our ears: 'She is my sister.' This, if it was as true as his words, violates Leviticus 18:9. Is this the place to mention Lot and his daughters? Or rather, Lot's daughters and their father. Either way, he was (all too) passive in this story in Genesis 18–19. I'll presume you know the story or will look it up. This violates the primary injunction of Leviticus 18:6: 'None of you shall approach any one of his close relatives to uncover nakedness.' Both sisters did just that. But perhaps Israel was comforted by the fact that they had already disavowed these relatives, these Moabites and Ammonites.

The Pentateuch makes it clear that God is deeply and personally interested in marriages of his people – even their sexual lives. Why? Of course, there is nothing God is not interested in for his people. But God is particularly engaged in the marital and sexual life of his people because sexual intimacy is a dramatic metaphor of the relationship of God to his people. Positively, we see this in Deuteronomy 10:20 where we are told, 'You shall fear the LORD your God. You shall serve him and hold fast to him'. The Hebrew behind 'hold fast' is the same verb Moses used in the Marriage Text: '*cleave* (hold fast) to your wife'.[6] Negatively, we perceive this in Leviticus 19:29 (where God opposes prostitution), and in Leviticus 20:10–21 (where God presents his taxonomy of punishments for various kinds of sexual immorality), and many other such commands scattered throughout Numbers 5 and Deuteronomy 21–25. Our sexual life and our marriage is no small thing to God. Marriage is the image, the drama, and the metaphor that God chose to represent our relationship to him. And it is personal for him. But at the end of the Pentateuch, it is clear: we are failing.

The Prophets: The Trauma of Marriage

Using the order of the Tanakh (Law, Prophets, and Writings), we move from the Law (Torah) into the Prophets (the *Nevi'im*), the

'N' in 'TaNaKh'. These include many of what we would call the historical books; under the heading of 'former prophets' we discover Joshua, Judges, Samuel, and Kings. Following these, we find those we consider prophets, including Isaiah, Jeremiah, Ezekiel, and the twelve 'minor' prophets. In the Prophets we will see a clear development and intensification of the failure of human marriage, and God's clear intention to use marriage as a metaphor for his nature and character.[7]

If the marriages in Genesis have been a bit 'too real', and too painful, the marriages in Judges – only glimpses – are tragic. The very idea of Israel acting the whore started in Exodus 32 when God responded to their idolatry (adultery) against him with the golden calf. Here, even as God replaced the Ten Commandments (the law broken by the people and the tablets shattered by Moses) and then renewed the covenant, he declared the danger: defeat the inhabitants of the land, drive them out, lest you also whore after their gods. Then, later, in the repeating of the Law, anticipating the death of Moses, God declared that this will in fact happen. Israel will 'whore after foreign gods' and they will be driven out – like Adam (Deut. 31:16).

I am impressed that many of the stories preserved in Judges are stories about marriage – or rather the failure of marriage.[8] Consider Samson. His marriage to a Philistine woman from Timnah ends in disaster for all (Judg. 14–15). Then he visits a prostitute (Judg. 16) – an anti-marriage. Then he has a dalliance with Delilah, his 'lover', though it is hard to discover any evidence of love between them.[9] Delilah is offered 1,100 pieces of silver (or perhaps several times this amount, if she received this amount from each of the conspirators) to betray Samson. She does so, eagerly and repeatedly and even with Samson's knowledge (and support!). Samson actually participates in his own destruction: 'cut my hair' (16:17). So then he is captured, mutilated, and later allowed one more opportunity to serve God. If Samson is in the list of the faithful in Hebrews 11, it is not because of his marital and sexual example.[10] And although God used Samson's failures to accomplish his own ends, yet these failures (particularly in regard to marriage) serve only to point to the need for Another who would be the Faithful One (a theme in Judges and Samuel) and the grace of God to us who are unfaithful to him.

There is an interesting follow-on story in Judges 17, the story of Micah. Often overlooked is that his mother, from whom Micah stole *precisely* 1,100 pieces of silver, could very well be Delilah; she is never named. Is it a coincidence that the 1,100 pieces of silver in Judges 17 matches the amount promised to Delilah in Judges 16:5? Perhaps this exact amount is here as an identifier for the reader! And if she is Delilah, then the author may be introducing Micah as Samson's illegitimate son. While this identification cannot be asserted, it is at least a strange contextual coincidence. If she is Delilah and Micah is Samson's son, then all that follows (the trauma of Judg. 17–18) is a result of a failure of Samson to enact faithfully the metaphor of marriage established in the Marriage Text; he did not display God's nature and character. If not, the conclusion is hardly different, just less emphatic.

Moving forward in Judges – forward, not upward – we are presented with the case of the Levite and his concubine in Judges 19–20. Here we discover another failed marriage. I think a case can be made that the point of the story is not primarily the problem of homosexuality (yet this evil haunts the story as well), but instead the failure of the Levite and Israel to see their own guilt in the terrible events. This story is perhaps like Paul's transition from Romans 1 to Romans 2, what Richard Hays called Paul's 'sting operation'. After inciting the church in Rome against the terrible evils of tortured sexuality and immorality (Rom. 1), he turns on them: 'You however have no excuse, because you who judge are doing the very same things!' (Rom. 2). The point may be the same. In this story, a Levite is in search of his 'unfaithful' concubine who has returned to her father's home in Bethlehem. What does the ESV translation 'unfaithful' mean? This Hebrew word, *zanah*, has been used in Exodus and Judges with the meaning 'whoring'. The Septuagint, the Greek translation of Jesus' day, selected the word 'anger' to translate the Hebrew: 'she was angry at him'. Both are possible and, in context, returning to her father's house seems more consistent with 'anger'. That said, the resolution does not matter to this point – either 'works'.

His 'marriage' with his concubine has failed. After regaining his concubine (hardly a 'reuniting with'), he is still angry with her – deadly angry. We are told that the Levite sent his concubine out to be raped, in order to save himself. Hours later, when the neighbours are done with her, he makes no move to help her, leaving her to die in the street. When morning comes, he discovers her collapsed on the threshold of the house, but he shows no compassion (Judg. 19:25–28). Taking her home, flopped over his donkey, he then distributes pieces of her body to all of Israel. Seeing only the offence of his hosts, the House of Benjamin (their homosexuality, lack of hospitality, and abuse), Israel responds and destroys Benjamin. But notice that God almost destroys Judah in the process (read the story of the costly battle in Judg. 20). This is not merely about Benjamin's failure. The concern in regard to the concubine is God's concern against Israel; God is *angry* with them all for their *zanah*, their *unfaithfulness*, but they are angry only at Benjamin. Is this not like us when we judge others, but do not judge ourselves? Here God is offended with Judah just as he is later offended at the Roman Christians. God's character and nature are mocked because of them. And as if to show the depths of their distortion of marriage, the conclusion of the story highlights a legal fiction which allows Judah to secure wives for Benjamin, further distorting marriage (read Judg. 21 to learn more about the strange deceit by which they 'fairly' provided wives for the few remaining Benjamites).

Marriage is not a minor theme in the historical books of Samuel and Kings, and in their synoptic parallel, the Chronicles.[11] Yet few, if any, of the marriages displayed here serve to reflect God's intended image of himself. Not Elkanah's marriage to two wives, not even their exemplary son, Samuel. He was a testimony, not to their marriage, but to Hannah's faith. Nor was Eli's marriage an exemplar, not if his sons revealed anything of the strength of his marriage or his obedience to Deuteronomy 6 ('teach these commandments to your children'!). Even Samuel's own marriage (1 Sam. 8:5) was no testimony to God. In what way did these families display God who is One-and-Many, and what praise did they offer God for his covenant-faithfulness?

David's own (many!) marriages were confused and disordered. While our insights are few and marriage is not the authors' emphasis, marriage is not a subject he avoided. We may be encouraged when we learn that his first wife, Michal, loved him (1 Sam. 18:20), and David and Abigail, his second wife, were quite impressed with each other – perhaps they loved each other (1 Sam. 25:39,42). And David was attracted to Bathsheba, but that is not the best news in regard to the holy imaging of God by marriage (2 Sam. 11–12). Then Michal was given to his friend by Saul (1 Sam. 25:44) – shades of Samson! Later, she was dragged away from a sobbing Paltiel, and Michal was restored to David (2 Sam. 3:13–16). But she mocked David when he worshipped (2 Sam. 6). Such marital 'problems' do not invalidate the possibility of imaging God's nature and character in marriage, but the constellation of events disclosed by the author are of little help to see marriage as the intended image of God. It only gets worse in the next generation. After David's moral failure with Bathsheba, he uttered the fourfold curse against himself, 'This man deserves to die; he shall restore the lamb fourfold' (2 Sam. 12:5–6). Then we watch the train wreck of his family played out in the deaths of his four sons: his firstborn of Bathsheba was put to death by God; Amnon was murdered by his brother for incestuous brutality; Absalom was murdered by Joab for treason; and Adonijah was put to death by his brother Solomon for overreaching. Does the misbehaviour and death of his sons reflect the failure of David's marriage(s) or failure to image God in his marriages? Not necessarily, but neither do they offer to us hopeful examples of imaging of God. They are unfocused distortions, but perhaps, in his unremitting repentance and perseverance with his family, the image remains.

Moving from the book of Samuel to the book of Kings, what need I say of Solomon with his 300 concubines and 700 wives (1 Kgs 11:3)? Indeed, according to 1 Kings 4:32 he wrote 1,005 songs, a Song of Solomon for each woman, perhaps? Surely not, even if we allow five extra as a rounding error or as 'spares' for wives that never materialized! But nothing in Solomon's approach to marriage sustains the image. God is building our grief. And indeed it can be increased even in monogamy: Ahab and Jezebel. Here is a marriage centred on greed and the power to exercise that greed, not on God's nature and character. These two combined their weaknesses to one purpose in order to murder Naboth and take away his vineyard. And they married their daughter, Athaliah, to Jehoram, the king of Judah (2 Kgs 8:18). Notice that from this point forward, the House of David is connected by marriage to the House of Omri, so Ahab and Jezebel are ancestors of Jesus who is the Christ (see Matt. 1:8). Throughout the historical books we find no examples of the glory of God in marriage.

Let me consider Isaiah (whose eponymous book centres around the year 700 BC), and Jeremiah and Ezekiel (whose books are set at the time of the exile(s), around 600 BC). These same books were preserved as Writings, holy Scripture, by God's people. As I mentioned in the introduction, it serves no purpose (to my point here) to wrestle with the issues of authorship or date, but I am considering these writings as they present themselves, and their particular focus on what Ray Ortlund calls 'the "tragic romance" between God and his people'.[12]

Isaiah uses many metaphors for the decayed and degraded relationship between God and his people. These include rebellion, sickness, uncleanliness, and the colour crimson. He makes the historical comparison with Sodom and Gomorrah. And he uses marital infidelity – whoring, 'How the faithful city has become a whore!' (Isa. 1:21). YHWH's people are his bride – his alone, belonging to no other. And all of this without leaving his first chapter! While the connection between adultery and idolatry is not dominant in Isaiah, the author returns to this theme again toward the end of the book. He calls Israel the 'offspring of the adulterer and the loose woman' (57:3).[13] Ray Ortlund paraphrases Isaiah's assessment this way: 'Claiming Abraham as their father will not do, for they show not that family resemblance, but quite another.'[14] Failed marriage is a metaphor that frames the people in this book. But in the middle of the reality of the failed marriage between God and his people, Isaiah declares that God is faithful (54:5a): 'For your Maker is your husband [*ba'al*, lord], the Lord [YHWH] of hosts is his name; and the Holy

One of Israel is your Redeemer [*ga'al*, redeemer]'. Here the assonance, the similarity of the vowels in these short two-syllable words (husband and redeemer), highlights the intense, unbreakable intimacy of the marriage of Israel to YHWH. He continues:

> 'For the LORD has called you like a wife deserted and grieved in spirit, like a wife of youth when she is cast off, says your God. For a brief moment I deserted you, but with great compassion I will gather you. In overflowing anger for a moment I hid my face from you, but with everlasting love I will have compassion on you,' says the LORD, your Redeemer (vv. 6–8).

Distinct from the human experience of unfaithfulness in marriage, God will stand as a faithful husband to his unfaithful wife, because he is not only our lord and master (husband), but our redeemer who has everlasting love that conquers the unfaithfulness of his people, his wife. In fact, he will rejoice over us: 'And as the bridegroom rejoices over the bride, so shall your God rejoice over you' (Isa. 62:5b).

Jeremiah takes the theme of infidelity, lightly used in Isaiah, and makes it central. Consider the first three chapters. Chapter 1 is Jeremiah's ordination. Chapter 2 is the beginning of God's words against his people. He begins in verse 2, identifying them, God's first and primary identification, as his people, a 'bride' whose love was devoted in her youth. But now she has lost interest in her husband, God. She has traded her God for other gods, acting the whore (v. 20). And to all her lovers, except God, she overflows with lust. She lusts for those who are not her Husband (vv. 24–25). So God brings charges against her: 'you have forgotten me!' His evidence is this: a virgin dresses to attract a mate and a bride dresses for her wedding, but God's people have no interest in remembering him at all (v. 32). Then in chapter 3, God wonders at his pursuit of his people who have been unfaithful – something not even permitted by the Law (3:1). Indeed, God declares that she has given herself to her lovers everywhere the eye can look (3:2)! She has polluted the land with her whoredom and God has withdrawn his common graces, such things as rain (3:3).

Then God points Judah to Israel whom he divorced – a warning (v. 8). Yet he calls her to come to her senses, acknowledging her foolishness (v. 12) and to 'return!' (v. 13, repent!). She has filled her life with her paramours: another man, many lovers, the Arab, stone and tree (idols), and foreigners. The list goes on. And on. And in this list, it is important for us to see clearly the mixing of human persons and lifeless objects, paramours and idols. Adultery and idolatry are considered alike, the same offence. God heaps allusion upon metaphor to convict his people of their adultery: faithless, treacherous wife, whore, orgies, shame, delusion, divorce, ravished . . . In chapter 3 alone, there are more than twenty-five references to Israel's failure in terms of her marriage to God. The very last verse (3:25) sounds a note of hope: 'Let us lie down in our shame, and let our dishonour cover us. For we have sinned against the LORD our God, we and our fathers, from our youth even to this day, and we have not obeyed the voice of the LORD our God.' The hope of confession. A picture of the future that does not happen in the lifetime of any of those listening.

Through the lifelong ministry of Jeremiah, which extended from Josiah through to the last king of Judah, the people do not respond to the call to return and live with their Husband. Jeremiah's accusation continues: 'In vain you beautify yourself. Your lovers despise you' (4:30). And 'they committed adultery . . . They were well-fed, lusty stallions' (5:8). 'They are all adulterers' (9:2). 'I myself will lift up your skirts over your face, and your shame will be seen. I have seen your abominations, your adulteries and neighings, your lewd whorings' (13:26–27a). 'The virgin Israel has done a very horrible thing' (18:13). 'For the land is full of adulterers . . . they commit adultery' (23:10,14). 'They have committed adultery' (29:23). 'All your lovers have forgotten you' (30:14). Jeremiah is well known for his many metaphors throughout his book. Among other reasons, God seems to have chosen him for his lively imagination. But the metaphor of marriage, and unfaithfulness to that marriage, is the metaphor to which he consistently returns. Now we turn to the Letter of Consolation, Jeremiah 30 – 31, which is cited repeatedly in the New Testament. Here in this text, Jeremiah reverses the terrible image of a failed marriage: 'Again I will build you, and you shall be built, O virgin Israel! Again you shall adorn yourself with tambourines and shall go forth in the dance of the merrymakers' (31:4). Restored, God's people return to the joy of their marriage to God – and God has restored, impossibly; she is *virgin* Israel. And interestingly, from this point on – in a book well known to be non-linear and disjointed in its historical flow – Jeremiah does not return to the theme of 'faithless Israel' or 'whoring'. This word of restoration of the bride is his last in that regard.

Ezekiel addresses the faithless bride of God in chapter 16 in three movements: unwanted (vv. 1–5), betrothed (vv. 6–7), and then married to YHWH (v. 8). He calls Jerusalem an abandoned child, cast out because of her abominations. Indeed, historically, Jerusalem was 'birthed' by the people of the land, not desired by the Canaanites and ignored by Israel during the conquest (Josh. 15:63). Only much later did Jerusalem come to represent the people of God. God explains that in this way: 'Live!' (Ezek. 16:6). Perhaps this is when God sent David to own her (2 Sam. 5), and betrothed her to God with the ark of the covenant (2 Sam. 6) – interestingly, at the cost of his wife, Michal. Jerusalem is not God's and represents his covenant to his people. Then, in Ezekiel's next movement, YHWH marries his bride (v. 8) and clothes her in beauty, transforming her (vv. 9–14). But this third movement of marriage is not the last movement in this drama. She trusted her beauty and did not cherish her husband YHWH (v. 15). She went whoring, using her wedding gifts to consort with idols (vv. 16–22). There is much more, just like this. In fact, the faithless, whoring, idolatry – the adultery of YHWH's Jerusalem bride – receives the weight of words of Ezekiel. But not the last word: 'I will establish for you an everlasting covenant . . . and you shall know that I am the LORD . . . when I atone for you for all that you have done' (vv. 59–63). This message at the core of Ezekiel, and other similar references not noted here, declares the same metaphor as Isaiah and Jeremiah: idolatry of God's betrothed is adultery against her husband YHWH. But that is not the end. The God who is faithful to his covenant will persevere with his chosen and beloved

whore. She will become his faithful bride; she will remember her
shame with grief and will be made faithful to her LORD and husband.
And, extending the metaphor, Jerusalem would not be barren but
have daughters – no longer her sisters, nor as a result of the covenant,
but by God's grace – the North and the South. And her new situation
would both humble her and give her eternal reason to marvel at her
Lord, YHWH.

Last among the prophets, let me address Hosea, the first of the
Minor Prophets, the first in the book of the Twelve. Hosea is at once
a living parable and the declaration of its meaning. The parable is
the life of Hosea who is told to marry a 'wife of whoredom', Gomer.
The temporal flow of this command is not quite clear. Is she now a
prostitute as he marries her, or is God speaking of who she will soon
be? Perhaps this is not as clear as we would like, yet the main point
is clear, starkly clear: Gomer represents God's relationship to faithless
Israel, 'for the land commits great whoredom by forsaking the LORD'
(Hos. 1:2). In brief the story of Hosea and Gomer is this: they marry
and she conceives a son, 'Jezreel', whose name is a reminder of the
place of God's discipline of his people.[15] Then another child is born,
'No Mercy'. And a third, 'Not My People'. Soon (how 'soon' or
how 'long' did it feel to Hosea?) Gomer leaves Hosea to run after
her lovers (Hos. 2), as if they were the reason for her happiness and
provision. But her real treasure was the only man who actually loved
her, Hosea. She did not prize, but rather despised, her treasure. The
next move is the shock for us. In Hosea 3, God commands Hosea
again. Parallel (or anti-parallel) to the first command in Hosea 1:2–3,
God commands: 'Go again, love a woman who is loved by another
man' (v. 1).[16] Yet, this act of restoration was not merely against all the
expectations of the reader, then or now; it was also against the Law
of Moses. In Deuteronomy 24:1–5 God prohibits taking a woman
back after she has been taken by another man.[17] Yet, this is just what
God wants in the case of Israel. Once again, in obedience, Hosea lives
out the next act of drama before God and Israel with Gomer. Hosea's
love was not blind – he was to 'love a woman who is loved by another
man *and is an adulteress*'. As at the beginning of the story, God makes

it explicit that this is about him and Israel. So also here: 'even as the LORD loves the children of Israel, though they turn to other gods and love cakes of raisins' (Hos. 3:1). But this turn in Hosea's drama follows the literary revelation of God's turn to his people in 2:14 as we saw earlier: 'I will allure her'. Shocking enough in itself, this is all the more shocking because it follows the connecting word, 'therefore', which causally links what went on before in Israel (adultery) with the current action of God (wooing in the desert)! Why does Hosea say 'therefore' as if we should understand? What has he told us that would make him think he has established a ground for what happened next? Do we understand?

Our marriages, even our failed marriages, are dramas. Even in our fallenness our marriages should display God's relationship with us – his covenant-faithfulness. And indeed, against the Law of Moses, Hosea bought his wife for the price of a slave and brought her to his home. He had no illusion about her feelings for him, nor about her maturity, nor even her repentance. This action was unilateral, a drama to display God's character and obedience to his command. Hosea brought Gomer into his house, but did not pursue intimacy, at least not yet. Not for many days.

The Writings: The Display and Disappearance of Marriage

Using the order of the Tanakh (Law, Prophets, and Writings), we move from the Prophets to the Writings (the *Ketuvim*), the 'K' in 'TaNaKh'. These also include many of what we would call the historical books which include Ruth, Esther, Ezra, Nehemiah, and even Chronicles; along with these we find the poetical and wisdom writings. Here again we see a clear development and intensification of the failure of human marriage and God's clear intention to use marriage as a metaphor for his nature and character. As we start into the Writings, I remind the reader that I am only sampling, rather than proving or even surveying. I am displaying some of the material in the Tanakh which may help us reflect on the thesis: marriage displays

God's nature (he is One-and-Many) and his character (he is faithful to his covenant promises).

I want us to think first about Ruth, the (Moabite) daughter-in-law of Naomi. Their circumstances are grave after the death of Naomi's husband, Elimelech. This is followed by the even worse tragedy of the death of both of her sons. Now, Naomi is a true widow, a woman with no family to support and protect her, and worse, living in a foreign land. Yet, her two daughters-in-law are faithful to her, travelling with her to Israel. Part way. For before they arrive, perhaps at the border of Moab and Judah, she makes a serious attempt to turn them around: 'Return to your mother's house!' and 'I have nothing to give you!' If she convinced Orpah, she did not convince Ruth. Ruth, faithful to her mother-in-law and YHWH, travelled on with Naomi. There, gleaning among the fields of Boaz, a near relative and kinsman-redeemer, Ruth is welcomed, provided for, and protected. More than doing his duty, Boaz seems quite taken with Ruth (someone might be tempted to see even romance in Boaz's remark about the younger men, 3:10). Most significantly Boaz does his duty as kinsman-redeemer and he is shown to be eager to show faithfulness to Ruth. This is in contrast with the unnamed man who refuses to redeem her because of the cost (4:1–9). It may be that the refusal of the author to name this failed redeemer is a slight; he is the only significant character unnamed in this story. Perhaps the lack of name highlights his failure. Perhaps in the light of Deuteronomy 25:9–10 we should name him One-Sandaled-Fool. The removal of the 'sandal' was not *merely* transactional, as it seems to have become in Boaz's day (4:7, 'custom'). Though fully able to redeem, this man fails. He was unwilling. Moses commanded that for this refusal, the elders should spit in his face! Cowardly and selfish, One-Sandal has shirked his duty. In contrast, Boaz acts as the man of God, faithful to Ruth in the way God is faithful to us. Boaz rescues the weak. Here is a glimmer, not merely of cherishing, but also of God's covenant-faithfulness, contrasted with the failure of the fool – both in the context of marriage. Here in Ruth and Boaz is an example of a good marriage that displays God's covenant-faithfulness. Here is a surprising oasis in Moab.

If we read the Psalms expecting to find this theme of marriage, and with it the adultery of Israel and her idolatry toward God, we are disappointed. Certainly, we might turn to Psalm 115, 'Not to us, O LORD, not to us, but to your name give glory, for the sake of your steadfast love and your faithfulness!' (v. 1). Here God's covenant-faithfulness is celebrated over and against the traumatic event of the golden calf, Israel's seminal move to idolatry. They betrayed their redeemer. This occurred just after hearing God's own voice declare the Ten Commandments and just as Moses was receiving the stone tablets. God mocked the idols and declared their judgment: 'Those who make them become like them [deaf, mute, unfeeling, and immovable]' (v. 8). They will become like what they worship. But God does not declare himself as Israel's husband, nor Israel as a wayward wife, an adulteress. And it would be reasonable to find such references here, for it was in Exodus 34, as Moses was receiving the replacement stone tablets after the calf of shame, that Israel was first called a 'whore'. But there is no such reference here. And there are no similar references to marriage to YHWH, immorality, fornication, adultery, or anything like that all through the Psalms. Except only one: Psalm 106. At the end of Book 4, we discover Psalms 103, 104, 105, and 106. This sequence is introduced as 'of David' (only Psalm 103 is attributed) and all of them begin with similar invocations and codas which tie them together: 'Bless the LORD, O my soul' (*Barak YHWH* in 103 and 104) and 'Praise the LORD' (*Hallelujah!* in 104, 105, and 106). Psalm 103 first declares the grounding truth of God's covenant-faithfulness to those upon whom he bestows his mercy. Here is no metaphor of marriage, but rather that of Father (v. 13). Psalm 104 recounts creation, 'He set the earth on its foundations, so that it should never be moved' (v. 5). Following creation, Psalm 105 recounts the story of the patriarchs and the exodus: 'To you I will give the land of Canaan as your portion for an inheritance' (v. 11). Following the exodus, Psalm 106 rehearses the mighty deeds of the Lord which were often ignored by his people; instead of worshipping YHWH, they rebelled. Verse 36 charges, 'They served their idols' – that is, the idols of the land to which the Lord had delivered them.

The psalmist concludes in regard to their failure: 'Thus they became unclean by their acts, and played the *whore* in their deeds' (v. 39). But their failure is not the end. God responds as a faithful husband: 'For their sake he remembered his covenant, and relented according to the abundance of his steadfast love' (v. 45). In fact, there is one other place where this same root is used that is translated here by the esv as 'whore'. Psalm 73:27 says, 'you put an end to everyone who is unfaithful to you.' Here the esv translates the word as 'unfaithful'. And in the context of the absence of marriage imagery in the Psalms, that might be better in Psalm 106 as well. We are left with a meagre contribution to a biblical theology of marriage. Perhaps fruitful suggestions can be made as to why, but not by me, or at least not now.

However, a complete reversal, we find the opposite in the Song of Songs. The first observation is this: throughout this song about romantic and marital love there is no mention of procreation. This poem, rather than considering purposes of marriage, considers instead the movements of the heart in romance and marriage. That is an offence to the trope that romance is a late invention of the western imagination. That charge is not without significance, but the charge may also be without precision. This canonical love poem finds romance with all its terror and challenges in the marriage of Solomon. But what kind of reading of this poetry is intended: merely poetical, or historical, typological, or allegorical-theological? In his introduction to his commentary on the Song, Dennis Kinlaw writes:

> History began with a wedding (Gen 2:18–25) and will climax with the Marriage Supper of the Lamb (Rev 19:6–10). It would seem no accident then that the Lord began his earthly ministry blessing a wedding. John the Baptist, when quizzed about Jesus' ministry, described it in nuptial terms (John 3:29–30). Jesus himself, when interrogated as to why his disciples did not fast, pictured his stay among us in terms of a wedding announcement party. A case can easily be made that the biblical philosophy of history is to be described in nuptial terms. Thus idolatry and adultery are used synonymously

across the length of Scripture . . . In a sense there is almost an Edenic quality to much of the Song of Songs, almost as if it were a commentary on Genesis 2:18–25.[18]

If so, this argues for an allegorical-theological reading. Arguing for a similar reading of the Song, Tremper Longman III writes, 'the allegorical approach was not wrong in insisting that we read the Song as relevant to our relationship with God'.[19] While the Song is historical-poetical, reflecting the place of marriage and sexuality for this poet who names himself a great king, it is also analogical-theological, teaching us about God and his relationship to us. This does not elide the real and historical features of the text, as if we could overlook this history or as if it had no real meaning in its time and genre. Instead, we must also read it as analogical-theological in its canonical place in the revelation of God. In the Song we perceive God's passion for us and understand the place of marriage – even romance – in the connection between God and his people.

The Song has its first place in the history and culture of the author. Reflecting on this historical context, I offer my reading of this text as the story of the king and his bride (précised in Table 3.1).[20]

Table 3.1 Structure of the Song of Songs

1:1–3:5	Imagining Future Delights: the time of waiting while recalling the betrothal
3:6–3:11	The Coming of Delight: the return of the groom for the wedding
4:1–7:13	The Struggle for Delight: three cycles of love's desires and love's anxiety
4:1–5:1	Cycle 1 Approach–Anxiety–Delight
5:2–6:3	Cycle 2 Anxiety–Approach–Delight
6:4–7:13	Cycle 3 Approach–Anxiety–Approach–Delight
8:1–8:14	Perseverance in Delight: an open question . . .

This biblical theology of marriage is not a commentary on the Song. Still, let me observe a pattern in these cycles. Intimacy is terrifying work. And it is just at this point of terror, as we observe the struggles of this couple to move into the true delight of intimacy, that idolatry and adultery are juxtaposed. The 'beloved', the woman, is eager for intimacy in the opening lines of this poem. Recalling the betrothal banquet, she longs for the return of her 'lover'. Even then, her dream in chapter 3 reveals how her desire for intimacy is moderated by her fear of intimacy. After the wedding – notice that it is here alone that the word 'bride' is used, neither before or after – Solomon allures his beloved, his bride, perhaps on the night of the wedding. He observes and describes her beauty, reflecting her beauty back to her. However, in 4:12 he sees that she is drawing back in her anxiety. He calls her 'a garden locked'. But she conquers her anxiety and moves toward her lover and delight: 'let my beloved come to his Garden'. In verse 1, the lover does just that and the chorus celebrates. The second cycle is like the first, though it begins with anxiety. Her dream of chapter 3 is revisited with deeper fears exposed – deeper perhaps because the intimacy of marriage is now experienced. In this centre cycle, the woman, called by the chorus, speaks to herself the truth of her desire for her lover. In her self-counsel, by looking at the truth of how delightful he is, she calms her soul and again the lovers find delight: 'My beloved has gone down to his garden . . . I am my beloved's and my beloved is mine' (6:2–3). The last cycle is the longest, merging aspects of both of the previous. It begins with the approach as the lover describes his beloved. At first, she was drawn to him (6:11a), but when she discovered his eager desire for intimacy (6:11b), she panicked (6:12). But the lover calls her back with one of the most beautiful and alluring verses in Scripture: 'Return to me, return to me, O woman of Solomon, return to me, return to me, that we may look upon you.'[21] She is drawn back as he describes her beauty once more. Her response is shown in 7:10 when she declares for intimacy and delight in the consummation of desire: 'I am my beloved's, and his desire is for me.' That truth is hard to hold on to. In fact, just as the Gospel of Mark ends on the word 'fear' in the best texts, so also this 'gospel' ends with ambiguity: will this couple persevere in the delightful experience of intimacy, or will they be drawn apart by their fear of intimacy?

This text (analogically, if not primarily) points to the reality of our desire for, and anxiety about, intimacy with our Lover and Saviour. So how, in that context, does this poem fit into the revelation of the nature and character of God in marriage? First, if God intends Christology, not merely anthropology, in this text, then God's characteristic covenant-faithfulness includes a component of 'passion', not merely 'com-passion', and his desire is intimacy with us. And if this text represents truth(s) about God's relationship to his people, then this fits well with the many texts like Hosea which speak of God's desire to 'allure' his people away from idolatry/adultery. Second, when we witness the human fear of intimacy and desire, especially in response to the eager desire of the Lover, we may see another, less obvious, motivation toward idolatry: fear of intimacy. While there are many reasons couples find an escape in adultery, one of those reasons is to avoid intimacy. Sex with someone you are just getting to know, someone who does not yet demand more of you than you want to present, is less intimate and less scary than a sustained relationship. Decades-long intimacy is more demanding – and rewarding. The same is true for our relationship with our holy God: it is more scary, more demanding, and more rewarding than shallow 'religion' or the easy escapism of idolatry (adultery). So, the last chapter of this poem – a chapter confusing to all readers and commentators, at least at face value – reveals the challenge of persevering in the cycles of approach-anxiety-intimacy. If this is about Solomon, with 700 wives and 300 concubines, perhaps it was easier for him to drop the role of lover and pursuer and start a new and therefore less demanding relationship – at least initially less demanding. In our marriages we have the opportunity, the privilege, of being pursuing lovers, and responding beloved, showing off to each other, the world, and even to God, a drama that portrays his character. And in the intimacy of two persons, refusing to be separated by their differences, we show off God's One-and-Many nature. The Song reveals the challenges and the wonder of this drama.

The Tanakh ends with the book of the Chronicles of the Kings. There is very little here to help us understand the connection between marriage and God's nature and character. There are many uses of the verb 'forsake' (*azav*), as in 'if you forsake him, he will cast you off for ever' (1 Chr. 28:9). Here is the image of an immoral woman who forsakes her husband (Prov. 2:16–18). Since 1 Chronicles describes the reign of David, this word is mostly absent. It occurs here as a charge from David to Solomon. Later it occurs ten times in 2 Chronicles of the Kings of Israel (7:9; 10:13; 13:10; 15:2; 21:10; 24:20,24; 28:6; 29:6; 34:25). Another key word, 'unfaithful' (*ma'al*), occurs more frequently.[22] On occasion it overlaps with one of the other two terms. Significantly, in 1 Chronicles 5:25 we find an intersection of the verb for the act of whoring (*zanah*) and unfaithful (*ma'al*) used of Israel, the Northern Kingdom. Of these northern tribes, mostly absent from Chronicles as compared to the book of Kings, God says, 'they broke faith with [acted unfaithfully against] the God of their fathers, and whored after the gods of the peoples of the land'. For that reason, they were removed by Tiglath-pileser of Assyria. Also once in 2 Chronicles (21:11–13, and only here), 'whoring' is used of Judah, led into this by King Jehoram (v. 11) and repeated twice in verse 13, noting that this was just like the Northern Kingdom. But I would expect much more in the last book of the Old Covenant. These few explicit hints of the connection between adultery ('whoring') and idolatry are perhaps more precisely *echoes* rather than hints, as if the very connection itself is fading toward the end of this aging, battered, starved, and fading-away Old Covenant.

It is worth mentioning a strange connection between idolatry and marriage in Ezra-Nehemiah, also among the Writings. There is a very strange drama in Ezra; he becomes irate about intermarriage of the people and forces them into divorce! After a return to the Land, Nehemiah had secured the walls. Ezra came to teach the people. Among other things, he commanded the priests, whom he had set apart: 'You are holy to the LORD' (Ezra 8:28). And echoing the language of the Garden command to 'work [cultivate] it and keep' it (Gen. 2:15), Ezra commanded the priests, who resided again in the Land (imaged by the Garden in Genesis), to 'guard and keep' the temple vessels (returned by Ezra) and so the whole of the Law of God. But they quickly failed! They did not keep themselves holy (separated from the people of the land and their abominations, Ezra 9:1) and so they were not 'guarding and keeping'. How had they failed? They had married the daughters of the idolatrous peoples – the sin of Solomon. Ezra called this faithlessness, three times (vv. 9:2,4; 10:6). Repenting, they agreed to put away their foreign wives (10:11). The connection between marriage and idolatry is made in this strange way, with an ending that is surprising to many citizens of the New Covenant: divorce. So important is this that it is repeated in the book of Nehemiah, when he 'cleansed' the people of Israel from their foreign, idolatrous wives (Neh. 13). While Chronicles is the last 'word' in the Old Covenant (according to the order found in the Tanakh), these books of Ezra and Nehemiah reveal to us the end of the timeline of the Old Covenant. Ezra recorded in his book, by name, those who had married against the Law. And Nehemiah (perhaps written by Ezra) declares: 'because they have desecrated the priesthood and the covenant . . . thus I cleansed them from everything foreign' (13:29–30).

If these last of the Writings are a muted echo of the nature and character of God, the echo is clear. This last story connects idolatry, adultery, and even marriage to God's faithfulness even when we are unfaithful. What will happen next?

The Meaning of Marriage in the Old Testament

The Torah, the Prophets, and the Writings all 'confuse' the human sin of idolatry with adultery. In this 'confusion' of terms is found the reality that God images his covenant-faithfulness in marriage. There is something progressive to be seen. Genesis defines and displays marriage, and shows its failure after the Fall. Exodus defines and displays leaving God by the metaphor of marriage in the tragedy of the golden calf (Exod. 34). The Prophets display our failure at keeping the laws of Leviticus with each other and condemn our unfaithfulness to God repeatedly and intensely in the same terms of marital corruption. In fact, adultery and idolatry, and similar terms, are freely interchanged as if they are synonyms. Adultery, the treason of a person who is married (or engaged) when they seek intimacy outside the bounds of that marriage, is regularly used as a synonym for idolatry, the sin of a person created by God to delight in him who exchanges the glory of God for a lie of greater pleasure in that which is created. But they are not identical. Spiritual adultery is only a subset of all the human examples of idolatry. Idolatry can be considered as adultery only when it is committed by a person who is pledged to God, only by one of the covenant partners. And at just this point, the covenant partner fails to image God's nature, his One-and-Many delight in the other, but instead the covenant partner displays a self-focused individuality. At the end of the Old Covenant, imaging has dimmed and is almost invisible.

4

Discovering God's Trinitarian Covenant-Faithfulness in the New Testament

As I followed the groupings of the Tanakh in the investigation of the Old Testament, I will follow an analogous order in the New Testament in which the gospels parallel the Torah, the epistles the Prophets, and the book of Revelation the Writings. As with the OT, I will be assaying rather than proving; sampling rather than comprehensively testing. My proposal is this: the Marriage Text in Genesis 2:18–25 is the appropriate anchor for a biblical theology of marriage in which it reveals God's nature, as One-and-Many, and his character, as faithful to his covenant people.

The Torah of the NT: The Johannine Centre of Marriage in the Gospels

I will begin this biblical-theological study of marriage in the New Testament in the gospels, which are sometimes considered the New Covenant analogue to the Torah. Specifically, I will focus on the Gospel of John to the exclusion of significant passages in Matthew (including Matt. 19) and elsewhere. Some of these will yet be addressed in Part Three. I hope that the reasons for this will become clear in what follows. I will try to show that John positions his gospel at the very centre of a biblical theology of marriage which is anchored in the Marriage Text, intentionally following Genesis, especially Genesis 1–3.

Many are aware of connections between the Gospel of John and Genesis, including the famous opening words of both: 'in the beginning'. Let me offer several other examples. In John 5, the Evangelist (John the author of the gospel is called the Evangelist, rather than the Baptist) reflects on the crowning sabbatical account of the seventh day (Gen. 2:1–3) when Jesus declares that God's work of creation is ongoing: 'My Father is working until now, and I [too] am working' (John 5:17). Also, some have read the healing of the paralytic in John 5 and of the man born blind in John 9 as a paradigm for Jesus' creative work; Jesus completes creation by healing both men.[1] Also in John 20:22 we read, 'He breathed on them and said to them, "Receive the Holy Spirit"'. Here in the life-giving breath of the Spirit from Jesus to the disciples, we hear an echo of Genesis 2:7, 'the LORD God formed the man of dust from the ground and breathed into his nostrils the breath of life and man became a living creature'.[2] N.T. Wright notes the connection between the resurrection of Jesus and the 'first day of the week' (John 20:1,19). He perceives an intentional reference to Genesis and the first day of creation, the first day of a new creation.[3] Others have noticed a significant connection between the use of 'life' throughout the gospel and the emphasis on 'life' in Genesis 1–3.[4] The connections between John and Genesis are many.

While these connections (and others) reinforce the ideas I will consider, I am showing a deeper connection, or at least attempting to. The connection I am suggesting is that John 1–2 follows the events of Genesis 1–3, as if Genesis 1–3 was John's 'outline' for writing his opening chapters. See Table 4.1.

Table 4.1 Comparison of the outlines of Genesis 1–3 and John 1–2

Genesis 1–3	John 1–2
Creation / Genesis 1:1 – 2:3	Incarnation / John 1:1–14
Preparing of the Garden / Genesis 2:4–17	Preparing the wilderness / John 1:15–34
Search for helpers / Genesis 2:18–20	Search for disciples / John 1:35–51
Garden marriage / Genesis 2:21–25	Cana marriage / John 2:1–11
Expulsion from Garden / Genesis 3:1–24	Clearing the temple / John 2:13–22

The question, of course, is whether I am imagining this, or whether this mapping is intended by John. If I am right, this connection offers an explanation for the unique centrality of marriage at the opening of John's gospel. If so, then perhaps John is revealing to us the trinitarian nature of God in marriage as One-and-Many and his character as the God who is faithful to his covenant with his chosen bride – an intermediate stop in the biblical-theological development on our way to his conclusion in the book of Revelation. Following the outline above, I will lead us in an investigation of the detail. If it seems like too many details, it is because the claim is unique to this project and needs to be established in the details.

Creation and incarnation (John 1:1–14)

The Evangelist, John, begins his work with the grounding connection to Moses, 'in the beginning'. This first connection between John and Genesis is no overreach and is obvious to all. John then proceeds to exegete the person of Christ from within the Genesis account and claims: 'the Word was with God', 'all things were made through him', 'in him was life', 'the light shines in the darkness', and 'the darkness has not overcome it'. These all not only point us to creation, but go beyond to the central place the Word had in creation.[5] In so doing the Evangelist teaches us about the relationship of God the Father and God the Word while also connecting this Word to creation as its author. This is not only an exegesis of Genesis, but a distinct advance on what Moses wrote. John Chrysostom (349–407) saw this same advance and wrote of John's gospel: 'compare the approach of the Son of Thunder: when humankind had advanced along the path to perfection, no longer did he have them move by this lower way, but led his listeners to a loftier teaching.'[6] In his colourful way, Chrysostom is rightly saying that John told us more than Moses did: Jesus was there at creation, as creator! This is more commonly called *progressive revelation*. The Evangelist has 'fleshed out' (literally) the One-and-Many picture of Genesis 1&2, clarifying for us the fuller trinitarian image in Christ. In doing so, he also anticipates the new creation ministry of the Word. But this beginning is not merely a connection to 'The Beginning' to give weight to his gospel or to the central figure of his gospel – though it is that. Even more, it is a call to us to be attentive to how he will display Christ, the New Adam in creation (both accounts), as well as in the Marriage Text, and the Fall narrative.

Adam was given 'birth' by God, with the help of neither a man nor a woman. John emphasizes the similarity of Christ's birth. In the final movement of John's introduction (vv. 12–13), where he juxtaposes creation and incarnation, we find an intriguing bridge: 'children of God, *who* were born, not of blood nor of the will of the flesh nor of the will of man, but of God'. Some early church Fathers even amended this text from 'who were born' to read, '*he* was born'.[7] In this way, they not only display John's anticipation of our 'virgin birth' (explained by Jesus to Nicodemus in John 3), but also an affirmation of the virgin birth of Christ. In this textual amendment which seems to point clearly to Jesus' virgin birth, they had no extant textual support. Yet they do seem to have caught John's drift. John seems to focus on God's unique place in his birth: a child of God by the will of God, an allusion to the virgin birth that focuses on God more than on Mary. And in this allusion to the virgin birth, 'by the will of God . . . the Word became flesh', John may be alluding to Genesis: 'let there be' an incarnation! This new creation by God's Spirit is not merely descended from Adam, not *merely* the Seed; he is also God by God. Do we hear an echo of the Genesis 'And it was so' when the Evangelist declares, 'the Word became flesh'?[8] And it is then no surprise when the author responds joyfully to this new creation: 'we have seen his glory!' – an echo of 'and it was good!' And we hear even more. 'Glory' is a word that in the OT revealed the presence of the Holy Spirit. So also, 'glory' here was intended as an indicator that Jesus' coming declares the presence of the One who is tabernacle and temple.[9] This One tabernacles with us. And having discerned his presence in glory, we may see more. When the author of the Gospel of Luke celebrates the birth of Christ, he famously records the words of the angels: 'Glory to God in the highest, and on earth peace among those with whom he is pleased' (Luke 2:14). Glory in Luke is linked to God's blessing which has arrived among us. Also, when Solomon's temple is dedicated, we read, 'When all the people of Israel saw the fire come down and the glory of the LORD on the temple, they bowed down with their faces to the ground on the pavement and worshipped and gave thanks to the LORD, saying, "For he is good, for his steadfast love endures for ever"' (2 Chr. 7:3). Here too, glory results in blessing. Yes, it is a blessing declared over this new creation, but here it is from us to God. So, when they saw God's glory, they declared that *God is good*. Perhaps this is the form of John's blessing in this text; he implicitly blesses God when he mentions glory. That is when he writes, 'we have seen his glory', he then erupts in joyful blessing, 'glory as of the only Son from the Father, full of grace and truth.' Our glorious God is *very good* and he is now among us.

Preparing the Garden and the wilderness (John 1:19–34)

Genesis 2:4–17 is God preparing the Garden for Adam.[10] In parallel and in distinction to Genesis, the Baptist is going ahead of the second Adam. In parallel, he is preparing a place for Jesus: 'I am the voice of one crying out in the wilderness, "Make straight the way of the Lord"' (John 1:23). In distinction, he does so not in the Garden, but in the wilderness. Both preparations include a significant focus on water, specifically rivers.

In John, we are told that the Baptist's testimony took place at 'Bethany across the Jordan' (John 1:28). But there is no Bethany (known to us) on the other side (the eastern side) of this river – assuming a western perspective. D.A. Carson proposes that John was baptizing at Batanea, called Bashan in the OT. He points out that such a difference is not unusual because we can observe a great diversity in the spelling of proper nouns in the first century.[11] Perhaps. It may also be the case that this name highlights the place name for his readers. They know that Bethany is decidedly *not* on the 'other side'. So, they might wonder why the Evangelist would highlight a non-existent

'Bethany'? The answer may lie in the meaning of the name itself. One likely etymology for Bethany is 'house of affliction'. But a more 'literal' meaning is 'house of figs' and this is not without merit.[12] John may be calling attention to something, figs. Consider that figs are the *only tree* mentioned in the Garden by name (Gen. 3:7). And Adam & Eve used the leaves of the fig tree as a covering for their sin – a rather inadequate covering! Then notice that it is just here, near 'the house of figs' (Bethany), that John the Baptist is baptizing for forgiveness of sins. And it is here that he is testifying to the Lamb of God who takes away the sins of the world. This proper noun may have a proper fit.[13] The Baptist has prepared the Wilderness for the second Adam.

Search for helpers and disciples (John 1:35–51)

Barth noticed this connection between John and Genesis as well. Reflecting on Genesis 2:18 and Jesus' calling of his first disciples, he wrote:

> Why could not man be alone? . . . because the man Jesus, the Son of God, whose earthly existence was envisaged at the creation of heaven and earth, and the Son of Man whose manifestations and work were envisaged in the election of Israel, was not to be alone. Because in His own followers, in the Church which believes in Him, He was to have His counterpart . . . His helpmeet.[14]

While Adam's search would prove frustrating, Jesus' search succeeds.

The drumbeat of John's narrative in this section is the counting of days: 'the next day' (1:29), 'the next day' (1:35), 'the next day' (1:43), and then, finally, 'on the third day' (2:1). Below I will examine possibilities for John's specific intent in counting days up to the culminating wedding feast. Here it is sufficient to note that nowhere else in John does he write of days so that they tick like a metronome, echoing the meter so familiar to readers of Genesis 1, if not the enumeration. With each day, God is preparing this place more thoroughly for the second Adam to serve as the appointed prophet, priest, and king. Interestingly, the early Garden was not full of the kinds of cultivated plants that would exist after the Fall, for there was no water and no Adam: 'no bush of the field . . . no small plant of the field' (Gen. 2:5).[15] But here in the Evangelist's 'creation account', they were in the 'wilderness', outside the Garden where only cultivated plants and weeds grow (John 1:23). And unlike the early Garden, when these plants were not yet growing, there was abundant water in this wilderness, a sign of hope (John 1:26): Adam is about to arrive. But unlike the Garden, there was sin in the wilderness – sin that urgently needed to be dealt with (John 1:29).

In this anti-Garden setting, the wilderness, Jesus will now, like Adam before him, seek for fitting helpers. It is significant that John introduces Jesus in a way that also connects him to the Tanakh, beyond the Garden texts of Genesis 1–3. In his introduction of Jesus, the Evangelist (and so also the Baptist) connects Jesus to the OT sacrifice: 'Behold, the Lamb of God' (John 1:29,36). The reason that John identified Jesus as 'the Lamb of God' is not wholly clear.[16] There are many possible antecedents: God's creation of sacrificial animals (hinted at in Gen. 3:21), the Levitical offerings (Lev. 1–3), John's conquering lamb of Revelation (introduced in Rev. 5 and throughout his book), or the morning and evening sacrifice of a lamb (Exod. 29:38–44). All of these, and others, are possible antecedents, taken individually or even together. Yet, certainly, we should give prominence to the sacrificial lamb of the Passover.[17] From a biblical-theological perspective, if not a linguistic one, the Passover lamb fits, necessarily, for this is the Lamb who was slain, whose blood protects his people from the wrath of God against our sin. If this is correct, then this Lamb is pointing a way out of Egypt and to the land of milk and honey; the Lamb points the way out of the wilderness and back into the Garden.

We should also notice that like Adam, the second Adam is introduced by the Baptist, alone. This is not fitting; not good. But in contrast to Adam's initial and unsuccessful search for helpers, Jesus' search was abundantly successful. He finds not one, but many helpers. As noted above, Adam was looking for a fitting helper in the context of the

Garden temple, as its priest. So Jesus does, both as the priest and as the temple (anticipated in John 1:51 and affirmed in 2:21). In John 1:51 we find Jesus interacting with Nathanael when he declares that Nathanael will see 'heaven opened, and the angels of God ascending and descending on the Son of Man'. Jesus is connecting his story to Jacob's vision in the place that he called Bethel ('house of God'; Gen. 28:12). By this place name, 'house of God', he names what he witnessed as the opening of heaven. The 'greater things' which Jesus speaks of here declare that he is not only greater than the forefather of the Jews, Jacob, but also greater than the temple! So just as Adam in the first Garden-temple went in search of a fitting helper, Jesus, the new Adam and the new Temple, goes in search of helpers. And Jesus finds five.

On the third day, Jesus found two helpers, those who turned away from following the Baptist and now followed Jesus. They included an unnamed disciple and Andrew (by name, John 1:40). Andrew found his brother Simon and brought him also to Jesus (John 1:41–42). The next day, the fourth, Jesus found and called Philip, who found and brought Nathanael (John 1:45). Just as Adam did with the animals in order to name them, so did Jesus. He noted the character of these men and gave them new names (John 1:42,47). And these helpers are more than mere participants, more than mere servants. These men, and all of the twelve who would be called as fitting helpers, were with Jesus to know him. This connection may raise an alarm, for I seem to be making a connection between the intimate marital knowing (*yada*) of Adam & Eve (Gen. 4:1) and this 'knowing' of Jesus and the disciples. I am indeed. But sexuality is wholly subordinate to intimacy, a shadow of true intimacy. It is a pointer to true intimacy, rather than the other way round. And further, sexuality is neither essential to all intimate knowing, nor to the semantic domain of *yada* (Hebrew for 'know', or its nearest Greek synonym, *gnosko*). Indeed, in John 14:9 we read, 'Jesus said to him, "Have I been with you so long, and you still do not know me, Philip?"' It is for knowing Jesus that these helpers have been called; these helpers are with Jesus in order to know him intimately. Now, with fitting helpers found, named, and with him in order to know him, we prepare for a wedding, but not that of Jesus.

Garden marriage and Cana wedding (John 2:1–11)

This wedding is unusual, a departure from the other gospels, and recorded only in John. It is also unusual because of the emphasis which John places on this account; it not only stands as the inauguration of Jesus' public ministry, but it is the first of the seven signs which are a framework for this gospel.[18] This first sign occurs 'on the third day', counting from the last day mentioned in 1:43. As already noted, this numbering echoes the days of Genesis 1 and anticipates the last sign, the resurrection.[19] D.A. Carson counts exactly seven days in this text: an unnumbered first day in which John responds to the delegation (1:19–28), a second day when John introduces Jesus for the first time (1:29), a third day when he does the same with his disciples with him (1:35–42), and a fourth day when Jesus calls Philip and Nathaniel. The wedding then takes place on the 'third day' (2:1), the third day counting inclusively from the previous event. So, counting all of these days, the wedding takes place on the sixth day from the beginning of the search for helpers. However, Carson also notes that on the third day counting as above, 'they spent that day with him' (1:39, NIV), ending at 4 p.m. This may allow (or even necessitate) that Philip's introduction to Nathaniel was on the following day, therefore adding one day to the count. If this is correct, then the wedding is on the seventh day, Shabbat.[20] What was the author's intention in so carefully enumerating these days: whether six days or seven? Certainly, his enumeration of days makes it clear that he had a point to make, for he does so nowhere else in his gospel. As Carson says, 'This analysis is not grasping at straws'.[21] If the reader counts seven days, then perhaps the author intended that the first sign be performed on the Sabbath, accounting for a full creation week.[22] If the reader rightly counts six days, then this means the wedding takes place on the sixth day, and so the same 'day' as the marriage in Genesis 2. Whichever system of counting is the case, we find here an analogical reflection of creation.

But again, this is not Jesus' wedding. In regard to that, his time has not yet come. This wedding is proleptic, or it anticipates and looks forward to, a future culminating event: the Marriage Feast of the Lamb. Carson observes that the unusual exchange between Jesus and his mother in verse 4 (γύναι; οὔπω ἥκει ἡ ὥρα μου, 'Woman, yet comes my hour' or 'Woman, it is not yet my hour') might help us in this case. Jesus, who is not here as the bridegroom, is not responsible for providing all the wine for the guests, though that day is coming as the Baptist's introduction in John 3 makes clear (3:27–30); at that time, Jesus will be the messianic bridegroom.[23] If this is correct, this unusual exchange between mother and son establishes this text more closely with Genesis. Jesus' warning not to worry about the future, but to trust him, points to what is yet to come. The marriage in John provides an intended link between the *typical* marriage of the first Adam (a type of all human marriages) in Genesis and the *telic* marriage of the second Adam in Revelation (the culminating marriage to which all marriages point).

This first sign, the miracle at the wedding feast of Cana, also echoes creation in its form and language. First, this follows the pattern of 'forming and filling', but in reverse. In Genesis 1:2 God identified the challenge of creation as being 'formless and empty'. Then Moses presents his structured response in which he first forms the heavens and the earth over three days, and then fills the earth over the next three days.[24] So the Evangelist shows us a similar structure in this miracle, as a reversal of forming and filling in which the jars are first explicitly 'filled' ('to the brim') and only then is the water 'formed' into wine ('turned into wine'). In another way this is parallel to Genesis in which God speaks the command, 'let there be', and this is followed by the declaration 'it was so' and/or 'the earth brought forth'. So here Jesus commands, 'Fill the jars', and this is followed by 'they filled them'. Notice also that Jesus did not touch the water or the jars, but commanded and it was so; by his word alone he filled and formed. And like Genesis, there were no witnesses to this miracle, only those who observed the effect after the fact. Moses relates in Genesis what neither he, nor any person, witnessed, yet he testified to the effects which are enduring and pleasing to all. At the wedding, when Jesus turned water into wine, no one observed the miracle itself, not even the servants who heard the command and did the filling. They did not see the creation event inside the jar. And the master of the banquet could only enjoy the pleasing (and confusing!) effects (John 2:9–10). But somehow the disciples, who are not displayed in the picture, are told (by the servant?) of this new wine. For them this creation miracle is indeed a sign that they can discern and believe glory revealed to them (1:15), but to others it is merely good wine. The connection of this quiet sign to creation in Genesis is made complete by the exclamation of the master of the banquet, who tasted the wine and declared, 'you have saved the best till now' (NIV). How this is like the coda of Genesis, 'and it was good'.

It is also worth noticing that Jesus created his wine in ritually pure stone jars. Just as the creation of Genesis was created good, what was created here was good in the sense that it was ritually pure. There is at least one more parallel. In the Garden, at the inauguration of the first age, God provided an abundance of water which flowed into the Garden to water it, and flowed out as four rivers (Gen. 2:10–14). In the gospel, at the inauguration of the new age, John calls our attention to six stone jars which each held a large volume of water ('two or three measures'). Jesus then created a lavish abundance of new wine for a new age. The parallels to Genesis are pure, rich, full, and flowing.

Recorded only in this gospel, the decisive significance of this event is revealed to us in John's conclusion: 'This, the first of his [miraculous] signs, Jesus did at Cana in Galilee, and manifested his glory. And his disciples believed in him' (John 2:11). It is certainly here that the hidden glory of John 1:14, 'we have seen his glory', is perceived by a very limited 'we', only his disciples. To understand the significance of this small audience, it may help to return to the initial and (to many) confusing exchange between Jesus' mother and Jesus when the hospitality crisis was first discovered: 'When the wine ran out, the mother of Jesus said to him, "They have no wine." And Jesus said to her, "Woman, what does this have to do with me? My hour has not yet come." His mother said to the servants, "Do whatever he tells you"' (John 2:3–5). Many proposals have been put forward to make this exchange understandable. Typically, it is noted that Jesus' use of 'woman' is not disrespectful, but indicated a changed public relationship, and that by his response, he was indicating that it was not yet time for his public ministry. That has merit, but it does not explain why his mother then told the servants to 'Do whatever he tells you' (v. 5). Most significantly, it does not explain why Jesus did what he said he would not do![25] I propose that this exchange, at the beginning of the marriage story (v. 4), anticipates the conclusion at the end (v. 11); Jesus revealed his glory, but *only* to his bride. When Mary first speaks, she reveals her anxiety, 'They have no [more] wine.' Is she anxious for her friends, that they might not be embarrassed by this lack? Perhaps. Or is Mary more anxious *about* Jesus? That is, rather than attempting to provoke him into a miracle, was she instead afraid of what a miracle from Jesus might mean? Would Jesus respond with a miracle, reveal his glory to the whole wedding party, and be put to death *then and there*? Surely his coming death, and her pain, was on her mind. Though not recorded in John, Mary must have kept in mind Simeon's prophecy, 'a sword will pierce through your own soul also' (Luke 2:35). Did John know of this prophecy? Notice that this prophecy might explain a mother's anxiety whether or not the author of John's gospel knew that she knew this prophecy. He was an historian, reporting events, not their author. Yet, if he wrote his gospel later than the other gospel writers, he probably did know. In either case, Mary knew. Perhaps Jesus perceived Mary's anxiety that in revealing his glory he might be taken from her immediately? His answer, 'My hour [time] has not yet come', may indicate just that; Jesus was attempting to calm his mother's fears. N.T. Wright makes this same point, connecting Mary's exclamation to a fear of Christ's death:

This is only one of two occasions that we meet Jesus' mother in the Gospel, the other being at the foot of the cross (John 19:25–27). This is important, because Jesus' strange remark in verse 4, 'My time hasn't come yet', looks on, through many other references to his 'time', until at last the time does come, and the glory is revealed, fully as he dies on the cross.[26]

This phrase was a normal expression of Jesus (or the narrator) to indicate the time of his death. Though crowds often grew restless (dangerous!) around Jesus, he declared that the *time had not come* for him to die (John 7:6,8,30; 8:20). And later, in the positive sense, he declared that *the time had come* for him to die (12:23; 13:1; 16:32; 17:1). Perhaps this perspective sheds light on Jesus' next statement: 'Woman, what is this to you and to me!' (my literal translation).[27] Is Jesus saying, 'Do not worry about the future'? A very similar phrase was also used by the demoniac, Legion, in Luke 8:28 (and Mark 5:7) and a lone demon in Luke 4:24. In the mouths of these demons this phrase represents a harsh challenge and an abrupt dissociation – as it is often understood in this context between mother and son. But demons may not be the best place to turn for hermeneutical help to understand similar words in Jesus' mouth. The Gospel of John may be of more help to us. When ministering to Peter after the resurrection, and to correct his over-inquisitive interest in the *future* status of the author of the Gospel of John, Jesus said (literally): '*What* [is this thing] *to you? You* [to] *me* should follow' (John 21:22).[28] If the smooth translation of the first statement to Peter is, 'What is this thing to you?', compared with Jesus' statement to his mother, it is missing 'and to me'. But notice that this appears in the next phrase in John 21:22. While the construction is distinct (John 2 uses an explicit pronoun, 'to' (*pros*), rather than the implied 'to' of the dative case in John 21), still it is very much like what Jesus said to his mother. Strikingly, both are similar direct addresses of Jesus to a person he loves, both are at a turning point in his ministry, and both are mildly chastising corrections against anxious concerns for the future. To Peter, Jesus corrects his desire to know the future status of the author

of the Gospel of John. To Mary, Jesus seems to correct her concern
that Jesus might reveal his glory to all and so die later that day. And
notice that in both the concern is about death. There is a bit more:
the following phrase in Jesus' words to Peter translates as, 'Follow
me!' This phrase is intended to redirect Peter into the only place of
comfort: trust and focus on Christ. So also to his mother, Jesus offers
a word that could be understood as comfort: 'my time has not yet
come'. So, on Jesus' lips, both phrases are a correction against assuming responsibility for that which is God's alone, the future, and also
in the second phrase, it is a call to trust Jesus. Satisfied, and relieved,
Mary instructs the servants, 'Do whatever he tells you.' This makes
more sense.[29] If this is the right reading of the interchange between
mother and son, now the conclusion in verse 11, 'he manifested his
glory' [but only to his disciples] who 'believed in him [as a result]', is
the anticipated fulfilment of his correction and promise to his mother.
The first observation is that this interchange sets up the concluding
point: Jesus' glory is revealed here for only his bride to see – her alone.

Now John pronounces the benediction, 'This, the first of his
signs, Jesus did at Cana in Galilee, and manifested his glory. And
his disciples believed in him' (2:11). Perhaps this final verse of the
marriage in John may echo the benediction in Eden at the end of
Genesis 2:25. That event enjoyed a 'revealing' benediction: 'And the
man and his wife were both naked and were not ashamed' (v. 25). Yet,
in both John and Genesis the peaceful coda should make the reader
anxious about the future. As a great playwright said, 'If in the first
act you have hung a pistol on the wall, it must be fired in the next!'[30]
What will disturb this revealing peace? Moses points out the coming
disruption by a connecting word. The word for 'naked' in Genesis
2:25 is a homonym for 'crafty' in Genesis 3:1, 'Now the serpent was
more *crafty*'. Same word. The marriage benediction anticipates the
coming of the snake. A shadow moves into the garden to disturb
the peace. We see something similar in John 2:11 when the apostles
delight in seeing Jesus, uncovered, as it were. Like Adam & Eve, who
are revealed to each other (and to the reader) as pure and glorious, so
Jesus stands 'naked' to the disciples: he 'manifested his glory'. We see

that he is the tabernacle with no covering to hide the glory of the Father from whom he came.[31] But the tension set before us is reversed. In the first Garden, and after the marriage, we anticipate a fall from glory to shame. But here we should anticipate that the glory of Jesus will yet be revealed, not just to the disciples, but to the world. And because the world is not in the light and refuses to come into the light (John 3:19–20), they will attack the light, as if to put it out. Just as his mother feared. And Mary's heart will be pierced. And ours.[32]

Now, perhaps, we can understand the choice of the author of the Gospel of John to place the wedding in his narrative at this point. It does indeed parallel Genesis 2. Following the creation there is a search for fitting helpers. For both, God provides. Following the provision, there is a wedding. At the conclusion of the wedding, all is well, but we are being prepared for a change, a painful change which in the first place brings condemnation and death to all, but in the second will, through pain, bring justification and life for his bride. And, while in Genesis the wedding is a culminating event, a climax, for John it is proleptic, anticipating the future marriage of the Lamb.

Exile from the Garden and the temple (John 2:13–22)

This event, like the wedding at Cana, stands uniquely at the beginning of the Gospel of John. Unlike the wedding of Cana, this event (or one like it) is known in the synoptic gospels, but all three synoptics place this event at the end of Christ's ministry. Yet, the author of John's gospel places it here, at the head of Christ's ministry. Did this event happen at the beginning or the end of Jesus' ministry? Or were there two (or more) similar events? For this investigation, the point is moot – John crafted his gospel so that it stands here.[33] The theological question persists: what impact did John intend on his readers by reporting this event here in his narrative? Surely, it must fit into his stated goal in John 20:30–31, 'that you may believe that Jesus is the Christ'. Perhaps congruent with that primary goal, the Evangelist intends us to hear the echo of Genesis 1–3.

Going up to Jerusalem at the time of Passover, Jesus enters the temple courts. Here we will witness the Fall and the exile, again. The temple court is filled with merchants and money changers, and animals as well (like the Garden?). Acting the priest (the one who 'guards' the temple from what does not belong in the temple), Jesus makes a whip out of cords and drives them all from the temple area. Unlike Adam who failed as a priest, Jesus chases the religious leaders ('sons of their father the devil' and 'a brood of vipers') out of the temple. When the Jews demanded of Jesus a sign, that he might show his authority to act in this way, they were too late! Indeed, they had just witnessed the sign, the cleansing of the temple! This is his second sign, promised beforehand in Malachi 3:1–3 and Zechariah 14:21. It had been fulfilled as they watched, but they missed it. Even so, Jesus is willing to offer more: the explicit sign he promises is intentionally disorienting to those without faith: 'destroy this temple and in three days I will raise it up'. He speaks of his death and resurrection, the last of the seven signs in John. What is the connection to Genesis 1–3? There are several. First, by the placement of the temple incident immediately after the marriage, the author – or Jesus himself – raised a distinct connection with the Fall of Genesis. Second, the sellers of goods were overwhelmed by their desires and disobeyed God, as did Adam & Eve. Consider Adam who failed to drive the tempting serpent from the Garden, while Jesus succeeded, driving what is unclean from the Garden/temple.[34] Finally we see the parallel of Adam & Eve who are driven from the Garden in Genesis 3 and the sellers whom God drove out of the temple. We might also notice the distress of the religious leaders, their repulsion at the very idea that this newly restored temple, forty-six years of work and not yet complete, might be destroyed (John 2:20)! If they were mocking Jesus' hubris that he could raise it again in three days, they were probably horrified at the idea that such a work of beauty and grace might be corrupted. What a parody. They cared greatly about this Jerusalem temple, which was indeed a renewed and great creation, recently restored by Herod.[35] But the temple points to a Garden temple, and all creation, which languishes even today under corruption to decay

(Rom. 8:18–23). For this, they gave hardly a thought. And worse, the true Temple stood among them, and they would soon tear him down with zeal.

In explaining this event, the Evangelist summarizes by saying that after Jesus was raised from the dead, the disciples believed the Scriptures, and the words he had spoken (John 2:22). The word he had spoken is clear: 'I will raise it in three days'. But which scripture(s) are fulfilled? Perhaps prophecies in general and all of them together in the light of John 14:26 where Jesus promises that the Holy Spirit will teach them about him with clarity. But this 'fulfilment' must include the first prophecy about the redemptive work of the Christ: Genesis 3:15, the *protoevangelium*. Moses wrote, 'I will put enmity between you and the woman, and between your offspring and her offspring; he shall bruise your head, and you shall bruise his heel.' This Jesus accomplished when he died and rose to life, when the Temple was destroyed and raised in three days. First and foremost, it is *this scripture* (Gen. 3:15) which was fulfilled by the Evangelist's words, 'and they believed the Scriptures'.[36] John is pointing first to Genesis 3. And this scripture is fulfilled in the coming of the Seed by the childbirth that would come through marriage. And this childbirth is a testimony to the character of God: he is faithful to his covenant.

In the beginning of his presentation of the Christ, the author of John is following the arc of the Genesis creation story(s) to the climax, to the biblical-theological vector of marriage. In this, he is interrupted, as was Moses in Genesis. There is an ejection from the Garden temple. This temple must now be torn down and rebuilt. That project now holds John's focus for the rest of his gospel. The telos of the marriage will not be encountered until John writes of his Revelation. But even so, John never loses sight of this goal. In the very next chapter of John, in the fourth and final introduction of Jesus by John the Baptist (John 3:29), we encounter Jesus as the bridegroom: 'The one who has the bride is the bridegroom. The friend of the bridegroom, who stands and hears him, rejoices greatly at the bridegroom's voice. Therefore this joy of mine is now complete.' Jesus is the bridegroom. And Jesus has already discovered his bride in his fitting helpers who represent the foundation of the church and the whole of the people of God. So, now in the progression of John's story, the bridegroom reclaims the Garden, the temple. In doing so, he makes space for himself and his bride.

This work comparing John with Genesis is not complete. I will not complete this task here. I must leave it for later, or to another, to investigate more parallels between John and Genesis as they apply to marriage. Let me hint at directions that may be fruitful. These fitting helpers will be with him for ever, in heaven, but there is work to do first. Chosen, but at this point in Jesus' ministry they are not yet his bride or even his betrothed. However, John 6 makes it clear that his marriage to the apostles is arranged by his Father. He declares in verses 37 and 44 that those the Father sends, and only those the Father sends, come to him. In light of John's declaration that Jesus is the bridegroom and we are the bride, this sounds like an arranged marriage. Indeed, Jesus is pleased with the Father's will in this, and will never cast out (divorce?!) those God has sent him, but raise them up on the last day. Indeed, they will not turn from him, specifically because he has chosen them (vv. 69–70). Jesus is faithful to his covenant – but he has not chosen all as his bride (v. 71). These chosen ones he will instruct for some time, preparing them and himself for his death – the bride price. And before his death, at a banquet, he will seal them to himself as his betrothed. Recorded in John 13, they drink the cup of the New Covenant with him at what we now call the Lord's Supper. But at that same banquet, one of their number was cast out; he was sent away from that betrothal feast, not betrothed to Jesus. Jesus fed him with a dipped morsel and then he was cast out from the feast, betrothed to another; Judas was betrothed to Satan who entered him. It is worth considering Jesus' high-priestly prayer in John 17. Here Jesus uses language which is very like that which is found in the Marriage Text when he speaks of his goal for those God has given to him: our union with him in the Trinity. He prays 'for those who will believe in me . . . that they may all be one, just as you, Father, are in me, and I in you, that they also may be in us . . . *that they may be one even as we are one*' (John 17:20–22). How closely this echoes the desire of Genesis, 'they shall become one' (Gen. 2:24). Then by his death, Jesus crushed the serpent's head, paying the bride price to the Father. He then left to build a home for his bride to dwell with him (John 14:1–3). And soon he will return for his bride. By God's covenant-faithfulness to his betrothed, the One-and-Many nature of God becomes our reality, when we, though still many ourselves, are one with him, as he is one. Marriage is the metaphor that points to the telos, the culmination of history.

The Prophets of the NT: The Ephesian 'Confusion' of Marriage and Theosis

I move now to the epistles, which may be considered a parallel to the Prophets in the Old Testament. But again, I will not study them exhaustively or even in any way that approaches a complete study. There are many texts in the epistles which touch on marriage and I am not dealing with most of these. Such texts include Romans 1 and 7; 1 Corinthians 7 and 11; Colossians 3; and 1 Peter 3. I will return to some of these in Part Three, the doctrinal (dramatic and 'ethical') section of this book. But as I wrote above, the point of this investigation is not an *exhaustive* examination of the Marriage Text against *every* text that touches on marriage. Instead I have a modest goal: to establish reasons for considering the Marriage Text as a ground for a sound theology of marriage and to promote further investigation. To this end, I want to consider Ephesians 5, a most significant text on marriage which is explicitly connected to Genesis 1–3. Let me display this critical text, verses 22–33, in full:

> [22]Wives, submit to your own husbands, as to the Lord. [23]For the husband is the head of the wife even as Christ is the head of the church, his body, and is himself its Saviour. [24]Now as the church submits to Christ, so also wives should submit in everything to their husbands. [25]Husbands, love your wives, as Christ loved the church and gave himself up for her, [26]that he might sanctify her, having

cleansed her by the washing of water with the word, [27]so that he might present the church to himself in splendour, without spot or wrinkle or any such thing, that she might be holy and without blemish. [28]In the same way husbands should love their wives as their own bodies. He who loves his wife loves himself. [29]For no one ever hated his own flesh, but nourishes and cherishes it, just as Christ does the church, [30]because we are members of his body. [31]'Therefore a man shall leave his father and mother and hold fast to his wife, and the two shall become one flesh.' [32]This mystery is profound, and I am saying that it refers to Christ and the church. [33]However, let each one of you love his wife as himself, and let the wife see that she respects her husband.

Ephesians 5 is famous in part because Jerome (347–420) 'tricked' the church into categorizing marriage as a 'sacrament' when he translated 'mystery' (Greek, *musterion*) with the Latin *sacramentum*. He translated Ephesians 5:32, 'this sacrament [mystery] is profound'. Arguably, other options were before him. But if numbering marriage among the sacraments was an historical accident, a 'trick' of translation, it may have been a move in the right direction for other reasons. I will consider this in the next chapter. Here my main concern is that Ephesians 5:22–33 is one of Paul's most detailed teachings on marriage, one that is also clearly grounded in Genesis, specifically on the Marriage Text.

What is this great mystery pointing us toward? One scholar, Matthew Godshall, has noticed what he calls the re-contextualization of Genesis 2 in Ephesians 5 by which it takes on for Paul's readers 'a new significance in the light of the inauguration of the "age to come".' That is, while the Marriage Text was connected to creation – as Barth would say, it is the climax and conclusion – so Paul 'has reoriented the marriage union around the eschatological reality of Christ's union with his Church'.[37] Paul has reversed its direction. Godshall's argument is important here, focusing on the distinction between 're-contextualizing' over and against 'reinterpreting'. He writes:

Paul is, therefore, not reinterpreting by claiming that Genesis 2:24 is referring to Christ and the Church, but rather, he is re-contextualizing it by interpreting the verse in the new eschatological context of the oneness Christ shares with his people. He does this in order to show that Christian marriage has a role to play in providing a 'sneak peek' of the eschatological union of all things in Christ.

In our marriages we are putting on a forward-looking drama. Godshall argues that Paul is making a parallel between Adam's 'vows' ('bone of my bones, and flesh of my flesh', Gen. 2:24) and Paul's claim that we are 'members of [Christ's] body' (Eph. 5:30). The next phrase, 'therefore' (or 'for this reason'),[38] points backwards to our position in Christ. Then it follows that the 'this' of 'this mystery' points, not to the marriage in Genesis or even our own marriage, but rather to our integration into Christ's body. The next phrase is offered by Paul as a clarification: 'I am saying that it [this, the mystery] refers to Christ and the church' (v. 32). I think Godshall is correct, syntactically. But Paul is doing more. He has told us something in an intentionally intriguing way. Paul's discussion of marriage, and the re-contextualization argument with its explicit need for clarification, is not intended to remove the mystery of Genesis, 'two shall become one flesh', nor that of our own marriage. Indeed, the very next movement in his argument returns us to human marriage (v. 33). Rather, the reorientation that we experience when we understand what has happened in our betrothal to Christ, so that we are now members of his body even as we wait for our ultimate marriage to him, only enhances the mystery of Christian marriage which acts as a 'sneak peak' of what is to come with Jesus.[39] This, too, is a glorious mystery. I am saying that it refers to Christian marriage as well. This is the glorious 'confusion' of human marriage and theosis – the coming together with God as one.

What is theosis? Perhaps it can be understood, tutorially, by examining the profound and glorious mystery of human marriage. In Genesis, we learn that marriage represents the One-and-Many unity which is in God. This dramatic portrayal is shared, if dimly (ever so dim!) by Lamech and all of us who followed him, and by all marriages. But now in Christ, Christian marriage specifically shares in what the Orthodox Church calls deification, theosis, or Christification.[40] In accord with the high-priestly prayer of John 17, we are to participate in the Oneness of the Many in the Trinity. The Western Church sometimes is apprehensive about this doctrine, especially about the name 'deification'. But this is just what Paul is reaching for when he says that we are part of Christ's body and that our uniting in him in marriage is the end for which we were redeemed. No, we are not to become God or gods, but to be united with the Trinity. Oliver Crisp explains this well as he reflects on Edwards:

> The Spirit unites us to God in Christ in 'infinite strictness,' yet not so that we lose our identity, becoming 'part' of God as a drop of water becomes part of the ocean into which it is poured. To use a distinction Edwards does not (but that is consistent with what he does say), in theosis we creatures are invited to participate in the divine life but not in the divine essence. Union does not imply fusion.[41]

This is just the point of the Ephesian mystery.

This unity is so strong that Jesus can say, 'they shall be one as we are one'. This oneness is now dramatically portrayed by two people in Christian marriage. Together they display our future and present reality; together they participate in the One-and-Many reality of God in Christ. This is the great privilege that is thrust upon us sinners who dare to marry! This is the drama the church shares when we support families – true for us all, whether we are single, divorced, widowed, engaged, married happily, or married unhappily.

In light of this (indeed as Paul intended, for this passage is first about human relationships as v. 21 explains), it is even more important that we fulfil the marital vows of Adam: '[you are] bone of my bones and flesh of my flesh!' (Gen. 2:23a). Paul, reflecting on this text, wrote: 'In the same way husbands should love their wives as their own bodies. He who loves his wife loves himself. For no one ever hated his own flesh, but nourishes and cherishes it, just

as Christ does the church, because we are members of his body'
(Eph. 5:28–30). When husbands strive to fulfil these vows to their
wives for all to see, they are dramatically portraying the care of Christ
for his bride, the One who 'loved the church and gave himself up
for her, that he might sanctify her' (5:25–26). In one magnificent
text, Paul has drawn together both themes from the Genesis Marriage
Text, re-contextualizing them to Christ: God's character of covenant-
faithfulness to us in Christ, and our participation in the One-and-
Many nature of God through Christ.

The Writings of the NT: The Culmination of Marriage in Revelation

Last, at least for this New Testament biblical theology, I venture into
the Revelation of John. As the gospels may parallel the Torah, and
the epistles the Prophets, so Revelation is like the Writings. Before
venturing into such a contested book, let me review a taxonomy of
approaches to the Revelation of John. Depending on your background,
you will identify with one or another of these approaches. I will not
try to convince you of the best approach, but rather hope to assure you
that I am aware of the various approaches and how they affect our discussion of marriage. These include: preterist (in which the Revelation
only describes the fall of Jerusalem in AD 70 or the fall of the Roman
Empire in the fifth century AD with no prophetic connection to the
eschaton, to last things), historicist (in which the movement through
Revelation displays the successive events of church history), futurist
(in which the book offers essential predictions of the time immediately
before the eschaton), and idealist (in which the book portrays the
symbolic conflict between good and evil, timelessly, or in the eclectic
or modified form, also portrays the events of the second coming of the
Messiah). These may be investigated at length elsewhere.[42] My own
position aligns closely to Gregg Beale's modified-idealist position. In
brief, while the text makes reference to historical-future (to the author)
events, many/most of the references are 'trans-temporal', making

reference to the battle that continues in the time between comings. Historical references then have multiple referents; they are fairly identified with many different events. Moreover, all of these events are said to culminate in the return of Christ. For example, Revelation 19 may foresee, correctly, the fall of Rome in the fifth century. Yet, I understand the marriage feast of the Lamb to be a future event to which Revelation 19–22 witnesses. Further, I understand this feast to be the inaugurating event of eternity. Indeed, canonically, it is most significant that the wedding feast of the Lamb is the event toward which Genesis 1–2 reaches and in which it finds its completion. The canonical arrangement is quite purposeful; the placement of the Garden marriage at the beginning is paired, historically and theologically, with the marriage of the virgin bride and the Lamb, closing the arc. While this overlaps with real historical fulfilment(s) and the general battle between good and evil, I am compelled by canon to see a future and culminating fulfilment as intended by John in his Revelation.

So then, I see the book of Revelation as the intentional terminus of the arc that began in Genesis 1–2. In Revelation 19–22 the meaning of the metaphor of marriage is fulfilled. The reader may recall that they are two: the imaging of God's One-and-Many nature (his trinitarian nature) and God's character (his covenant-faithfulness to his people). Both find their culmination here at the terminus of the canon.

If we make our way through Revelation to the wedding feast in the last chapters of his writing, we encounter these ancient themes of idolatry and adultery which are so prevalent in the Tanakh. However a person may interpret the seven letters to the churches, two of them prominently feature a connection between idolatry and adultery, Pergamum (2:14) and Thyatira (2:20–21). The word here, and most often in Revelation, is the more general word 'immorality', rather than 'adultery'. However, adultery seems to be implied by inclusion in the broader term. The issue seems to have been teachers (false teachers!) who permissively encouraged participation in the local cult of idolatry which included both food offered to idols and sexual immorality. In this they are like Balaam and Jezebel of old. And this is also adultery, because their teaching seems to be an encouragement toward general participation, not merely that of the unmarried youth of the church. The church, even those who did not participate, also failed to oppose the tarnishing of the image among them. In doing so they failed to enact God's drama, accepting any theatrical travesty, uncritically. Even here, the connection between idolatry and adultery continues.

In Revelation 9:21 'immorality' is again charged against God's image-bearers. Indeed, it appears here at a key turn in the book: a pause after the description of the seals and trumpets of God's wrath and prior to both the two witnesses (ch. 11) and the recap of the history of redemption (ch. 12). Here we are told that humankind refused to repent. As proof, their idolatry and immorality (adultery) is exposed by the judge. Then in 14:8, we are shown Babylon the Great who has fallen, the one who incited idolatry (not mentioned in this text, but established thoroughly elsewhere) and sexual immorality. In 17:1–6, this same image and similar description is repeated. This continues in 17:15; 18:3,9; 19:2. But here in chapter 19 that idolatry and adultery are ended: 'Hallelujah! The smoke from her goes up for ever and ever' (Rev. 19:3). Now we are ready for the culmination of all of history.

Recall that the first sign of the incarnate Messiah was at the wedding of Cana (John 2). At that time, Jesus said, 'my hour [time] has not yet come'. Among other meanings (some suggested earlier in this chapter), perhaps there was an undertone that the wedding in Cana was not Jesus' wedding; it was not yet his responsibility to provide unlimited wine for his guests. But at the end of time, at the wedding feast of the Lamb, it will indeed be his time to provide. In fact, he will serve us at the wedding feast ('Blessed are those servants whom the master finds awake when he comes. Truly, I say to you, he will dress himself for service and have them recline at table, and he will come and serve them', Luke 12:37). In Revelation 19, John turns to the fulfilment of the first sign of his gospel, the wedding feast of the Lamb. Now we have the first glimpse of that wedding – at least of the bride. In verses 6–10 we 'hear' a great multitude praising

God for his salvation! The 'hallelujah' sounds first for the judgment of the false bride (the great prostitute, vv. 1–2) and again (vv. 3–4), confident that we have seen the last of this adulteress. Then the true, virgin bride appears and the 'hallelujah' erupts yet again, from everyone who stands with the Lord our God. She 'has made herself ready' and 'it was granted her to clothe herself with fine linen, bright and pure', a fulfilment of OT prophecies and anticipated already in the Revelation. And an angel declares, and commands John to write, 'Blessed are those who are invited to the marriage supper of the Lamb' (v. 9). Then suddenly, just as we anticipate seeing the marriage feast and the marriage, the scene changes – dramatically.

The invitation to the wedding supper is juxtaposed with a very different feast. While the bride has been feasting on Christ ('this is my body') and will soon be feasting with Christ, waited on by him, perhaps in fulfilment of Psalm 23, Jesus now sets a table before the bride in the presence of her enemies! In fact, he serves up her enemies to the birds of the sky: 'Come, gather for the great supper of God' (Rev. 19:17). And the carrion birds feast on the defeated foes of the warrior Lamb (v. 21). While in John's first recorded sign (John 2), the Messiah provided unlimited wine, here he provides an unlimited meal of flesh: 'eat the flesh of kings, the flesh of captains, the flesh of mighty men, the flesh of horses and their riders, and the flesh of all men, both free and slave, both small and great' (v. 18). Revelation 15:1 declares that this sign is 'the last, for with them the wrath of God is finished'. With the pouring out of those bowls, the stage is set for the full conquest of God's enemy, Babylon – all who oppose him. This sign continues to unfold from Revelation 17 to 19. Here is the completion of what began there. This defeat of God's enemies, the completion of that last sign, is the last explicit sign in history. Now comes the final judgment of Satan and his followers (20:7–15). And then the wedding!

There is a paucity of detail about the wedding feast and very little about the flow of the events. Still, in glimpses and fragmentary references, much is on display. In the new creation, the bride is portrayed as a holy city, the New Jerusalem. She is 'prepared as a bride adorned for her husband' (21:1–2). John is connecting this glimpse as following his first sight of her in 19:7–8 where it was granted to her to clothe herself. And as is the case for married couples in all cultures, there is a home prepared for their living together. This home is God himself: 'Behold, the dwelling place of God is with man. He will dwell with them' (v. 3). Then in verse 21:9, we are again introduced to the bride, our third glimpse: 'I will show you the Bride, the wife of the Lamb.' What the angel showed John was a city, the New Jerusalem. It seems to be a reprise of 21:2. But this time there is much detail, including that she has 'the glory of God' (v. 11), probably another reference to her adornment. We must notice that the bride, this city of God, is composed of both Israel (after which her gates are named, vv. 12–13) and the church, for her foundations are named after the Twelve, the apostles (v. 14). Indeed, after our survey of the metaphor of marriage in the OT and NT, we should be careful to identify the bride, not simply as 'the church', but as the people of God.[43] She herself is many and one, as Paul asserted in Ephesians 2:14, 'he has made both one'. Many have suggested understandings of the various characteristics and measurements that follow in verses 16–27. We are certainly to be instructed by these details, but they do not lie in the main path for this investigation of marriage.

Interestingly, readers do 'stumble' across two more references to the 'immoral' and the 'idolaters', shocking to us after seeing the bride arrayed for her wedding! Were we not told that we were done with this lot in chapter 20? Did we not sing 'hallelujah', not only that we saw the bride arrayed for her Lover, but that we saw the last of the false bride! The first of these unwelcome returns of the 'immoral' is found in Revelation 21:8, 'But as for the cowardly, the faithless, the detestable, as for murderers, the sexually immoral, sorcerers, idolaters, and all liars, their portion will be in the lake that burns with fire'. But notice that these 'adulterers' are not 'here' – and that is the very point made in John's reference to them. God is declaring that the eternal separation has already begun and will forever continue: 'their portion will be [for it already is the case] in the lake that burns with fire and sulphur, which is the second death'. The second and last reference is in Revelation 22:10–11,14–15, 'let the filthy still be filthy [now]' and 'outside are . . . the sexually immoral'. One possibility for understanding why John returns them to 'the stage' is that beginning with verse 6 ('these words are trustworthy and true') we have returned to John's own time before the return of Christ (22:20, 'Surely I am coming soon'). This is a word to the church in John's day. This seems likely. Yet there is more, for in verse 15 we are also called to witness the eternal divide. We are told that 'the immoral' are (will be) outside the gates of the eternal city. They will never enter. The bride is inside. And the bride and the Spirit call, 'Come!' (v. 17). But they, the immoral idolaters, cannot come. This is a witness to the final fixing of places, an ultimate and concluding reality that will not change. This is in distinct contrast to Eden, which was created and allowed for an instability, a movement out of Eden (and, conditionally, back in). Then, everyone was inside the Garden wall, but a threat hung over them: 'Do not eat!' They ate. The first meal of the Bible was with the serpent. And following the fatal feast, everyone in the Garden was driven outside the Garden wall where death would reign. Guards were set that they might not return to eat of life. Then God, who worked for us without ceasing, and Jesus with him, unfolded his plan to bring his bride back inside the Garden; he did this over thousands of years. His work was displayed as complete in the incarnation, death, and resurrection of Christ. It promises to resolve in the ascension and return of Christ for his bride. And in that resolution we discover an eternal fixity of place which is distinct from the instability associated with the original Garden. The new Garden, now the Garden-City, is no longer a place where there is movement in and out. Those who are in stay in, and those who are out stay out. Indeed, our last view of the bride is with the Spirit when she makes one last call for those who are invited to enter: 'The Spirit and the Bride say, "Come." And let the one who hears say, "Come." And let the one who is thirsty come; let the one who desires take the water of life without price' (Rev. 22:17). Even now the Spirit calls to all who will hear; he calls through the church. The door to this wedding feast stands open. Whoever has ears, let him hear what the Spirit says to the churches! But soon the door will close and the wedding feast will move to consummation. Then there will be no divorce, no instability: 'I will never cast [them] out,' says Jesus (John 6:37–44). His promise is now fulfilled; our place is secure in him.

God is vindicated in this marriage of the Lamb and his bride; he is faithful to himself and to his covenant, and God has drawn the many into the oneness of the Trinity. Eternally.

The Culmination of Marriage in the New Testament and the Whole of the Canon

This biblical-theological investigation reveals marriage as a key metaphor, even the golden thread which God is using to sew his story together from Garden to Garden-City. Marriage is a sanctifying drama, a witness to God's One-and-Many nature and a prophecy of the new creation fulfilment of God's faithfulness to his bride. In our rebellion, yet God remains faithful, giving his life to present his bride, restored as a virgin bride. In our weakness, marriage displays the one-and-many reality, perhaps even a three-in-one reality. Malachi said of marriage: 'Did he not make them one, with a portion of the Spirit in their union?' (Mal. 2:14–15). And soon, in the culmination of redemptive history, the bride and groom will be revealed. They live happily ever after.

Interlude: Historical Theology

I have been following an overarching outline of exegesis, theology, and doctrine: Part One, Part Two, and doctrine should follow here. Soon. But before I do, I want to insert an interlude. In doing so I am positioning this material as a conclusion to the theological section and as an introduction to the doctrinal section. Of course, historical theology could be placed alongside biblical theology. Yet, in this instance, in this particular investigation of historical theology, I want to consider the specific effect that the Reformation had on our understanding of marriage as (or not as!) a sacrament. From this will follow my proposal that we reconsider that move, reversing it. And also, speaking specifically to my evangelical brothers and sisters, I would restore marriage, not as an 'ordinance', but as a 'sacrament'. To do so, I will redefine sacrament, but faithfully grounded in its historical roots. This proposal will colour, though not dominate, the investigation of the doctrine of marriage, the drama that the Spirit intends for us to engage as the people of God. For that reason, because it is both 'theology' and 'doctrine', I want to give it a transitional place, between (biblical) theology and doctrine.

5

Historical Theology: Revealing Marriage as a Sacrament[1]

I have proposed that the Marriage Text (Gen. 2:18–25) is the ground of a biblical theology which displays God's nature, One-and-Many, and his character, faithful to his covenant. I have displayed, rather than proved, that this proposal fits both the Old Testament and the New Testament. Now, in this historical interlude, I want to consider reinstating marriage as a sacrament, that is, with sacrament 'properly' defined.

Defining Offence and Sacrament

'Why would you want to change a perfectly good word like "ordinance"?' So a fellow theologian erupted when he heard my plans to challenge the exclusive use of 'ordinance' and to reconsider the term 'sacrament'. I understand. 'Ordinance' is not merely a term of art among some evangelical Protestants, but a distinctive. Historically, the association of sacraments with *saving* grace is so strong that the retreat to 'ordinance' continues with little or no discussion. Yet, among many Protestants, 'sacrament' is an apt term for baptism and the Lord's Supper. I want to rehabilitate this term for the broader Protestant Church. To do so, I want to explore a definition of 'sacrament' that may be historical, biblically consistent, and still satisfying to Protestants, especially Reformed, evangelical Protestants. But not only. Since the Reformation, all Protestant Christians have accepted the exile of marriage from among the sacraments – even from the ordinances. If 'sacrament' is a worthy term, it may be that marriage should be included as a sacrament. I think that Luther and Calvin may have done us a disservice by removing marriage from among the sacraments and (also, as I will show) from the domain of the church.

'Sacrament' is an old word, with a rich, multidimensional meaning, attached to it from centuries of use. Its historic and common roots are well known: a military oath and the sum which litigants deposit with the courts.[2] Tertullian was perhaps among the first to use the Latin word *sacramentum*, in a religious context referring to the deep mysteries of God which are associated with faith, including baptism.[3] Later, in the early fifth century, the word was ordained by Jerome in the Vulgate. Specifically, he used the term eight times to translate the NT Greek *musterion*,[4] but only one of these uses was in the context of any of the sacraments later enumerated by the church. This singular instance was in Ephesians 5:32 where he translated the Greek word as *sacramentum*. Even more influential is Augustine whose definition is cross-claimed by many traditions: 'sacraments are the visible signs of invisible realities'. But there is no evidence that by this he made reference to a specific set of sacraments, nor does this common attribution exist in this simple form in his writings.[5] It is worth adding that Augustine insisted that what made the sign (sacrament) efficacious for the believer was the word. He wrote of John 15:1–3:

'Now ye are clean through the word which I have spoken unto you.' Why does He not say, 'Ye are clean through the baptism wherewith ye have been washed,' but 'through the word which I have spoken unto you,' save only that in the water also it is the word that cleanseth? Take away the word, and the water is neither more nor less than water. *The word is added to the element, and there results the sacrament, as if itself is also a kind of visible word.*[6]

In this he is followed by Calvin and others. What began as an oath (connecting us to the command of God) took on the added dimension of association of a sign which points to the deep mysteries of God, effective in the life of the believer, because of the word preached.

'Ordinance' is also an old word referring to something commanded. For many evangelicals, particularly those baptistic evangelicals of my tradition, this is the essential term which represents the Lord's Supper and baptism. However, in comparison with the sacramental rites of the church, it is singly dimensioned. The *Oxford English Dictionary* (*OED*) testifies to the use of 'ordinance' as a synonym for 'sacrament'. That is, by referring to this one characteristic of 'sacrament' – God's command – 'ordinance' made reference to the whole. The *OED* cites several examples of such usage from the fifteenth to the twentieth century. But that changed in the last hundred years. In fact, during the twentieth century the *OED* limits the use of the term 'ordinance' to the 'baptistic church' and as a substitute term. No longer a synonym, it is a term of distinction over and against 'sacrament'. Of course, many other Protestants use the word 'sacrament', including Anglicans and Lutherans, and Wayne Grudem understands them even now as synonyms.[7] But among baptistic evangelicals, the accepted term is 'ordinance': 'ceremonies that Jesus commanded his church to perform'.[8] Millard Erickson is conventional in this regard: 'Since [baptism] was ordained by [Christ], it is properly understood as an ordinance rather than a sacrament.'[9]

The encyclopedia of the Roman Catholic Church (RCC), *New Advent*, defines 'sacraments' in this way: 'outward signs of inward grace, instituted by Christ for our sanctification'.[10] This definition echoes Augustine. However, the second edition of the Catechism defines sacrament thus: 'The sacraments are efficacious signs of grace, instituted by Christ and entrusted to the church, by which divine life is dispensed to us.'[11] While both definitions are still used, the emphasis in the second is that the sacraments *in themselves* effectively cause grace to flow to the recipient. This conferring of grace was codified about one year after Luther's death during the seventh session of the Council of Trent (March 1547). Then, and to this day, sacraments were declared to be seven in number and also to confer grace explicitly.[12]

Martin Luther had no objection to the term 'sacrament' and it continues in general use today by Lutherans. He did reject most of the seven sacraments of the RCC, accepting only the Lord's Supper, baptism, and penance, arriving at this list by the use of two filters – 'a divine promise' and 'a sign':[13] a *sacrament* is 'a word of divine promise, which must be believed in by him who receives the sign'.[14] Fundamentally, this means Luther rejected the Roman understanding of the operation of faithless grace through the sacrament. He did not reject the sacraments as means of grace, but as either the unique means of grace, apart from the word, or a means of grace which could be faithlessly received.[15] Berkhof offers a helpful definition: 'A sacrament is a holy ordinance instituted by Christ, in which by sensible signs the grace of God in Christ, and the benefits of the covenant of grace, are represented, sealed, and applied to believers, and these, in turn, give expression to their faith and allegiance to God.'[16] It is worth noting that this definition maps well on to the fourfold definition of the *New Advent Encyclopedia*, quoted previously: a sign, of grace, a commandment, and sanctification. To see this we must understand 'benefits . . . expression to their faith and allegiance to God' as sanctification, distinct from justification.

In Book 4 of the *Institutes*, John Calvin distinguished between or-dinances and sacraments. He writes, 'Marriage is a good and holy ordinance of God; and farming, building, cobbling, and barbering are lawful ordinances of God, and yet are not sacraments. For it is required that a sacrament be not only a work of God but an outward ceremony appointed by God to confirm a promise.'[17] This helps us see both terms in active distinction. For Calvin, much influenced by Augustine, a sacrament is: 'a testimony of divine grace toward us, confirmed by the outward sign, with mutual attestation of our piety toward him'.[18] And like Luther, Calvin rejects the idea that sacraments are a cause of grace apart from the work of the Holy Spirit to regenerate, citing Augustine for support. Calvin says that there is a parallel between the Word and sacrament, so that both are received with God's mercy and grace. But grace is received not merely because the sacrament is *received*, because they are received *in faith*, thus *confirming* our faith by grace, rather than *conferring* grace apart from faith.[19] This asserts significant distance in his thinking between the concepts of 'confer' and 'confirm'. Further, whatever profit we have from the sacraments is only by the power of God's Spirit[20] so that in no way do they impart grace *in themselves*, for he called such magical ideas 'diabolical'.[21] So, for Calvin, sacraments do not confer grace by any means, *per se*, but rather sacraments act as mirrors in which we may contemplate God's grace.[22] Sacraments are wonderful and rich, distinguished from ordinances, which are merely commanded by God for our good. Calvin would define them this way: sacraments are ceremonies confirming a promise, ordained by God, which reflect God's grace into the life of the believer by the action of faith, the Word, and God's Spirit. In distinction, ordinances are singly dimensioned, referring only to the command, when compared with the multidimensional concept of sacrament. Also, like Luther, Calvin restricted the number of the sacraments, retaining baptism and the Lord's Supper, and rejecting all others, including penance, which Luther also rejected later.[23]

In summary, 'sacrament' is a term which was retained by the Reformation and, when properly understood, offers a rich, multidimensional understanding of these treasures given to the church by Christ. This is distinct from the term 'ordinance', which came into use recently, is used only among a minority of Christians, and is singly dimensioned (referring only to the command). As such, it ignores much of the richness of these gifts: the drama of the signs, the mirrors of God's grace, and their role in our sanctification.

So, let me make a first approach toward a definition acceptable to evangelical Protestants: *a sacrament is a sign which mirrors the grace of God, which is ordained by God for our sanctification.*[24] Contra Trent, and faithful to the distinction of the reformers, sacraments do not confer grace in themselves. And sanctification may be understood in the words of Berkhof: 'the benefits of the covenant of grace . . . are represented, sealed, and applied to believers, and these, in turn, give expression to their faith and allegiance to God.'[25] Or, said with a nod to Calvin, sanctification arises as the work of God in the life of the believer as he or she contemplates the grace of God in the sacraments as in a mirror. This seems to reflect the intent of the reformers without the explicit errors codified at Trent. I propose that the richer term, 'sacrament', is the more valuable. Now we turn to the historic Protestant exclusion of marriage as a sacrament.

Excluding Marriage from the Sacraments and the Church

The careful definition of 'sacrament' leads necessarily to a reconsideration of what actually should be numbered among the sacraments. Today, the seven sacraments of the RCC are a larger superset of the Protestants' two: baptism and the Lord's Supper.[26] Let's consider here the specific judgment of both Luther and Calvin in regard to excluding marriage.

Luther understood marriage not as a sacrament, but as a public estate. Michael Parsons writes that Luther understood marriage as 'the word and ordinance of God within the temporal government of his rule. Its nature, therefore, is outward and physical. Its realm is not that of the church, but that of civil affairs.'[27] Luther rejected marriage as a sacrament in *Babylonian Captivity of the Church*, writing, 'Nowhere do we read that it was instituted by God in order to symbolize something, although we grant that all things done in the sight of men can be understood as metaphors and allegories of things invisible. Yet metaphors and allegories are not sacraments, and it is of sacraments that we are speaking.'[28]

Here Luther distinguishes between a symbol and a metaphor. A symbol is explicitly made so by Christ himself, whereas a metaphor is discerned by inference. Next, Luther objects: 'There has been such a thing as marriage itself ever since the beginning of the world, and it also exists amongst unbelievers to the present day. Therefore no grounds exist on which the Romanists can validly call it a sacrament of the new law.'[29] This point is not a minor one. First, marriage cannot be a sacrament if real marriages are engaged by believers and unbelievers alike. And marriage cannot be a sacrament if it was instituted under the Old Covenant, and not in the New.

John Calvin also rejected marriage as a sacrament. He did this on at least four grounds.[30] First, it was lately adopted as a sacrament under Pope Gregory X (1210–76). He writes, 'All men admit that it was instituted by God; but no man ever saw it administered as a sacrament until the time of Gregory.'[31] Second, as noted above, he rejects it as a sacrament because if marriage is a sacrament, then everything is. Third, he rejects marriage because it is a ceremony without a promise. And, finally, as Luther also objected, its inclusion by the RCC is based on the misapplication of Ephesians 5:32. Marriage is not numbered among the sacraments for the Reformed.

While Luther and Calvin had differing understandings of the meaning of the sacraments, they retained two: baptism and the Lord's Supper. They agreed that marriage was not among the sacraments. Five hundred years later this position is a distinctive of the Protestant Church over and against the RCC.

But Luther and Calvin's work was not complete in regard to marriage. They exiled marriage not only from the sacraments, but also from the domain of the church. Luther declared marriage to be not of the divine estate, but of civil government. At a theological level, marriage is excluded because of his understanding of two distinct kingdoms: temporal and spiritual.[32] John Witte writes that Luther came to see marriage as 'an outward, physical, and worldly station',[33] and also, 'marriage was subject to the state, not the church. Civil law, not canon law, was to govern marriage', and for Luther, 'marriage was subject to the prince, not the Pope'.[34] There were perhaps other, less theological forces at work. Among his reasons for this was the terrible state of marriage in Germany which occasioned the writing of 'On the Estate of Marriage'.[35] It was, perhaps, only reasonable to assume that the civil government which protected him would also be a good repository for reformed marriage. Calvin, also, divested the church of the primary authority in marriage, investing it with the civil government. Witte writes that for Calvin, 'marriage required the coercive power of the State to preserve its integrity. But it also required the spiritual counsel of the church to demonstrate its necessity.'[36] This makes sense for Calvin, who trusted his own civil government, for by 1555 in Geneva he had successfully purged the city council of opposition. Of course, he could have left marriage fully within the church, notwithstanding that he had demoted it from sacramental status. But perhaps it seemed that the church lacked the authority to govern and preserve it. Marriage, in exile from the church to the state, came under great forces which were already moving to make government a poor choice to secure marriage. The Enlightenment would secularize all things in the public square, including marriage.[37]

It should also be observed that Luther and Calvin did something quite unprecedented in removing marriage from the church and putting it under the state. The state's authority over marriage is quite new. Stephanie Coontz writes, 'Some things that people believe to be traditional were actually relatively recent innovations. That is the case for the "tradition" that marriage has to be licensed by the state or sanctified by the church.'[38] For the first time in history, marriage was no longer under the family or religious community, but under the governing authority of the state.[39] Whether this transfer was caused primarily as a result of the influence of the reformers is not essential to the point. There can be no doubt other cultural changes contributed. But they were very influential and accomplished their purposes. And with some irony, we should notice that the RCC made no movement in this direction, yet they were also caught up in this movement of marriage toward the state. So, over the next several hundred years, without the agreement of the RCC or other religious groups, the actions of Luther and Calvin led to, or were concurrent with, forces which removed marriage from the family and religious community and placed it under the state.

Of course, the idea of governmental control of marriage was not wholly new at that time. What was new was that control *actually* passed to the state. For example, the West could look back to Rome, which made a significant attempt to require a state marriage licence. The Christian emperor Justinian (527–65) required a state marriage licence to protect inheritance when he allowed aristocrats to marry between classes. However, he soon had to relax his own ruling as unenforceable.[40] In fact, marriage licences, issued by western governments, only became common after the middle of the nineteenth century.[41] Reasons for government involvement seem to include supporting parental authority over minors, enforcing racial purity,[42] and perhaps taxation. Until the middle of the nineteenth century, in the United States, cohabitation, with no licence and no church ceremony, was recognized as a marriage.[43] What is new is that the state authority over marriage has become law and seems normal to us. In the context of a Christian marriage the words, 'by the power vested in me by the State of Minnesota, I now pronounce you man and wife', are so familiar that we forget how novel they are. And this has effects. As the state took greater responsibility, the church's influence over marriage weakened. That is not to say that this change is fundamentally wrong. The state has provided protections for marriage partners and protection for the children of the marriage, and also for the inheritance of property.

I now ask, what if we evangelicals, who hold to the singly dimensioned term 'ordinance', revived the multidimensioned term 'sacrament'? And what if marriage was brought into the number of the sacraments by evangelical Protestants? I want to explore possible advantages of both.

As I propose reviving the term 'sacrament', and restoring marriage among the sacraments, let me state working definitions. First, sacrament: *a sign, a dramatic enactment, which mirrors the grace of God, which is ordained by God for our sanctification.* Second, marriage: *the uniting of two, a man and a woman, into one, representing the image of the One-and-Many God and also his divine covenant-faithfulness.*

Let me make two initial comments in regard to these definitions. First, it is not my desire to abolish the use of 'ordinance'; it is a perfectly good word. But let 'ordinance' be used as a part for the whole, and let 'sacrament' be revived as a synonym which points to the larger picture, which is displayed in the definition above. And if we use the term 'sacrament', we do so without the baggage of Trent, as did Luther and Calvin who resisted 'magical' reflections, which assume or claim that any sacrament could confer saving grace. But, someone could object, why consider a term in need of pedagogical maintenance? Precisely *because* the use of the richer term 'sacrament' *invites* explanation and teaching. Teaching is the opportunity, not the problem. Moreover, 'ordinance' may be too thin a description of so great a gift from God without the support of the richer term. Yet, whichever term we use, let us engage each other with the sign and enact the drama of God's work in our lives.

Second, let me address my use of 'drama' in association with 'sign' in this definition. 'Drama' is not intended in its trivial use which we associate with entertainment. On the contrary, how much more appropriate is the term 'drama' to describe the ordained acts of eating and drinking to display the death of Christ, immersion in water to enact his death, drawing up from the water to enact his resurrection, and living out the two-in-one display of God's covenant-faithfulness within marriage? In the sign, the drama, we mirror the grace that stands behind the sign and to which the drama gives witness. We do this because we are commanded by God. But more than that, and in participation, we are drawn into the sanctifying work that the Holy Spirit brings into our lives through these sacramental acts.

Now perhaps it is time to answer the question above: is there sufficient reason to revive the use of the term 'sacrament'? I think we have much to gain by reviving the use of the word 'sacrament'. If we did, it would not be a theological shift, but a revival of a useful and biblical idea. Moreover, it would be an opportunity for instruction because the use of 'sacrament' may enhance our understanding and exercise of the commanded ordinances.

That leaves us with the more difficult question, and the one that is most important for this study: if the term 'sacrament' is called to duty among evangelicals, as well as among all Protestants, would it make sense to include marriage among the sacraments? To address this, I will consider the objections of the reformers and also the apparent lack of symmetry between the two Protestant 'sacraments' (ordinances) of baptism and the Lord's Supper on one hand and marriage on the other.

As we consider these objections, I will be comparing marriage to our working definition of a sacrament, and propose a modification of this definition, which may actually be implicit in our understanding of 'sacrament' (or 'ordinance'), but not expressed.

Symmetry of Marriage, Baptism, and the Lord's Supper

Does marriage fail as a sacrament for lack of symmetry with baptism and the Lord's Supper?[44] This objection has several parts: marriage lacks a sign, marriage lacks a promise, marriage is not given to all within the church, and marriage is a creation ordinance which is not uniquely given to the church.

First, let me consider Luther's objection that marriage, unlike baptism and the Lord's Supper, lacks a sign. He wrote:

> [N]or does the rite of matrimony contain any hint that the ceremony is of divine institution . . . Nowhere do we read that it was instituted by God in order to symbolize something, although we grant that all things done in the sight of men can be understood as metaphors and allegories of things invisible. Yet metaphors and allegories are not sacraments, and it is of sacraments that we are speaking.[45]

Luther is not deprecating metaphors, but rather noticing that marriage engages no sign or symbol such as water, bread, or wine. But is that the best way to understand the sign? Instead of considering a sign to be an earthly element, should we instead consider the elements to be properties ('props') in a drama, and the sign to be the drama itself? The properties, or the elements, are the physical and tactile objects, which are indeed important. They are important because they can connect the physical to spiritual through the sensory. But while there is no such property in the marriage drama, the intimate physicality of marriage, distinct from the ceremony, may provide the same kind of sensory connection. Indeed, this is hinted at even in the declaration of unity in Genesis 2. If this is so, then the *sign* in baptism is not water, but baptism itself. Such seems to be the implication of Romans 6:3–4 which describes baptism as a drama of the death, burial, and resurrection of us in Christ. Similarly, in the Lord's Supper the bread and cup are properties used by the church to enact the drama of Christ's self-giving for us in which we must partake in order to live. The corporate enactment of the Lord's Supper is the sign, not the wine and the bread. If I am correct, then it would be the drama, and the physical experience of the drama, which is the sign, not physical properties themselves. And although marriage is an ordinance or sacrament between two people and God, it is also observed by all, and so it is sacramental for the whole community, a sign of God's covenant-faithfulness. So then, marriage does not lack a sign, for when it is enacted by God's people, it *is* the sign, pointing to God's faithfulness.

Second, let me consider both Luther's and Calvin's objection that marriage, unlike baptism and the Lord's Supper, lacks a promise. The argument above tells here as well. The promise of baptism is that if we die with him we will live with him; the enactment in the water points to this promise. The promise of the Lord's Supper is our forgiveness in the new covenant; drinking his blood and eating his flesh point to this promise. But what is the promise in marriage? It is this: the promise of God's faithfulness to return for his bride. This hardly needs support, but we could consider the intended confusion of terms among the prophets in their use of the words 'idolatry' and 'adultery', the story and prophecy of Hosea, the description of Israel in Ezekiel 16 and then, again, as Oholah and Ohaliab in Ezekiel 23, the image of the bride in the writings of John, and Paul's teaching on marriage in Ephesians 5. The promise of marriage is the covenant-faithfulness of God to his church; the wedding ceremony, and the marriage lived out, point to that promise.

Third, consider the objection that marriage, unlike baptism and the Lord's Supper, cannot be participated in by all. Table 5.1 may be helpful in following this argument.

Table 5.1 Comparison of the participants in, and frequency of, celebration of the sacraments

Baptism	Marriage	Lord's Supper
One participant / many observers	**Two** participants / many observers	**Many** participants / many observers
Once	**Once** (until death of one spouse)	**Often**
Required of all believers	**Open** to all believers, but not expected or required of all	**Open** to all believers on any given occasion of its celebration

Notice that marriage falls between baptism and the Lord's Supper in its distinctions, rather than in opposition to both. In just this sense, the limited participation and singular frequency fills out the symmetry, rather than breaking it. Still, it might be observed that such an explanation is not emotionally satisfying, at least for those who might desire to participate in marriage but for one reason or another cannot or should not. Returning to the idea of sacraments as a sign, or drama, sacraments (and so marriage) are fundamentally enacted by the whole church. While two people may have the starring role, yet the company of the church includes gaffers, musicians, stage hands, lighting crew, and also the leading roles – though not the director, a role reserved for the Spirit. While our participation and specific role may be fluid, changing from performance to performance, no member of the cast should complain that they do not have the starring role in a particular performance or any performance. One is baptized. Only the confessed and prepared take the Lord's Supper. And only some marry. Disappointment may be understandable, but perhaps Romans 12 could apply here in regard to the body of Christ and its parts! This shifts the sacrament from a focus on the individualistic performances to the corporate witness. This is not a minor point and it may point to a deep connection between the sacraments: sacraments are not private, nor should they be considered to be so. They are always fundamentally community-oriented, signs of God's favour and reflections of great truth. If marriage is a sacrament, it is participated in by two, but it is a testimony of God's faithfulness to the whole community – married, unmarried, single, widowed, and divorced – and enacted by them all. Indeed, a marriage is not a wedding, and all participate in the faithful enactment of every marriage performed as the church.

Fourth, and last, in regard to the apparent asymmetry of marriage in relation to baptism and the Lord's Supper, if marriage is a sacrament, what do we say of the rest of the world who also marry? Certainly these marriages cannot be sacramental by intent or in effect. It must be agreed that marriage was given in Genesis 2 as a creation ordinance, so it is a grace both to the world and to God's people. Marriage is a common grace to the world. Where it is honoured, it is God's ordained means of procreation: both the community and the couple benefit from chastity and the foundational family structure it provides. This was the common perspective of Luther and Calvin.[46] There is also no tension in agreeing that Christian and non-Christian marriages are valid marriages before God and offer goods to the world. This is the implication of Paul's argument in 1 Corinthians 7:12–16. Here Paul gives instructions to Christians who find themselves married to unbelievers. No situation limits the possibility of the sacramental reality of marriage for believers. Baptism and the Lord's Supper are not given to the world as sacraments, but they are given to the whole world in a different way by God. Everyone takes baths, and all people consume bread and wine; so what distinguishes the Lord's Supper from a meal and baptism from a bath? The distinction is in the Spirit and the Word as the reformers so often declared. Moreover, sacraments are distinguished by the gathering of the people of God and their intent. Is this not also what distinguishes the marriage contract for unbelievers from the covenantal sacrament of marriage of God's people?[47]

I want to follow this point further. Baptism was a significant sign in Christ's day of other things: John baptized, but this was not the trinitarian baptism commanded by Christ as an ordinance or a sacrament. Paul himself makes a distinction in Acts 19 between John's baptism and that in which the Holy Spirit is central. And the Jews had their *mikvot* (ritual baths) before and after Christ. Though Jesus gave us a sacred meal of bread and wine, the evil spirits also gave people 'sacred' meals of meat and drink, which is one of the issues that seems to have prompted the writing of 1 Corinthians. Though Christian baptism and the Lord's Supper are not unique (not distinguished as practices of bathing and eating) to God's people, this parallel participation of others in the same activity resulted (and results) in no confusion as to the meaning and expression of the Lord's Supper or baptism for God's people. So also, marriage can be sacramental for God's people, even though those outside the people of God also marry. Marriage is a sign and contains a promise, and it comes by the Word and the Spirit – for God's people. It displays the image of God as One-in-Many and God's covenant-faithfulness to his people. So, marriage is a sign pointing to God's covenant-faithfulness and could be considered very much like baptism and the Lord's Supper, which share common practices with the world.

Marriage, a sign which points to a promise, is sacramental to participant and witness, and while it is a creation ordinance for the whole world, it is also a sacrament for God's church. In this, marriage is like the other ordinances; asymmetry fades.

Is Everything Sacramental?

Now we turn to the final concern: is everything sacramental? If we include marriage among the sacraments, then is this category broadened beyond all bounds? Let me restate Calvin here: 'Lastly, there is matrimony, which all admit was instituted by God, though no one before the time of Gregory regarded it as a sacrament. What man in his sober senses could so regard it? God's ordinance is good and holy; so also are agriculture, architecture, shoemaking, hair-cutting legitimate ordinances of God, but they are not sacraments.'[48]

He makes two arguments here: historical and definitional. I have responded to the historical argument. In regard to Calvin's definitional argument, let us recall the terms Calvin used to define a sacrament: ceremonies, ordained by God, which reflect God's grace into the life of the believer, the action of faith, the Word, and God's Spirit. If this is a fair representation of Calvin, the exemplar activities which Calvin brings forward as parallel to marriage do not track. They are not commands (not ordinances of Christ) but goods, and they are associated, not with ceremonies, but activities and trades. But are these objections merely strawmen? Marriage, as has been shown above, is a command, is initiated in a ceremony, and contains all the elements of a sacrament.

But if marriage is 'in' and 'shoemaking' is out, what other God-ordained dramas might be numbered among the sacraments? I suggest that the ordinances which we do recognize are the commands which are uniquely grounded in the great events of the salvation history of God's people. Each points to one or more of the three great acts of God in salvation history of creation, redemption, and restoration. Each of these acts of God is spoken of as both an act of creation and a crisis (or turning point). Baptism rests on redemption and restoration: redemption because it connects us to the death of Christ in our immersion, and restoration in the promise of resurrection in our coming up out of the water. The Lord's Supper connects us to the death of Christ (redemption) and also to the wedding feast of the Lamb (restoration). So, baptism and the Lord's Supper are not only ordained by God in Christ, but they connect us with the great turning points of salvation history, though not necessarily all three. Table 5.2 may help show this graphically. It displays the chiastic structure (the outline) of the Bible through three Creation & Crisis events.[49]

Table 5.2 Chiastic outline of the Bible around three Creation & Crisis events

Chiasm of the Bible		
1	Creation of heaven and earth	
1'	The fall of humanity	Old Covenant
2	Incarnation of Christ	
2'	Death of Christ	
2	Resurrection and Creation of a new people	
3'	The judgment	New Covenant
3	Creation of new heavens and new earth	

Note: ' (apostrophe) indicates Crisis.

Marriage is just as deeply connected to these turning points, perhaps more so, for it connects to each of these Creation & Crisis events of redemption. The connection to creation has already been established (Gen. 2). Specifically, this seems to be a connection to our participation in the image of God, two becoming one, so reflecting God who is One-and-Many, and also anticipates the biblical theme of God's covenant-faithfulness displayed in marriage. We can see a deep connection to redemption which is displayed in the words of John the Baptist who calls Jesus the bridegroom (John 3) and Jesus' own parable of the wise and foolish virgins (Matt. 25). This is made more explicit in Ephesians 5. Here Paul commands men to 'love their wives as Christ loves the church and gave himself for her'. This is God's covenant-faithfulness to us and it invokes all that preceded it in the Old Covenant in this regard. Apart from any historical translation errors (*sacramentum*), marriage is still tied to redemption because it is intended to display the selfless love that Jesus has for his people. In fact, the concepts are so intertwined, Paul cannot (does not want to) keep them fully separate through any phrase within this text. Finally, marriage connects us sacramentally to renewal in the Revelation of John (19:7; 21:2–9; 22:17). When Christ returns, his people are to be joined to him as a virgin bride. And we will celebrate with him in the wedding feast! We will be the bride. He will be the Groom. And we will be united with him for ever. If ordinances are also sacraments, not only because they offer a sign pointing to a promise, mirror God's grace, and engage us in sanctification, but also because they connect us to the specific promises of creation, redemption and restoration, marriage may be the chief of the sacraments.

So, let me return to the definition of a sacrament, now complete when limited by the filter of salvation history: *a sacrament is a sign, a dramatic enactment, which mirrors the grace of God, which is ordained by God for our sanctification, and which displays God's great acts of salvation history.* So defined, I propose that 'sacrament' is a helpful term for the evangelical Protestant Church, along with the term 'ordinance'. Further, this definition of sacrament enriches the term 'ordinance', which in modern usage was in danger of becoming too flat to contain the grandeur of these things. And how much more is this true in the case of marriage which in our tradition does not even aspire to ordinance, but is considered by evangelicals as an 'institution'. I propose that if we understand marriage as a sacrament (or an enriched ordinance), we will value God and marriage more highly.

Now, with this proposal as a backdrop, I want to explore how we might be intended to live out this drama of marriage, this sacrament of marriage, before God and by his Holy Spirit. If the goal of the drama is to reveal God's nature and character, this demolishes ethics. Rather than rules which govern marriage, we will have dramatic purposes and goals which we are privileged to display in our own marriage and to encourage in the marriages of others. This I will now explore.

Part Three

Doctrine: What God Does through Marriage

So far, I have examined the exegesis and biblical theology of the Marriage Text, Genesis 2:18–25, as God's *locution*, his words, and God's *illocution*, his meaning and intent. That is, the Marriage Text is intended to reveal two truths about YHWH, his nature as One-and-Many and his character as faithful to his covenants. We saw how this is developed and revealed in both the Old and New Testaments, culminating in the ultimate marriage of the Lamb and the virgin bride. I have also proposed a definition for 'sacrament': a dramatic sign, commanded by God, which mirrors his grace, and sanctifies his people – sacramental because it connects us to God's three-part Creation & Crisis chiasm of the Bible (Table 5.2). In contrast with Luther and Calvin, and with all of Protestant tradition since the Reformation, I have also proposed that marriage is such a sacrament. Now I turn to the doctrinal *perlocution*, the effect, that God intends for his people by his initial marital speech-act recorded in the Marriage Text and the arc it traces through the canon to its culmination in Revelation.

What is doctrine? Again, I acknowledge my idiosyncratic use of this term. I retain this use because of the helpful pattern and symmetry it offers. As I explained earlier, our word 'doctrine' is not quite the same as 'theology' but is more like the idea of teaching which is always linked to obedience – the behaviour we display as a result of instruction. So, as we move from exegesis to theology to doctrine, we are discovering the dramatic display that God intends for his people through marriage. Doctrine is connected to the idea of sacrament, a dramatic portrayal of a sign that points to God and his purposes. This makes marriage a privilege and a participation with God in his purposes – a drama that reveals him to the world. That is how I want to explore God's intent for marriage, a dramatic privilege given to God's people – something we 'get to do', rather than a burden or ethic that we 'must do'.

6

Pursuing the Doctrinal Drama Intended by the Spirit for the Church

Stated simply, the doctrine is this: marriage, which is rooted in the Marriage Text, calls us to this sacrament in order to display God's nature and character and, by the enactment, to sanctify us. This is a glorious privilege; it is an opportunity to image God's nature and character for his glory and for our sanctification and joy.

So who am I writing to? As I mentioned earlier, I believe that the drama (and sacrament) of marriage is an issue for all of us: married and divorced, single now and always single, parents and children, widows and not-yet-married, old and young. How the church lives out the sacrament of marriage affects us all. How are we doing? There are many distinct readings of divorce and remarriage statistics within the church. Most people are familiar with the oft-cited 50 per cent divorce rate. Not all agree. Shaunti Feldhahn, a marriage researcher, calls these commonly reported statistics fundamentally flawed interpretations.[1] Using the available data rather than new research, she argues that the often-reported statistic that 50 per cent of all marriages fail misconstrues the very data that was used to arrive at these numbers. This rate, she argues, is based on a projection rather than the actual rate of divorce. That is, the data reports the current divorce rate of one-half the marriage rate, but it is a numeric fallacy. The rate at one point in the data cannot be extrapolated as if it is the average rate over the whole sample. In fact, on Feldhahn, this data suggests instead a divorce rate of closer to 30 per cent of marriages when looking at all marriages over time.[2] Feldhahn further argues that the data reveals that among those who attend Christian worship regularly, the divorce rate is half of that of the general population. We do not have to resolve this discussion. The reported divorce rate among those who are committed to Christ is reasonably bounded between 15 per cent and 50 per cent. Knowing that churches are composed of committed and casual Christians, we could estimate a 30 per cent overall divorce rate for those in Christian churches. What would that mean for the average church member's experience of divorce? By the numbers, that would mean that a family with two children who marry will experience one divorce within their nuclear family. Of course, statistics are not 'smooth', so that they literally affect one family in every three. Statistics are 'lumpy', so that divorces occur in groups, more within one family and less in another. More than that, divorce is not limited to the divorcing couple. In fact, one divorce in a family of three couples directly and deeply affects all three of those couples, and several others. Even optimistic divorce rates would mean that *most Christian families* will suffer direct experience with divorce within their family over a span of three generations (including in-law relationships). When I preach on marriage, I find that most (all!) families in my church are immediately affected by divorce and remarriage. So, marriage is an issue which is important not only to the couple at risk, but for all of the church: parents and children, in-laws and outlaws, widowed and divorced, single and engaged. Even those who never marry. Whether or not we are married, or will marry, divorce among our friends and relatives affects each of our lives. And if I am right that marriage is a sacrament, divorce affects our ministry and the gospel. Yet, while it affects us all, the point of the Bible, and this book, is not to create a better marriage ethic or a stronger commitment to stand against 'divorce'. It is a call to stand for something wonderful – the privilege of displaying God's drama.

Reflecting on the Very Possibility of a Christian Marriage Ethic

Jacques Ellul (1912–94) was a sociologist, a philosopher, and at root a Christian (even an 'anarchist' – a longer discussion, but I will return to this later). In his book *To Will and to Do*, he argues that there is no such thing as a Christian ethic. I cannot investigate Ellul's whole argument here, nor will I attempt to, but I do want to summon him as a witness. I need his help to communicate a point that is very difficult for some to grasp, but critical to my project: there is no possibility of a 'bare' Christian marriage ethic. That is, there is no such thing as a 'Christian ethic' (or morality) stripped of a relationship to YHWH. Nor would one be of any value.

Let me begin with the clear grounding that Ellul offers when he considers Adam's fall: 'In scripture, there is no possible knowledge of the good apart from a living and personal relationship with Jesus Christ.'[3] He argues that biblical morality is always bound up with our disobedience toward a Person. If there is such a thing as a natural morality, it is not a bridge back to the Garden. Morality (or ethics) offers no opportunity to raise ourselves up to God. Rather, true (not 'bare') Christian 'morality' and 'ethics' are never separated from the Person, but obedience arises from faith and is deeply personal. Said another way, obedience is only obedience when it is an expression of faith which flows out of a connection to the Person, YHWH.[4] In fact, divorced from a personal relationship God, Christian 'ethics' must be wholly rejected: 'Christianity is an "antimorality." Not only can it not rise to any morality which would be faithful to the revealed truth, but it is also destructive of all morality . . . Revealed truth is antimoral, and . . . as soon as a Christian morality is developed, just so soon is it called into question, and before long, destroyed.'[5] Let me parse this. People, all people of every religion or irreligion, like to reduce revelation not merely to propositions, but to rules: 'Do this!' But such reductionist tendencies create terrible monsters when they make Christian ethics. Such an ethic is 'bare', with no meaning and no value in the Person. As such, 'bare ethics' undermine the gospel, our joy, and they even obscure reality. But Revelation is antimoral and personal, tearing down the impersonal and moral structures of reductionist religion. Such is the poison of 'bare ethics' and such is their end before the Person. Still, this does not mean ethics, even 'bare' ethics, have no value whatsoever: 'Ethics can never cease to bear witness to the reality from which it proceeds, to wit, the word of God.'[6] True. But there is no such thing as a 'bare ethic', divorced from God's person, which is valuable to a human person(s), as an ethic.

James Rogers, a friend and Professor of Political Science at Texas A&M University, says 'the marriage relationship images the union of humanity with Jesus. Our "divinization" as the Orthodox put it, our being taken into intimate union with God himself, is the whole purpose of creation.'[7] Reflecting on its sacramental place in our lives, he writes, '[In] our union with Christ's body (his flesh) in baptism, in the Supper, and in the eschatological marriage of the last day . . . we literally become one flesh with Jesus because we are united with his body and blood in the sacraments.' Rogers rightly says that an attack on marriage is an attack on the image of God – hence so many sexual sins in the Bible receive the death penalty. But he does not desire, for that reason, to reduce our engagement with marriage to an ethic of what we must do. Instead, marriage is an opportunity to enact a drama that displays the image of God. As such, Rogers reminds us that the rules for marriage (and so ethics and sacraments, too!) are something that is, colloquially, a 'get to' rather than a 'have to'. That is because 'divine "ethics" [how God tells us to live] and divine "ontology" [who God says he is] are treated as inseparable throughout the Scriptures'.[8] That is, Christian ethics cannot be separated from the real and personal God. This is the message of Proverbs 8, 'For whoever finds me finds life.' This is just the point. Biblical commands cannot be reduced to an abstract or 'bare' ethic, divorced from the Person we pursue in the commands. There is no such thing as a 'marriage ethic' (or any Christian 'ethic') divorced from the pursuit of God.

In keeping with the spirit of Ellul, we can now see how it is that Christianity is 'anarchist': it undermines the cultural norms – even attacks them. Christians and non-Christians alike tend to create bare structures around ethics extracted from revelation without God. We are interested in 'what we need to do' (to live well, to get to heaven, to form a better culture) but not what we get to do in order to know and love God. Even the Decalogue, if published in its entirety with preamble and the first three commandments, refuses to be about 'not stealing'. Rather, it demands to be seen in relationship to YHWH our redeemer who wants first place in our lives. A true Christian ethic undermines the wish-dream of a bare Christian ethic; it is anarchist. We must deny a Christian ethic that can be exported without the Person. We are not offering the world an ethic, a way to live successfully, but demanding surrender to a holy God who loved us even when we were his enemies.

Last week one of our discipleship group pastors came to me, concerned about a couple in the group who were buying a house and moving in together. Both were professed Christians. They announced their plans to the group, anticipating congratulations. The group did their Minnesota best to be happy for them, but it was difficult to hide their surprise and ethical horror at the prospect that someone in the group would disregard God. Fair concern. But here is the problem: most of us want to fix behaviour that makes us uncomfortable. So, after discussion, privately and apart from the couple, some of the group decided that the best outcome would be to approach the couple in friendship and express concern. Trusting the positive relationships, they expected (with fair reason) that the couple would ask what they should do. They proposed that, since the home was already purchased, one of them should move in, while the other would continue to live elsewhere until they were ready to marry. While the outcome of this discussion remains in doubt, this is Minnesota and for the sake of relationship this just might work. *Even as it fails!* You see, this solution must fail because even if the couple agree, it reduces Christianity to a bare ethic. If this 'works', the only one served is the group who 'feel better' about the situation because they kept their friends from doing something 'wrong'. Rather than help them, they turn them into hypocrites. Hypocrites are not merely people who know the right and deceptively do the wrong. Hypocrites are those who are unconvinced of the right, and yet do so to make others comfortable. You see, even now, this couple does not hide the fact that they are 'sleeping together'. At the same time, they do not explicitly discuss this aspect of their moving in together. It is merely a plan for a living arrangement. But the discipleship group could choose to ignore this deeper reality since that issue is not as 'obvious' as moving in together. Such a solution would be a 'bare ethic', for it cannot draw the couple closer to God. If it turns them into hypocrites, it does the opposite. 'Bare ethics' is not a bridge to God. Apart from desiring God, ethics is a bad and deadly drama, for ethics do much for appearances and general comfort, but lead only to death apart from God. There is no such thing as a bare ethic which is, in truth, Christian.

Christians are right to declare what is good and true. That includes how to live with God. And this includes all the truth about the 'ethics' of marriage. But this is not exportable apart from God.

Too much of our teaching on marriage has been rule-based: thou shall not divorce! We cite Matthew and Luke. Sometimes 1 Corinthians or Malachi. Less often Genesis 2. However we interpret the divorce statistics, the church has not displayed the beauty of God with shining glory by enacting the sacrament of marriage in a way that would catch the attention of the world. I think that may be, at least in part, because we have reduced marriage, divorce, and remarriage to rules. This approach has not been pleasing to God or good for us. And it leaves us even more discouraged, hesitant to take the stage, but there is a drama to enact. The Spirit calls to us, 'The play must go on!'

Indeed, marriage is challenging! But God has called the full cast of the church – the married, divorced, engaged, single, children, widows, and 'extras' – to perform the drama of marriage as a high and glorious sacrament. With this call and privilege of the sacramental display, we 'get to' press on even in our weakness, and despite our failures. As with all challenges, when we see the goal, even our failures will not fail to deepen our delight in God and our desire to call the world to know our gospel. So the disciples understood when Jesus declared against divorce in Matthew 19. They replied, 'If such is the case of a man with his wife, it is better not to marry!' (Matt. 19:10). If the argument of this book is correct, then a biblical theology which is grounded in the Marriage Text of Genesis 2, as the conclusion and climax to the twin accounts of creation, might help us. If the two key meanings that flow from this biblical theology are the opportunity to image the One-and-Many God and the privilege of revealing God's covenant-faithfulness, then marriage is not a bare ethic, but a relationship with God and something we 'can do'. Even those who are not married (now or in the future) have the opportunity to support the drama because they delight in God. This sacrament requires the whole cast and a great vision of the Person for whom we perform the drama.

This biblical theology calls men and women who marry to take on the holy privilege of imaging God in their marriage and supporting the marriages of all in the church. This is part of the glory of the church. But some object: is marriage a treasure of the church? They remind us that this sacrament was given to Adam (the world), not Abraham (the people of God). Indeed it was given to Adam & Eve in the Garden and they were privileged to image God together in marriage. It was given to them because it was good to do so – failing to do so was 'not good'. The Fall does not destroy this reality. Marriage was a gift to all people, a common grace, but to the people of God it is a sacrament. This is the same for food, provided by God as a common grace, yet for God's people it is a sacrament of bread and wine to dramatically portray the sacrifice of Christ. So also, God gave water to cleanse the world, a common grace, but Christians receive a public bath of cleansing, a sacrament of water, to dramatically portray the pledge to God of a clean conscience. If motives for marriage have been distorted, just as motives for eating and bathing have been distorted, it does not destroy the reality of the goodness it has in imaging God for God's people. Though it might require us to warn each other about performing our marriages badly, just as Paul did to the Corinthians in their eating badly, to their detriment. Christians are called to wash, eat, and marry all to the glory of God, not merely because of the bare ethic of the law.

There is more. Not only is this imaging the trinitarian God, but marriage images his covenant-faithfulness (Hebrew, *chesed*) and his faithful love (Hebrew, *'emet*). So in marriage, Christians are not marrying merely for pleasure, but entering into a covenant before

God which represents God's faithfulness and love to his church. For a woman this is described as living in the beauty that God desires, to please God, and witnessing to her husband without words (1 Pet. 3). Her beauty comes not from what others say, by looking at the outside, but from what God says, witnessing her inner beauty. God is declaring this in the very real context of what Peter describes as a distorted marriage when she and her husband are not seeking God together. In 1 Corinthians 7, he calls spouses of non-Christians to stay in the marriage for the sake of their spouse and children. In doing so, the Christian spouse creates a holy temple space in his or her marriage for the sanctification and prayed-for deliverance of the family. For a man, this looks like mission-boldness. The man is a valiant warrior who serves his wife for her sake, not his own, to present her as the woman God created her to be. But men and women both fail. Sin distorts the drama. The performance dissolves. But even then – or just then – the (maturing or real) Christian spouse is called to perseverance for the sake of the spouse and the children. As Christ loves the church and gave himself for her, the husband is to delight in his bride and endure all – even rejection – without striking back (Eph. 5). Just as Christ will never drive away those the Father has given him, but will raise them up before God on the last day, so we are called to do with our troublesome spouse (John 6)! The husband is to take the pain on himself, and deliver her. The wife is to be fearless like Sarah with Abraham (1 Pet. 3). We are to be warriors who suffer all for the joy set before us – like Jesus – always completing our mission before the Commander (Heb. 12:1–3). This does not reduce any spouse to a 'project' any more than the church is a 'project' for Christ – rather he loves the church and gave himself for her. It demands real love, sacrifice, boldness, courage, planning, humility, gentleness, and a certain ruthlessness against distractions from the mission. Christian marriage is to testify to God's love and faithfulness to the church. That can only be seen through real failure and perseverance in failure.

This approach to marriage – rejecting our usual sadism and masochism – changes marriage from a rule-based approach (you must stay married!) to a glorious mission to image God's unity and sacrificial love in a real battle with glorious rewards. It is a mission, not just for the married, but for the whole cast of the church: it takes a village to preserve a marriage.

Chastity: The Drama that Anticipates and Governs Marriage

What is chastity? It is not the absence of sex. Some of the early church Fathers often spoke with intensity about chastity as the lack of sex before marriage and in marriage. In fact, there was a consensus that sexless chastity was the experience of the Garden.[9] This causes some to envision a symmetrically sexless heaven. Josiah Trenham observes, 'Methodius understood that after the Fall there was polygamy with close family members, then only polygamy, then eradication of polygamy and adultery, then monogamy as normative with "continence", then an introduction of virginity.'[10] The end point is that in eternity, 'finally earthly marriage will be done away with in the Kingdom of Heaven, and all will live as the angels'.[11] This fits with Jesus' teaching in Matthew 22.[12] Taken together, this might imply the great value of everyone practising sexless chastity now. In this way we might read Augustine whose many references to the sin of concupiscence, lust within marriage, are given as a (speculative) reason for the virgin birth.[13] But chastity is not the mere absence of sex, either before marriage or in marriage. Rather chastity means 'proper sexual behaviour', purity.

Augustine, despite his concerns about concupiscence, understood chastity as one of the goods of marriage, not lack of sexual union, but fidelity within marriage. Calvin rightly spoke of 'conjugal chastity'.[14] That is, sexual intimacy is to be honourably experienced within marriage. Chastity is not abstinence, but marriage rightly performed. Chastity is 'purity'.[15] One modern author wrote, correctly, 'abstinence is what chastity requires outside of a marriage relationship; and fidelity is what chastity requires inside a marriage relationship'.[16] The biblical call to chastity is a call to dramatic fidelity that upholds the good of marriage and points to the ultimate marriage of Christ to his bride.

How should we understand the Bible's call to chastity in relationship to the Marriage Text and a biblical theology of marriage? Chastity, and the connection of chastity with marriage, is not explicit in the Marriage Text, but Jesus makes it implicitly clear in Matthew 19 (which we will consider in some detail later in this chapter). Notice that in Matthew 19 Jesus connects 'one flesh' with the sexual union as does Paul in 1 Corinthians 6:15–16. To this we could add all the closely packed connections between adultery and idolatry we observed in the previous section. So, chastity could be defined as the work of protecting the drama of marriage by sexual purity in marriage and outside marriage (in the next section, I will address how this applies to singles, and the role of chastity among singles in the dramatic portrayal of the sacrament of marriage). If God represents the image of his Many-in-One nature by the sacramental drama of marriage, specifically by the purity of the sexual union, then it is part of that drama to live in purity whether in or out of marriage. So also, if God displays his character of covenant-faithfulness by the sacramental drama of marriage, specifically by our faithfulness to our spouse and sexual intimacy with them alone, then it is part of that drama to live in sexual purity whether in or out of marriage.

The implication of this is clear. Chastity may be the basis for good laws which make for a successful society. One would expect so, if it is based on God's character. But chastity is not a 'bare' ethic, and Christians should not teach it as an ethic. Rather it is part of the dramatic and sacramental observance of marriage. Indeed, even those who are not now, or never will be, participants in the sacrament of marriage are participants in the drama of marriage. Chasity is foundational. It is an essential part of the drama from the Fall to the renewal of all things at the marriage of the Lamb.

Singleness: The New Idea for a New Covenant

It is important to situate singleness within the sacrament of marriage as it develops in biblical theology. Though time and space do not permit me to develop a rich theology of settled-singleness, it is clear to readers of the Bible that something changed between the Old Covenant and the New Covenant. Singleness was unusual, perhaps even unacceptable, in the Old Covenant. There was no law against singleness, but there were no explicit examples of lifelong singleness among God's servants, nor laws covering permanent singleness. It was assumed that all would marry and have children. But that changed. In the New Covenant, two towering examples stand in distinction, even contrary to our expectations developed in the Old Covenant: Jesus and Paul. Both single. Both God's servants. While Paul may have been a widower (as some imply from 1 Cor. 7:8), he remained (or was) unmarried for the sake of the gospel. Singleness was the choice of Jesus for his entire earthly life. What changed? At least this: in the Old Covenant, the gospel was focused on the coming of the Seed (Gen. 3:15) and so marriage and childbirth were the means of God to bring about the coming of the Messiah and our salvation. This was accomplished with the advent and revelation of the childbirth of the Messiah (1 Tim. 2:13–15). But the New Covenant is focused on the childbirth of making disciple-makers (Matt. 28:18–20). Our God-ordained work is to be midwives for the birth of children of God by the Spirit (John 1:12–13; 3:1–8; Gal. 4:19). Paul (1 Cor. 7) and Jesus (Matt. 19) call us to consider singleness (as they did) for the sake of the kingdom, while declaring the continued importance of the sacrament of marriage in their teachings.

If singleness was unusual in the Old Covenant, it is a calling in the New, precisely because the mission has changed. But the sacraments have not. Singles (young singles, divorced, committed singles, widows, and widowers – all singles) are called to purity and chastity in their dramatic participation. Indeed, as cast members in the dramatic portrayal of the sacrament of marriage, the role of singleness is critical. They both protect marriage and help to display its importance. The chaste single life preserves the marriages of others, and attests to the intimate meaning of marriage – we are made for Jesus alone! So, the single who lives in chastity upholds the drama of marriage. This is true because chastity supports existing marriages, free from adultery. And it is also true in regard to fornication, the sexual unions between unmarried singles. For Paul declares that to be joined to a prostitute constitutes a marriage 'union' (1 Cor. 6:15–16).[17] Therefore, by extension (since the Corinthians did not immediately recognize sex with a prostitute as a 'union'), we should recognize that fornication also constitutes the same kind of 'union' between 'singles' – not joined in formal marital union. This means, on the basis of Paul's argument, that sexual union between singles constitutes a 'union', whether we explicitly recognize it or not. More positively, chastity supports the drama of marriage we are called to as God's people. This means that singles can support the drama, not only by upholding and encouraging the marriages of their brothers and sisters by positive support and encouragement, but also by their own purity. Indeed, we all have a vested interest in this, not only because we love one another, but because *each one of us and all of us together* are betrothed to the Bridegroom! We are together awaiting the ultimate and most important marriage to Jesus as his virgin bride. All marriages could point to this reality. Every Christian marriage should do so, sacramentally.

This should not be dismissed as a small thing among singles. If marriages in the New Covenant have a continuing and central role in displaying the nature and character of God, then every cast member, every gaffer, the publicist, the choreographer, the properties manager, the whole audio-visual team, and the stage hands (let us allow that God is the director and the Spirit is the stage manager) – the whole of the team, are essential (not merely important) to the dramatic performance of the sacrament. And chastity has a key place. Together, we all delight in the privilege of our supporting roles in God's drama.

The 'Problem' of Permission: Divorce for Any Reason? (Matt. 19)

What are the 'rules' for divorce? Or rather, how are we to live out the drama of marriage in a fallen world? It is now time to turn to Matthew 19:1–12. I have already pointed out the obvious: Matthew 19 draws on Genesis 1&2. In fact, Christ's blending of citations from Genesis 1 with Genesis 2 helps us to recall that the Marriage Text is a 'climax and conclusion' not merely to Genesis 2, but to the twin creation accounts. Jesus is first faced with the Pharisees' challenge: 'Is it lawful to divorce one's wife for any cause?' David Instone-Brewer makes the case that this is a particularly tricky cultural question, trapping Jesus between two rabbinic positions: one loved by the people and one loved by the legalists. The 'any cause divorce' is not unlike what we might call a 'no fault divorce' – the approach is different, but the effect is the same, easy divorce.[18] If Instone-Brewer is correct, this seemed to trap Jesus between supporting God's word or the popular tradition. The response of the disciples in verse 10 lends a vivid intensity to the trap the Pharisees laid. Jesus responds by citing the Word – and calling them out for failing to read it! He first cites Genesis 1:27 and then 2:24. There is something interesting to notice. Jesus repeats, three times, the phrase that completes the image of God in the creation of his people by the climax of marriage: 'the *two shall become one* flesh', 'no longer *two but one* flesh', and (by way of application, restates) 'What therefore God has *joined together*, let not man separate' (Matt. 19:5–6). This union of two in one is the central focus for Jesus – at least in regard to the question of divorce.

The religious leaders, seeing themselves defeated if they accepted Jesus' exegesis of this foundational text, turned instead to Deuteronomy 24 with shaky (or should we say, misleading) exegesis. They called this a 'command' to divorce, in keeping with their tradition. But Jesus responded with a challenge to their thinking: 'Moses (only) allowed' divorce (he did not command it!) and even such permission was only because of the 'hardness of your heart'. The latter is his second personal attack on them. The first was that as scholars of the Law, they did not read it! He charges that they are like Pharaoh of old – hardened by sin against God. Jesus then returns to the grounding text: 'from the beginning it was not so'.

What does Jesus intend for us in regard to marriage – and permission to divorce? Many other texts deal with the issue of divorce in the Old and New Testaments. I will not explore those here. Remember, my intention is not to establish a bare Christian ethic – though it would not be hard to do so: no divorce! If divorce is allowed for the hardness of our heart, it is not the way God intends the drama to be played. Divorce undermines the display of God's nature, One-and-Many, and God's character, faithful to his covenant. Asking about permission for divorce is not the right question! Instead, the question is how to faithfully enact the sacramental drama, the sign that points to God. If divorce is permitted for contractual reasons, such as impurity, it is not commanded for those reasons. In fact, Hosea, against the Law,[19] was faithful to his covenantal marriage in order to display God's character to Israel – at God's shocking command. If there is a time when the drama is so badly displayed that it must be stopped and the house dismissed with a refund, let it be so. But all our efforts, those of the whole cast in the church, should be to uphold the privilege God has given us to display his nature and character by the sacrament of marriage – however painful our sin. Of all that the Bible teaches us about marriage, perseverance is the focus, rather than 'how to get a divorce' or 'when to get a divorce'. We must persevere against our own inclination to selfishness and self-centredness, and be faithful to our covenant before God.

How do we respond? The disciples speak for us: 'If such is the case of a man with his wife, it is better not to marry' (v. 10). We insist on an escape hatch for marriage and, without it, why should anyone even bother to marry?! Why indeed? Jesus makes something clear. The alternative to marriage is not sex outside marriage. The alternative is to be a eunuch – though this is not for everyone: 'Not everyone can receive this saying, but only those to whom it is given. For there are eunuchs who have been so from birth, and there are eunuchs who have been made eunuchs by men, and there are eunuchs who have made themselves eunuchs for the kingdom of heaven. Let the one who is able to receive this receive it' (vv. 11–12). One point is clear: sex is for marriage only and if you cannot 'receive' this teaching on marriage, then you must be a eunuch. Another point is clear: whatever we do, our motivation should be 'for the kingdom of God'. That is, stay unmarried or married for the sake of the kingdom of God – for the sake of the drama of God's character that he intends to display through you. This is what marriage is about – this is why divorce is a failure. It is not mere ethics, but it is about a Person.

It is important to speak about divorce when there is abuse. The Pharisees were more interested in laying a trap for Jesus than in understanding. They posed the 'any reason' divorce issue – and this was what Jesus responded to. Not abuse. And banning the 'any reason' divorce was enough to panic his disciples! But what about the tragedy and the trauma of abuse – physical, sexual, and verbal? It is all too common and women are often most at risk; the husband, even if abused, is usually in less immediate danger. What more can we say than Jesus said? God gave us divorce for the hardness of our hearts, for the reality and tragedy of our depravity.[20]

But is abuse the reason for most divorces? It is not. The reason is rather as Jesus told us, the hardness of our hearts. As many have referred to this sinful dilemma, too many marriages are like 'two ticks and no dog'! What if all of us, married and single, did all we could to encourage and protect the drama of the marriages with which our lives intersect? Married or not, we must all do all we are able to do to preserve marriage because of the glory of God revealed in the dramatic sacrament of marriage.

The Necessary Question: Should Christians Remarry? (1 Cor. 7)

The letters to the Corinthians, like most of Paul's letters, were occasional, that is, prompted by specific events and concerns which Paul addressed. In 1 Corinthians 7, the occasion is this: 'Now concerning the matters about which you wrote: "It is good for a man not to have sexual relations with a woman."' In response, Paul speaks quite practically. In verses 2–5 he instructs married couples not to withhold sex from each other. He also addresses the issue of self-control in verses 6–9 which provides the background to what comes next: 'To the married I give this charge (not I, but the Lord): the wife should not separate from her husband (but if she does, she should remain unmarried or else be reconciled to her husband), and the husband should not divorce his wife' (vv. 10–11). In brief, Paul is teaching: do not separate or divorce, but if you do, do not remarry. But that is not Paul's last word on divorce or even remarriage in this text.

Here is the reason one should stay married, especially to an unbeliever: 'the unbelieving husband is made holy because of his wife, and the unbelieving wife is made holy because of her husband' (v. 14). This could be said concisely: stay married, as much as depends upon you, for the sake of your spouse's salvation. This touches again on the Marriage Text, not explicitly on God's nature, but on his character. God is faithful to his covenants for the sake of his name, but also for the sake of his people. His faithfulness is his glory, but it is also our only hope of joy.

However, there is a noted exception that is offered here. Verse 15 declares, 'But if the unbelieving partner separates, let it be so. In such cases the brother or sister *is not enslaved*. God has called you to peace.' For many, this is the key verse in this text because it seems to give permission for remarriage. But does it? It is interesting that the only other time in 1 Corinthians where Paul uses this verb, *enslaved*, the focus is the gospel: 'For though I am free from all, I have made myself a *servant* to all, that I might win more of them' (1 Cor. 9:19). It is just this, the kingdom hope of gospel witness in our family, that is the context for Paul in 1 Corinthians 7: 'For how do you know, wife, whether you will save your husband? Or how do you know, husband, whether you will save your wife?' (v. 16). There are several observations to make. First, when Paul speaks of 'made holy' (a completed action) in verse 14, it cannot be the same as 'will save' (an incomplete and future action). Verse 14, 'made holy', seems to speak of a holy environment that may eventually lead to salvation (v. 16), which is constituted by enduring in the marriage. So, verse 15, whatever it means, is sandwiched in-between a call to endure, in order to create a holy space in your marriage, in the hope of the future salvation of your spouse. And this is in the larger context of verse 12, which calls us 'not to separate', and verse 13, which calls us 'not to divorce'. Second, it is not wholly clear what is meant by the words, 'not enslaved' – words used of the believing spouse after an unbelieving spouse leaves (v. 15). I have already noted that connection to 1 Corinthians 9:19; it seems that Paul may be saying that even for the sake of the gospel, we are called to peace and cannot 'force' our spouse to stay with us. But is this permission to remarry? The oft-cited texts to clarify 'not enslaved' come at the end of the chapter in 1 Corinthians 7:39, and in Romans 7:1–3. These texts permit remarriage after death, as is declared or implied in many biblical texts in the Old and New Covenant. That is not at issue here and clearly permitted. But what about remarriage when the spouse leaves? In 1 Corinthians 7:39, Paul writes, 'A wife is bound to her husband as long as he lives. But if her husband dies, she is free to be married to whom she wishes, only in the Lord.' This is clearly permission for a widow to remarry and in verse 15 Paul uses similar language – but not quite. In verse 39 the key words are 'bound' and 'free'. If 'bound' means the same as 'enslaved', nevertheless 'free' does not appear in verse 15. Is it implied? Perhaps, but not clearly. Notice that verse 39 is not there to encourage remarriage. Paul continues in verse 40, 'Yet in my judgment she is happier if she remains as she is. And I think that I too have the Spirit of God.' So, verse 15, the 'exception clause', the only New Testament ground for remarriage, is very thin ground, if it is ground at all. It is thin because of context. It is thin because of syntax and vocabulary. It is thin because remarriage is not the point, but at best (if at all) a concession. And notice, nothing is said here about two Christians who cannot get along and divorce. For them, Paul would offer with Jesus a call to stay on the stage and enact the drama God wrote – the curtain is still up! Now, until Jesus returns, we are permitted to enact this drama which reveals the nature and character of God. The play must go on.

There is more in this chapter, 1 Corinthians 7. None of it could be read as intended to free us from enacting the drama of marriage, and might be construed as calling those who are single to stay single. It takes no great skill in exegesis to understand Paul clearly. But it does oppose our inherited worldview! Paul declares that we may be called to be single and are called to live in purity. Notice how important this is for us in the context of our culture – not only the Corinthian culture. Our culture assumes that it is not possible (and certainly not reasonable) to live without sex once we hit puberty! But God has been declaring since the beginning that sex is not to be our 'god' and God's people are to live under (self-, or is it Spirit-) control. God and Paul assume self-control is possible, even expected. That is a 'worldview' distinct from that of our culture. Sadly, it is also distinct from the view that many Christians have! Recall Matthew 19 when Christ explained his position: consider being a eunuch for the kingdom! What preacher could get away with that advice to a couple who wanted to remarry? But that is Jesus' answer. The point is this: if you are committed to the gospel, you are not enslaved to sex or even all of the real and good 'benefits' of marriage. The kingdom is not primarily about us, not sex, not even marriage. Certainly not remarriage. It is about God and his kingdom. Those who are called to enact the drama and sacrament of marriage have a great privilege. But for some, it is a call to sexual chastity and refusing remarriage, for the sake of the kingdom.

Again, as I did above, it is important to speak about divorce and remarriage when there is abuse. Should a woman (or a man) be free to seek divorce and remarriage under the tragedy and trauma of abuse? As I said above, a case can be made that Jesus says 'Yes' to such a divorce. Perhaps one could even fairly construe this as the meaning of 1 Corinthians 7:15 in this context. But does that provide sufficient reason to get remarried? The emphasis of this text (and all others) is 'No'. If remarriage is permitted, it is not Paul's primary point. This is a call to the priority of the gospel and the right enacting of the drama in difficult circumstances. So then, if your spouse does leave, what are the choices? Nothing prevents a rejected spouse from living singly and praying for the restoration of their former spouse who is in danger of hell. Perhaps there is another consideration. The Levirate marriage laws of the Old Testament (Deut. 25) provided for a childless widow to be married to her kinsman-redeemer (see Ruth!). This was to provide for the woman and for the enduring name of her husband. Perhaps poverty is a reason for remarriage. In 1 Timothy 5, Paul provided for the widows who serve God well – the older widows should be cared for by the church, while the younger widows should remarry. The issue for both was poverty at the death of their husband if they had no immediate family able to provide for them. The comparison, and there is one, between a woman abandoned by her non-Christian husband (1 Cor. 7:15) and a widow whose husband has died (1 Cor. 7:39) at least raises the possibility of remarriage in the face of poverty. But we, who have the privilege of enacting the drama, are to delight in the one who directs the play, eager to enact what he has called us to. Like kids in the elementary school, we fumble through the play, but our Father never misses a performance and wipes our tears when we get it wrong.

The Essential Foundation: What Can Christians Forgive? (Matt. 18)

It would be a mistake to deal with the 'ethics' of Christian marriage in a biblical theology without dealing with forgiveness. The immediate context in Matthew for Christ's discussion of marriage and divorce in chapter 19 is forgiveness in Matthew 18. Of course, the retelling of events will create context by the selection of the author and the sequence in Christ's life. Some events may be merely juxtaposed by accidental necessity. But Matthew is indeed a theologian and – like all biblical authors – an excellent one. If these contextual events do not share a theological thread in Matthew's intent, they at least share a theological proximity in regard to how we are to live out our relationships before God! Our hope of salvation, our union with Christ as his bride, is based on forgiveness. How much more is that the mutual case for human marriage?

Let me walk us through Matthew 18. It begins with a gospel of forgiveness in which we are called to come to God as children. It is also a severe warning against leading a weaker (weakened, younger) brother or sister into sin. Then, Matthew shows us how Jesus deals with forgiveness in three movements: interactive forgiveness, unilateral forgiveness, and the ultimate requirement to forgive. Interactive forgiveness is displayed in the steps that we would call today negotiation (18:15), mediation (18:16), arbitration (18:17a), and restorative consequences (18:17b). At each step either party could discover their error and ask for forgiveness (the first brother for his sins or the second when he discovered his incorrect accusation). Assuming that negotiation and mediation fail, the process goes to arbitration, and assuming that the charge of the first brother is sustained, the second brother is disciplined by exclusion from the life of the church. The exact nature of that isolation – a point of significant discussion – need not be discerned here. But we can note that the isolation is intended to result in restoration as Paul interprets this to the Corinthians (1 Cor. 5:1–5 leads to 2 Cor. 2:5–11). It is worth pointing out that the context of the (famous) phrase, 'where two or three are gathered in my name, there am I among them' (v. 20), is the establishment of discipline and the hope of forgiveness. God is with us in restorative discipline!

This discussion leads Peter to question Jesus about the smaller matters of life. How often should he simply forgive his brother (v. 21)? Perhaps seven times – a perfect number and generous! Jesus responds with a revision of the words of Lamech in Genesis 4. If Lamech called for seven-times-seven in retribution, Jesus calls for seven-times-seven in forgiveness – perfection squared! Of course, unilateral forgiveness may not be the same as unilateral restoration of a relationship – that takes two. But this unlimited and unilateral forgiveness is a radical idea.

Jesus, sensing the difficulty of his teaching, punctuated it with a story: forgiveness is not a good idea; it is required. The parable is clear enough and you can read it in Matthew 18:23–35: forgiveness is required of forgiven believers. He helps us feel how unthinkable it is for any forgiven person not to forgive another. It is then, in the very next movement of this gospel, that Jesus and Matthew turn to the problem of divorce.

What will we forgive in our marriages? What could lead us to say, 'That I could never forgive!'? Following this parable, in verse 37, Jesus makes the explicit connection that we face the wrath of God if we do not forgive. We should be terrified – given the context of the Lord's Prayer in Matthew 6 ('forgive us as we forgive others'), the parable of Hosea's life, and the reality of the cross – at the possibility that there is something we might not forgive in our marriage. Let me make this very personal for us: could I stand before God if I divorce because I am done with forgiving? Yes, there are times to bring our spouse to the church elders and declare that they sinned against us. And there is a time for church discipline if they will not listen – and if our complaint is sustained. But is there a time to give up on the drama which is intended to show God's covenant-faithfulness to us when we have (all too recently) committed spiritual adultery by desires for that which is not God? Have we not all exchanged our glory?! What will God do to us if we beat up our spouse for a 'day's wages' in the light of all God has forgiven us? Yes, there is even a time to call the police. And perhaps our lawyer. But we are indeed all – not just the offender – hard of heart too often. How do we know whether by our perseverance in the marriage (even if we are separated by necessity or the choice of the other) our spouse will come to know God? What are we willing to endure?

Forgiveness is not trivial. You cannot excuse your spouse for belittling you, ignoring your needs, failing to walk with you in your pain, or growing cold to you. These are not trivial things and they are not excusable. But they are forgivable – at cost. Again, we cannot afford to miss the culmination of the parable – Jesus does not explain all parables as he speaks them. He does for this one: 'so God will do to you' (see v. 35). The 'do to you' is a terrifying warning that God will not forgive us if we do not forgive others. But if we do forgive, and stay in the marriage, or refuse remarriage, choosing instead to remain the spouse-alone, praying for our errant spouse, then through us God makes our spouse 'holy' in hope (our hope and God's) that God 'will save' them.

The first rule of marriage is this: forgive your spouse. The continuing rule of marriage is this: forgive your spouse if God has forgiven you. The last rule of marriage is this: forgive your spouse as you expect to be forgiven. Forgive your spouse. You can even forgive the treason of destroying your intimacy. Of course, forgiveness does not mean trust – or if trusting, you trust them to do in the future what they have done in the past! Just as Israel did to God, and as you have as well. By our faithfulness to the drama of marriage, we can image the Bridegroom, who actively waits, keeping his covenant faithfully with us, the faithless. So we can forgive, pray, and wait for God to move in our disobedient, distant (or even hostile) spouse. This is not a Christian 'ethic', but this is a drama we share with Hosea, and with God who actively waited – or waits – for us.

Is It Marriage? The Challenge of LGBTQ 'Marriage'

Homosexuality is neither the main concern of the Bible, nor of this book. But neither the Bible nor this book can ignore the issue. How do we assess the issue? Book after book has been written, and this brief book could not even hope to summarize all of the arguments. Concerns include:

1. exegetical concerns: the paucity of the biblical material that addresses homosexuality, whether or not the Bible's concern is homosexuality or some other sin like failed hospitality or violence, the actual meaning of the words used for sexual sins (especially in Lev. 18 and 20), the meaning of 'natural' in Paul, and the relatively greater concern the Bible has for other sins;
2. theological concerns: whether or not there is redemptive movement in the Bible from historical opposition to homosexuality to enlightened acceptance, and the failure to understand the deepest truth about God and his love;

3. practical concerns: whether practical and real changes in our world affect the meaning of the Bible so that homosexuality may be primarily or exclusively related to genetic determination, the overwhelming need to give place to the value of diversity in our culture in order to thrive as humans living together in a broken world, and the inappropriateness of Christians determining the definition of marriage for a secular culture.

Many long books have been written on some or all of these concerns. I cannot write such a book here. But I can suggest a way through.

First, the very debate is a reminder that marriage is of critical importance. In my day-to-day experience, I am often confronted by the flippant challenge from unmarried couples who are living together: 'Why should we need a marriage licence? It's just a piece of paper.' I usually grant that to them for the purpose of the discussion, and also pursue them a bit further: 'Then why not get married? It is just a piece of paper!' Certainly they already have all the 'benefits' of marriage, but what 'stops them' is *precisely this mere* 'piece of paper'. Assuming they are my friends, and have not rolled their eyes and walked away, their next move is often, 'Well, I am just not ready for the commitment.' This is interesting in itself: they have already made the commitment. Either they do not recognize it or perhaps they refuse to admit it. They may actually be confused, as if they can protect their own feelings and potential future anguish by avoiding public (or even Godward) accountability – something they think they do not fear or regard. But their feelings imply otherwise. The paper and the public commitment loom large, but they are mistaken that protecting themselves from this 'paper commitment' saves their future feelings of pain when dissolving the implied 'marriage'. But the issue is reversed with many in the LGBTQ community. Indeed, they are tired of living together, unrecognized by the community as a 'family', and eagerly seek marriage. It is precisely the recognition that a 'mere piece of paper' affords which they desire. With the LGBTQ community, I have deep agreement: marriage is very important. And also with those who avoid marriage because of a 'mere piece of paper', I have deep agreement: marriage is very powerful.

Second, we come to the central question: is it marriage? The real issue with the LGBTQ community should be over what constitutes marriage. It may not be a marriage just because the state provides a licence. Consider Henri Blocher's observation:

> Why, however, should there be the differences between the man and the woman, and not simply the distinction between one person and another? Sexuality is certainly not necessary to being-with. True enough, but it necessitates being-with. The fact that the first company given by God to man in order to break his solitude was of the other sex reminds us that God does not institute an abstract otherness. He gives a neighbour and not merely an 'other'. He gives a concretely qualified presence, in the order he has decreed and not in abstraction. And the 'neighbourship' which is defined within God's order by sexual differentiation is of a most radical nature; every human individual, being either masculine or feminine, must abandon the illusion of being alone. The constitution of each of us is a summons to community. Genesis throws light on this privileged relationship.[21]

As a justice or compassion issue, it is hard to avoid giving support to LGBTQ couples who desire marriage. No one should deny security to anyone in the community, nor should anyone deny healthcare benefits to another because of their sexual orientation or beliefs about marriage, nor should critical legal protections be withheld from sexual partners for their adopted (or natural) children. It is good that these protections are granted by civil unions, without marriage. But again, it is not merely these protections which are desired – they are desired, but not only. The right to marry is also desired, and indeed this right to marry has also been granted. But is marriage something which can be defined by the state? In a previous chapter I have addressed this. In a way, the answer is yes. But in what way? The state has a right to create and enforce laws. But marriage may not be something that can be redefined. Or if it is, it may no longer be Christian marriage – or, indeed, marriage at all. This is like the example I examined in the Introduction – the mass of the electron. We can describe the electron, but we cannot create one *a priori*, from first principles, freely changing its mass as we like. Not only do we not know why the electron has the mass it does, but also we are not able to create one of a different mass.[22] It is what it 'is'; what 'it is' is not affected by our opinion. Could it be that marriage is the same?

First, it must be said that the best arguments for both sides have internal consistency and integrity, and both are true to their values. Both sides (or should I say, all sides) do their best to discern an answer that is both coherent (fits best at every point) and has integrity (does not undermine their own worldview). However, both have distinct perspectives on truth. One finds truth founded externally: marriage conforms to God's nature and character. Another finds truth founded contextually: marriage conforms to social norms and needs. It is fair to say that both can affirm that their position is coherent, has integrity, and is true in regard to their system. But internal consistency, integrity of the system, and conformity to values is only sufficient if there is no external norm.

What if there is a 'thing' called marriage which is neither founded in human systems nor established by human decision? Perhaps, like an electron, marriage is 'true' – something which does not and cannot draw its meaning from context and is not affected by opinion. What if the marriage of which we are speaking is a 'thing' which is as it is? I make no move to prove this, but merely raise the question. What if marriage is actually rooted in relationship to God, and draws its meaning only from God? Of course, it may not be so. But if that were the case, then no matter what the state says about 'marriage' and whatever laws it enacts about marriage, marriage is something that can no more be legislated than the mass of an electron. In this case, if Christians are true to the biblical 'thingness' of marriage, then Christians are doing one 'thing' and the state, though it refers to its 'thing' by the same name, is doing another and separate thing. Both bear the name 'marriage', but they are not the same 'thing'.

In the most liberal of worlds, the existence of state marriage (licensure) would not preclude the enactment of a Christian marriage. It might (or should) be the case that those who enact Christian marriage might also be required to get a state marriage licence. Still, the two could exist together happily, one having a meaning to the state and larger community, and the other only to Christians who chose it – believing what they do to be 'the thing'. But who would or should say they are identical?[23]

This liberal way of employing state marriage side by side with the enactment of Christian marriage by Christians might have a corollary: no Christian would (or should) tell the state how to define and employ state marriage in order to protect its citizens. Indeed, sometimes I think Christians do confuse our role, thinking it is our job to enforce Christian ethics on our world – as if that is what the world most deeply needs. I have addressed this earlier in the chapter, but there are a few points yet to tease out. Fairly, some have argued that Judeo-Christian ethics are good for any culture. Even a gift. If so, then let us demonstrate these 'ethics' and their fruit to the world by example rather than by fiat; let us value marriage ourselves. Indeed, Paul's famous 'sting operation' of Romans 2:1 may make the same argument. The Roman Christians were easily worked up against flagrant sin in Romans 1 – and with justification. God is the God of all, whether or not he is acknowledged as so. But in Romans 2:1 Paul writes, 'You have no excuse, for when you judge, you condemn yourself because you practise the very same things' (my paraphrase). This in no way undermines Paul's argument in Romans 1. Whatever he is condemning there (I would argue that Paul is condemning homosexuality, but this is not the place to make that argument), his turn against Christians does not minimize his opposition to the sins they are judging. Rather Paul is calling them to be so zealous for God that they first deal with their great sin. But the church, then and now, has not been zealous for holy marriages so much as for the idea of holy marriage and the ethics of marriage. This is the case whether we accept the common statistic of 50 per cent failures or Feldhahn's more encouraging 15–30 per cent.[24] We are more likely to side with the disciples' dejected exclamation (perhaps with hands and eyebrows raised!) in Matthew 19:10. When faced with Christ's determined position for marriage and against divorce, they declared (my paraphrase): 'Who should bother to get married if you are going to be so strict about it, Jesus!' In Romans 2:1 Paul is challenging us as he should. Will we battle *against* sexual sin and will we contend *for* marriage by living out the sacrament of marriage in our own lives (even supporting the painful marriages of our friends), so that the marriages of Christians exalt the nature and character of God – even if they do not make us happy? Our job is not to police the ethics of our neighbours, nor to legislate the good life – even though we are correct. We are to live a life of integrity that coheres to the nature and character of God because we are privileged to do so. We are not to choose the easy route of reducing Christianity to ethics. But does that mean we have no input on marriage as employed by the state?

Of course, in a democratic society we can, and perhaps should, lobby for good laws. But even if our western culture is democratic (perhaps there is some doubt), most governments in history and around the world are not democratic. What are those Christians to do? And even as we do export our ethics (and it is a gift because it is effective and a pointer to God), we must realize that ethics is not evangelism, but sanctified civics. Creating a world which is comfortable for us, or even 'good for them', is not an ultimate good. The ultimate good is to live a life that dramatically portrays God to the world – a sacramental and sacrificial life. That includes our sexuality, in our married or single life. This is the centre of the question, 'What about LGBTQ marriage?'

Conclusion

I have argued that Christianity cannot, must not, be reduced to an ethic. Perhaps this was Paul's meaning in Corinthians when he wrote,

'"All things are lawful for me", but not all things are helpful. "All things are lawful for me", but I will not be enslaved by anything' (1 Cor. 6:12; 10:23). An ethic is reductionistic, divorcing God's teaching from the person of God. Such a move states a relationship with God in terms that could be kept without knowing God. That does not mean we do not care how we enact God's sacramental drama – including marriage. Quite the opposite. It provides a Personal reason to get the drama right! To enact marriage is the work of the whole cast of the church, in whatever state we are found. And it is a privilege, not a legalistic command. When we fail, there is forgiveness from God. When we fail each other in the enactment, forgiveness must control us. Here is a clear enactment which displays God's nature and character to each other and the world.

7

If Marriage Is a Sacrament, What Does the Church Do?

I have considered the ethics of marriage. The point is this: rather than ethical norms, God has provided dramatic direction, in order that we may display his glory. If the last chapter was more about individual marriages, this one is about the church's role in performing marriages.

Whose Licence?

Speaking against divorce, Augustine observed by way of warning, 'marriage bears a certain sacramental character'.[1] Implied in his observation that marriage is sacramental, and in mine that it is a sacrament, may be this conclusion: the church should be the proper guardian of something so holy, not the state. It may be that for our sake, and for the world, we need to display and experience this very thing in our marriages. But we are not doing so. It has become axiomatic that marriages in the Christian church experience approximately the same divorce rate as all marriages.[2] Above all others, Christians have a deep motivation for succeeding in marriage beyond ethics or even our own happiness: dramatically portraying and delighting in the trinitarian God who pictures his love for us in the sacrament of marriage. But I need to be careful. If I am claiming that by calling marriage a sacrament, we will improve our marriages by this change alone, I am overreaching. If a sacramental understanding of marriage alone could protect marriages, Catholic marriages would be thriving in comparison to those of Protestants. Instead, I am considering a new way of thinking about our marriages, and a new way of relating to the state, that has the potential to cause us to think differently about marriage and our God's covenant-faithfulness to us. It would be my desire that this proposal results not merely in a change of terms, but in a change of the way the church lives out marriage, including the whole cast within the church: children, singles, divorced, widowed, and even those who experience gender confusion and same-sex attraction.

First, by restoring marriage to be among the sacraments, or at least sacramentally understood, I must be clear about what I am saying and what I am not saying. I am proposing that we think about marriage as a drama of God's covenantal grace enacted before the world; this includes the initiatory rite of the wedding and the marriage lived out, sacramentally. I have no doubt that we already teach and preach in ways that connect marriage to redemptive history, but, at least in some contexts, and as I discussed at length in the previous chapter, we may wrestle too much with the biblical permissions for divorce and remarriage. This interest is reflected, for example, in David Instone-Brewer's research on the biblical reasons for divorce. His work has been the seed for many important discussions. Here it is worth reflecting (again) on Matthew 19:3–6:

> And Pharisees came up to him and tested him by asking, 'Is it lawful to divorce one's wife for any cause?' He answered, 'Have you not read that he who created them from the beginning made them male and female, and said, "Therefore a man shall leave his father and his mother and hold fast to his wife, and the two shall become one flesh"? So they are no longer two but one flesh. What therefore God has joined together, let not man separate.'

The first thing we notice is that Jesus avoids their question. In fact, had they accepted his correction as an answer, the discussion would have concluded without addressing divorce, explicitly, except simply to say, 'let not man separate'. Let me paraphrase Jesus' answer this way:

'You want to know about grounds for divorce, but Moses wants to tell you what marriage means. If you knew what it means, you would not pursue this line of questioning. So listen to Moses!' Of course, they did not 'get it' and they pursued him further in a direction he was not eager to go. Could it be that our error is to stand with the Pharisees, instead of Moses and Jesus? Do we ask 'the divorce question' with the Pharisees, skipping over Christ's fundamental focus? Jesus responded by teaching the meaning of marriage, not grounds for divorce. Such an answer refutes even the question. Yet, sadly, we still pursue Jesus' answer in order to distil grounds, or lack of grounds, for divorce. But notice that the meaning of marriage is grounded in the two-in-one miracle of marriage which reflects the oneness and plurality in God and anticipates the oneness God intends between himself and his people. Paul expands on this mystery in Ephesians 5, showing us that marriage is intended as a display of his covenant-faithfulness to his people in Christ. This is preached and taught often, and yet so many do not hear. At least they do not hear in a way that causes change.

My argument above is that we restore marriage to be among the sacraments. If we do, this is a restoration, not a novel action. How might this help people hear again how holy and important it is? It will not do so as a 'bare' sacrament, a mere word-change without explanation. To a theologian and pastor, it may have rich meaning, but not for most of the church. But a word change may give the opportunity for instruction; a way to help people hear. How else can we help them hear? One way might be to institute a separation of church and state – an idea that also has very little of novelty in the West; indeed the very idea of a state-maintained marriage licence is relatively new. Recall that Stephanie Coontz and others have called attention to this: until the mid-nineteenth century the US courts routinely accepted cohabitation as a valid marriage.[3] So what if churches celebrated marriage (the ceremony and the enduring prac-tice) as a sacrament and did not participate in the state licence as a function of the church (or of church officers)? This practical step would certainly raise questions in the minds of the couple that a the-ological treatise on marriage as a sacrament would not! They would wonder, Why?! And then they may listen when we explain the meaning of the sacrament of marriage. Only God knows if they will hear.

But this is not only about helping people hear us on this issue. This is about the proper use of our authority over the perseverance of marriage that the Lord Jesus Christ has given to his church. In counterpoint, it should be observed that the Roman Catholic Church's (RCC) preservation of their authority in marriage, and divorce, has not ultimately preserved all RCC marriages. We should not confuse faithfulness with effectiveness. That the RCC may not have been effective is an analysis I am not prepared to address. That their governance over marriage has been flawed is historically true and a necessary effect of living in a world in which God's people are still flawed and still act with sin, including church leaders. But their position that marriage is the domain of the church may still be a right and faithful position which stands as a testimony to God's authority over marriage. We have the authority to display marriage as a sacrament and to reflect God's covenant-keeping grace for his people. This authority is ours to recover, if we understand marriage as a sacrament, separate from the state contract of marriage. We need not argue the state into agreement with us; we need only live out what is true.

Here is the place to say what I am not doing. I am not abdicating, giving marriage 'back to the state'. Quite the opposite, I suggest that we take it up again with all of God's authority. Said in another way, I must distinguish what I am proposing from any kind of libertarianism in regard to marriage. In this I agree with Jennifer Roback Morse, a self-affirmed libertarian, who argues that privatizing marriage is impossible, enhances the power of the state, and is unfair to children.[4] She is correct. Rather, I am arguing that we have no need to win a war of definitions; we 'own' marriage. Marriage is a sacrament of God's people and is given to us by God as a trust. The state should (not could) continue to debate and define the state laws of civil marriage. It is worth noting that in some countries, the United States included, all people, including Christians, have a right and responsibility to enter into that discussion. Good. But God's people are free to perform and live out the sacrament of marriage in the church without debate with the state. The interesting thing is that the state will not care; and in the United States they would not even notice. Far from giving it back to the state, I am proposing that we might unilaterally celebrate the sacrament of marriage. The state will continue to issue marriage licences. And our people should sign a state marriage contract as well, beyond the church. In fact, there is every reason to encourage those who are married in the church to also have a state marriage licence. We should not encourage anyone to deceive the state in regard to taxation. And perhaps there are still remnants of law which protect women and children in the case of divorce, though perhaps not as much as we think.[5] We must render to Caesar what is Caesar's and to God what is God's. But marriage, as I have argued, is a sacrament of the church. The marriage licence, and the state institution of marriage, is quite another thing. Could such a proposed break between the church and state help make this truth clearer to people, the people of God and the people who watch us to understand our God?

There is another unintended effect of such a break: it would change the tenor of the debate over the public definition of marriage. The foundations of the church – state partnership in marriage are crumbling over this definition because there is now significant cultural pressure to no longer define marriage as a unique relationship between one man and one woman.[6] In many contexts the debate is over, and the church has 'lost'. To the world, and at times to the church, instead of a covenant of grace which displays Christ's faithfulness to his people, marriage has become a mutually beneficial and temporal contract between partners. The issue of God's right to ordain marriage and the meaning of marriage is ignored by many even in the church and it is reduced to a contract. It seems the only question is: who can be partners? But we must remember that we are free to act unilaterally, allowing us to revive, reinforce, and support marriage in our own house, distinct from our participation in the public debate. We need not be limited by the debate. For even if we succeeded with legislation, we have not won the real battle; legislation does not change minds. Christianity is not ethical, but redemptive! The world needs Christ. To this end, the church has always been most effective when we live truth before the community – often while suffering for that truth. And if we endure in love, faithful and confident in God, we have an opportunity to define marriage by example, as a sacrament, instead of by legislation. And in that we show the glory and sufficiency of Christ, our bridegroom. We must use our influence, not our authority, to declare what is true and display what is true before the world!

I have attempted to revive, with amendment, the historical definition of 'sacrament': *a sacrament is a sign, a dramatic enactment, which mirrors the grace of God, which is ordained by God for our sanctification, and which displays God's great acts of salvation history.* I have also suggested that marriage could serve the gospel if we included marriage among the sacraments – not only the ceremony, but the daily drama, the *sacrament*, of living out the command of Christ in a way that displays his grace, not only for others, but for our own sanctification. I have tried to show that we need no permission from the state to define and practise marriage and, in fact, that our partnership with them may have been a mistake from which we need only to walk away. Marriage is whatever God says it is. We are free in Christ as we have always been. We are free to display God's truth and grace through the sacrament of marriage by the power of the Holy Spirit and in the community of the church. In this, God will be glorified.

Whose Marriage?

If this perspective has merit, it is not only that marriage is intended by God, sacramentally, but also that it belongs, first, to people who acknowledge and live for God; marriage belongs to the church. If so, then this ownership is without dispute, in this sense: the state does not care what the church does, as long as it does not interfere with the goals of the state. This means that if we do not participate in licensure, but leave that to the state, then we are free to uphold marriage as God defined it. If the state considers people married by the church, but without a state licence, to be living together, then they should also get a state licence before they move in together. Let no one give the appearance of evil. In the end, we have no one with whom to argue. Perhaps the public debate is a waste of time, at least until we are more intentional, as a whole cast (married, divorced, singles, widows, children, engaged, and even those brothers and sisters who suffer genetic and nurture-induced sexual miscues), as we enact the drama of the sacrament of marriage with all the excellence the Spirit allows to sinners who refuse to give up, even when we fail.

Conclusion: Marriage in Eschatology

I have led us through an investigation of the Marriage Text as the climax and conclusion to Genesis 1&2 and the anticipation of the trauma of Genesis 3. I have proposed that the Marriage Text is intended to establish marriage as a sacrament which mirrors the grace of God as it calls some (though not all) to the sanctifying drama which displays God's One-and-Many nature and his character of covenant-faithfulness. I have argued that marriage is not something under our authority that we can weigh and find wanting. Marriage cannot be redefined and adapted for our own purposes. Like the mass of an electron or the structure of a galaxy, marriage is not something we can change by our disapproval or modify by our will. Marriage and electrons are created realities. We can destroy an electron with an anti-electron, but we cannot create one with a different mass or different properties. So also, our subjective disillusionment with marriage is a self-assessment rather than a critique of marriage. Marriage is unaffected (and also unaffectable) by our feelings or debates. Marriage remains, like the electron, as something we can study, and gain understanding for our benefit, but cannot change. It is. But yet, like the electron, while we cannot change marriage, we might be able to destroy it. Nothing precludes the state from regulating a relationship they call 'marriage', but that does not destroy marriage, for that is not Marriage. It is left to the church to enact Christian Marriage and seek never to destroy the drama God intends by it.

Quite a few people are confused and disillusioned by the irrelevant power of marriage. God's people are not; or we should not be! Before God we have a privilege: to display this holy, sacramental drama. How will those who are married with contentment, and those married yet feeling alone, and the single and yet to be married, and also the divorced, widowed, sexually disoriented, or remarried . . . how will we all, the full cast of the church, enhance the performance of this sacrament which is intended to display God's nature and character? We will do so in the light of what is to come, in the light of our eschatology, the wedding feast of the Lamb. Every marriage, even bad marriages, point weakly but necessarily to this culminating event in history. By God's Spirit, the director of this drama, this is the power of marriage. It is far from irrelevant.

What If I Am Wrong?

My good friend Alexi (see the Preface) has changed his mind. He no longer sees his parents as the standard who lived out the truth of what 'marriage should be', but rather as an exception. Who is right, Alexi or me? As I close, let me ask the question that every author should consider. What if I am wrong? What are the danger(s) inherent in my ideas? Wrong ideas can and do undermine the performance of God's drama. If my ideas are wrong, how will they distort the drama intended by the Holy Spirit for the people of God?

Let me begin with the idea of sacrament. If 'sacrament' is adopted as a useful term, might the historical association of sacrament with *conferred grace* propagate theological error? Or if sacrament is adopted as a category for marriage, will those who do not marry feel excluded not only from marriage, but also from a sacrament? Moreover, if sacrament is adopted, would there be no end to the kinds of things which are considered sacramental? And if sacrament is adopted, would the term 'ordinance' be lost to the church? All of these are possible. Having done my best to address these challenges above (and even if I failed in that intent), still I think very little is at stake here, and much to gain. If we revive the idea of *sacramental marriage*, such a view of marriage offers us much: ordained dramas which mirror God's grace and sanctify us both as we participate in them and as we witness them in community. Our strong and biblical evangelical Protestant aversion to believing that external religious acts can confer saving grace will not waver as we practise the sacraments. If we are inclined to waver on grace alone, faith alone, and Christ alone, it will not be because we treat marriage sacramentally! And if marriage is restored to be among the sacraments, it could help us see the importance of marriage more clearly and deepen our delight in our covenant-keeping God. And if participation in the sacrament of marriage is given only to some within the church, and not to others, and this realization raises questions about the distinction between participation and witness, that conversation is an opportunity to understand more clearly that our call as the people of God is a call to hold the tension between the life of the individual and the life of the body.

I should also consider the bigger picture: the enactment of marriage as a sign to display God's nature and character. Although my theology is grounded in Augustine in fundamental ways, yet on this point I am at odds with him and with the many others who understand the Marriage Text and marriage to focus primarily on procreation. If they are right, this proposal fails. But this majority reading of Augustine may be thin. Wesley Hill writes, 'Augustine's view depends on our being able to follow the way he interweaves Genesis, Jesus' affirmation of the Genesis stories, and the later Pauline view that marriage not only fulfills the Genesis affirmation (Ephesians 5:31), but also gains its ultimate coherence when seen as an image or icon of Christ's love for the church.'[1] If Hill is right, then even Augustine sees marriage's ultimacy not in procreation, but in a display of God's covenant-faithfulness and love for his people. I think Hill is correct. If so, the difference with Augustine is one of emphasis only. Of more concern, if someone were to follow such a thin reading of Augustine, is the possibility that greater dangers would follow. The very idea that marriage is for procreation has led too many in our culture, with access to contraception, to just this conclusion. They propose, at least by their actions, 'marriage is for procreation, but singleness is for sex'. Not that Augustine would agree! But it seems that we have arrived at just this point in our culture: sex is assumed to be something 'divorced' from marriage. But if a person followed me into a belief that marriage is a sacrament which mirrors the grace of God and which calls us into a sanctifying drama which displays God's One-and-Many nature and his covenant-faithfulness, and marriage was not a sacrament, nothing is lost. Indeed, we are poorly served by a thinner reading of marriage.

Commencement: The Wedding Ceremony in Genesis 2:18–25

Marriage points robustly to the culmination of history in Christ. And we have the privilege of doing so as the cast members of his bride, the church. This begins by our right portrayal of the drama as first displayed in the Marriage Text. Such marriages begin with a wedding and there are deep connections between some wedding traditions and the Marriage Text. Though cultures differ and my primary perspective is rooted in the West and in the twenty-first century, not a few of these are transcultural.[2] We should first notice that Adam's marriage was arranged: 'So the LORD God caused a deep sleep to fall upon the man, and while he slept took one of his ribs and closed up its place with flesh. And the rib that the LORD God had taken from the man he made into a woman' (vv. 21–22a). If not in the West and if not so now in many places, most marriages were arranged by the parents. In fact, in this first marriage, the man is passive and God plays all the parental roles. He is creator of the man; he is his Father. God is also the Father of the woman when he creates her from the man's rib. In many traditions, the wedding begins with the call, 'Who gives this woman to this man?' So here in Genesis, we witness God as the man's 'Father-in-law' who presents her to the man as his bride: 'and [he] brought her to the man' (v. 22b). Today we may expect to hear the words, 'Her mother and I', but God serving also as the officiant and witness did not need to speak in this regard – he acted. Then vows are made, but in this first marriage they are spoken by the groom alone: 'This at last is bone of my bones and flesh of my flesh' (v. 23a). To some these words do not sound much like marriage vows, but they are! Paul seems to understand them to be so. In Ephesians 5 he offers his own exposition of them as vows when he says, 'In the same way husbands should love their wives as their own bodies.

He who loves his wife loves himself. For no one ever hated his own flesh, but nourishes and cherishes it' (Eph. 5:28–29a). The 'bone of my bones and flesh of my flesh' has become the very basis for how each man, as Adam promised at the first, must care for his wife. Every man must care for his wife as he does himself. The next element is the charge to the couple, given by Moses, speaking for God: 'Therefore a man shall leave his father and his mother and hold fast to his wife' (vv. 24a).[3] But who is Moses speaking to? This charge to the couple on the occasion of their marriage is given to all of us who attend this first wedding, the readers of Genesis. This charge is primarily for our edification rather than that of Adam & Eve, for Adam has no 'father and mother' to leave. This charge to the bride and groom is for us. Then the woman is given the name of the man. In this first wedding, she is given a name that reflects their unique connection and sounds like the name of her man: 'she shall be called *Wo-man*, because she was taken out of *Man*' (this homophone works in Hebrew as well as English).[4] In our day, this is echoed by the tradition, 'I now present to you Mr and Mrs . . .' Traditionally, she is given and accepts the husband's family name. Finally, there is the benediction – a good word over the couple: 'the man and his wife were both naked and were not ashamed' (v. 25). This beautiful and peaceful word was spoken over the couple in the Garden temple, their bridal suite. Yet it is also an alarming anticipation of the coming Fall. Indeed, this Marriage Text (ch. 2) is linked with the Fall (ch. 3) by both the words 'shame' and 'naked'. This brief comparison reveals many similarities and probably exposes some distinctions: no rice is thrown in this wedding!

With intention I have skipped a most critical part of the first wedding ceremony: the pronouncement of the marriage. In some traditions, it may sound like this: 'Now, by the power vested in me by the State of Minnesota, I now pronounce you man and wife.' The biblical pronouncement says nothing of the state (of course there is no state!), nor does it defend the authority of God to pronounce the union by citing an external power (never an orthodox idea). God simply declares, 'they shall become one flesh' (v. 24b). In many contexts,

Canada for example,[5] pastors act as the religious officiant (standing in for God), but the marriage is formalized for the state by an officer of Canada. At the core of the wedding announcement is a commissive: words which create a new state of affairs. By these few words a mysterious union is created, one which could be termed a sacrament. This created union is the core of every wedding and the basis of every marriage: the two (people) become one (essence) – even for those who do not know God. The two are declared to be one on God's authority in creation and by varied authorities in our traditions.

This new state of affairs, in which two are also one, is something not easily broken by people, if that is even possible. If a culture or a person can destroy a single marriage, yet marriage stands and is enacted by the whole church, a sacrament which displays glorious truth: God is One-and-Many; God is faithful to his people by his covenant. Every wedding and every marriage declares this truth (or highlights truth by failure) and every one of the people of God is called to strengthen the performance of this drama, in whatever state she or he may be found. Marriage is the first sacrament. Marriage is the central drama of Scripture, pointing to God's goal in Christ and the church. Marriage is the ultimate drama, the commissioning drama of eternity, pointing us toward the glorious day which is coming soon for the people of God. We will be his virgin bride! Every wedding is practice, grounded in the first wedding, pointing to the last. Indeed, there is no marriage in heaven, first and foremost, because Christ will be married to his virgin bride. And he will never drive her out, but will wipe away every tear and speak tenderly to her: 'my beloved!'

Bibliography

Aquinas, Thomas. *Summa Theologica*, ed. Kevin Knight (2008) www
.newadvent.org/summa/ (accessed 24 Oct. 2014).

Augustine. 'The Literal Meaning of Genesis', in *On Genesis: A
Refutation of the Manichees, Unfinished Literal Commentary on
Genesis, The Literal Meaning of Genesis*, 13, The Works of Saint Au-
gustine: A Translation for the 21st Century, 1 (trans. Edmund Hill;
Hyde Park, NY: New City Press, 2004), pp. 155–506.

———. 'On the Good of Marriage', in *Nicene and Post Nicene Fathers
1–3*, (ed. Philip Schaff; Grand Rapids: Christian Classics Ethereal
Library, 2001) pp. 397–413.

———. *Trinity* (trans. Edmund Hill; Brooklyn: New City Press,
1991).

———. 'Unfinished Literal Commentary on Genesis', in *On Genesis:
A Refutation of the Manichees, Unfinished Literal Commentary on
Genesis, The Literal Meaning of Genesis*, 13, The Works of Saint
Augustine: A Translation for the 21st Century, 1 (trans. Edmund
Hill; Hyde Park, NY: New City Press, 2004), pp. 105–154.

Barrett, C.K. *The Gospel According to St. John: An Introduction with
Commentary and Notes on the Greek Text* (Philadelphia: Westminster
Press, 1978).

Barth, Karl, *Church Dogmatics* (Peabody, MA: Hendrickson, 2nd edn,
2010).

Beale, G.K. *The Book of Revelation*, The New International Greek
Testament Commentary (Grand Rapids: Eerdmans, 1999).

———. *The Temple and the Church's Mission: A Biblical Theology of the Dwelling Place of God*, 17, New Studies in Biblical Theology (Downers Grove, IL: InterVarsity Press, 2004).

Berkhof, Louis. *Systematic Theology* (Grand Rapids: Eerdmans, 1941).

Blocher, Henri. *In the Beginning: The Opening Chapters of Genesis* (Downers Grove, IL: InterVarsity Press, 1984).

Block, Daniel. 'How Many Is God: An Investigation into the Meaning of Deuteronomy 6:4–5'. *Journal of the Evangelical Theological Society* 47/2 (2004): pp. 193–212.

Bonhoeffer, Dietrich. *Creation and Fall: Two Biblical Studies* (ed. John W. de Gruchy, trans. John C. Fletcher; New York: Simon & Schuster, 1997).

Brueggemann, Walter. *Genesis* (Atlanta: John Knox Press, 1982).

Calvin, John. *Calvin: Institutes of the Christian Religion* (ed. John T. McNeill, trans. Ford Lewis Battles; Philadelphia: Westminster Press, 1960).

———. *Commentaries on the First Book of Moses Called Genesis* (trans. John King; Grand Rapids: Eerdmans, 1948).

———. *Commentary on the Gospel According to John, Chapters 1–11* (trans. William Pringle; Grand Rapids: Eerdmans, 1949).

Carson, D.A. *The Gospel According to John*, Pillar New Testament Commentary (Leicester, InterVarsity Press, 1991).

Cassuto, Umberto. *A Commentary on the Book of Genesis* (Jerusalem: Varda, 2012).

Chapple, Allan. 'Jesus' Intervention in the Temple: Once or Twice?' *Journal of the Evangelical Theological Society* 58/3 (2015): pp. 545–69.

Chrysostom, John. *Saint Chrysostom: Homilies on Galatians, Ephesians, Philippians, Colossians, Thessalonians, Timothy, Titus, and Philemon*, 13, NPNF, 1 (ed. Philip Schaff; Peabody, MA: Hendrickson, 1994).

————. *St. John Chrysostom: Homilies on Genesis, 1–17*, 74, Fathers of the Church (ed. Robert C. Hill; Washington, DC: Catholic University of America Press, 1986).

Collins, C. John. *Genesis 1–4: A Linguistic, Literary, and Theological Commentary* (Phillipsburg, NJ: Presbyterian & Reformed, 2005).

Coontz, Stephanie. 'Taking Marriage Private', *New York Times* Op Ed, (26 Nov. 2007) http://www.nytimes.com/2007/11/26/opinion/26coontz.html?_r=2 (accessed 1 Sept. 2012).

————. *Marriage, a History: How Love Conquered Marriage* (New York: Viking, repr. edn, 2005).

Cooper, Betsy, Daniel Cox, Rachel Lienesch, and Robert Jones. 'Exodus: Why Americans Are Leaving Religion – and Why They're Unlikely to Come Back'. *Public Religion Research Institute* (2016) http://www.prri.org/research/prri-rns-2016-religiously-unaffiliated-americans/ (accessed 20 October 2016).

Crisp, Oliver D. *The Word Enfleshed: Exploring the Person and Work of Christ* (Grand Rapids: Baker Academic, 2016).

DeRouchie, Jason. 'The Blessing-Commission, the Promised Offspring, and the Toledot Structure of Genesis'. *Journal of the Evangelical Theological Society* 56/2 (2013): pp. 219–47.

Dever, William G. *Did God Have A Wife? Archaeology and Folk Religion in Ancient Israel* (Grand Rapids: Eerdmans, 2005).

Ellul, Jacques. *To Will and to Do* (Cleveland, OH: Pilgrim, 1969).

Erickson, Millard. *Christian Theology* (Grand Rapids: Baker Academic, 2nd edn, 2009).

Evdokimov, Paul. *The Sacrament of Love: The Nuptial Mystery in the Light of the Orthodox Tradition* (trans. Anthony P. Gythiel and Victoria Steadman; Crestwood, NY: St Vladimir's Seminary, 1995).

Feldhahn, Shaunti. *The Good News about Marriage: Debunking Discouraging Myths about Marriage and Divorce* (Colorado Springs, CO: Multnomah, 2014).

Frame, John M. *The Doctrine of God* (Phillipsburg, NJ: Presbyterian & Reformed, 1st edn, 2002).

Godshall, Matthew. 'Marriage and New Creation: The Re-Contextualization of Genesis 2:24 in Ephesians 5:31' (Evangelical Theological Society, Atlanta, GA, 2015).

Greene-McCreight, Kathryn. *Ad Litteram: How Augustine, Calvin, and Barth Read the 'Plain Sense' of Genesis 1–3*, Issues in Systematic Theology 5 (ed. Paul D. Molnar; New York: Lang, 1999).

Grudem, Wayne A. *Systematic Theology: An Introduction to Biblical Doctrine* (Grand Rapids: Zondervan, 1974).

Gundry, Stanley N., William Loader, Megan K. DeFranza, Wesley Hill, and Stephen R. Holmes. *Two Views on Homosexuality, the Bible, and the Church* (ed. Preston Sprinkle; Grand Rapids: Zondervan, 2016).

Hamilton, Victor P. *The Book of Genesis 1–17*, New International Commentary on the Old Testament Series (Grand Rapids: Eerdmans, 1990).

Heimbach, Daniel R. *True Sexual Morality: Recovering Biblical Standards for a Culture in Crisis* (Wheaton, IL: Crossway, 2004).

Hengel, Martin. 'The Old Testament in the Fourth Gospel'. Pages 380–95 in *The Gospels and the Scriptures of Israel*, Journal for the Study of the New Testament Supplement Series 104; Studies in Scripture in Early Judaism and Christianity 3 (ed. Craig A. Evans and W. Richard Stegner; Sheffield: Sheffield Academic Press, 1994).

Horton, Michael. *We Believe: Recovering the Essentials of the Apostles' Creed* (Nashville: Nelson, 1998).

Hunt, Rosa. 'Reading Genesis with the Church Fathers: Metaphors of Creation in John Chrysostom's Homilies on Genesis'. *Journal of European Baptist Studies* 12/2 (2012): pp. 21–33.

Instone-Brewer, David. *Divorce and Remarriage in the Bible: The Social and Literary Context* (Grand Rapids: Eerdmans, 2002).

Jerome. *The Homilies of Saint Jerome, Volume 1 (1–59 on the Psalms)*, The Fathers of the Church: A New Translation, 48 (trans. Marie Liguiori Ewald; Washington, DC: Catholic University of America Press, 1966).

Justin Martyr. 'Dialogues with Trypho'. Pages 194–270 in *The Apostolic Fathers with Justin Martyr and Irenaeus*, 1, Ante-Nicene Fathers (ed. Philip Schaff; Grand Rapids: Christian Classics Ethereal Library, 2001).

Kidner, Derek. *Genesis: An Introduction and Commentary* (London, Tyndale Press, 1968).

Kim, Paul. 'Critical Reinterpretation of Genesis 1:28: A Neglected Key to Unlock the Structural Coherence of the Whole Bible'. (Unpublished paper given at the Evangelical Theological Society, Atlanta, GA, 2015.)

Kinlaw, Dennis F. *Song of Songs*, Expositor's Bible Commentary 5 (Grand Rapids: Zondervan, 1991).

Köstenberger, Andreas J. *John*, Baker Exegetical Commentary on the New Testament (Grand Rapids: Baker Academic, 2004).

Lombard, Peter. *The Sentences Book 1: The Mystery of the Trinity* (trans. Giulio Silano; Toronto: PIMS, 1st edn, 2007).

Longman, Tremper, III. *Song of Songs*, New International Commentary on the Old Testament (Grand Rapids: Eerdmans, 2001).

Luther, Martin. *Lectures on Genesis: Chapters 1–5*, Martin Luther's Works, 1 (ed. Jaroslav Pelikan; Saint Louis: Concordia, 1958).

———. *Martin Luther: Selections from His Writings* (ed. John Dillenberger; Garden City, NY: Anchor, 1958).

Mbamalu, Abiola. 'Life in the Fourth Gospel and Its Resonances with Genesis 1–3'. *In die Skriflig* 48/1 (2014): pp. 1–5.

Menken, M.J.J. 'Genesis in John's Gospel and 1 John'. Pages 83–98 in *Genesis in the New Testament*, Library of New Testament Studies 466 (ed. Maarten J.J. Menken and Steve Moyise; London: T&T Clark, 2012).

Morris, Leon. *The Apostolic Preaching of the Cross* (London: Tyndale, 3rd edn, 1965).

———. *The Gospel According to John*, New International Commentary on the New Testament (Grand Rapids: Eerdmans, rev. edn, 1995).

Morse, Jennifer Roback. 'Privatizing Marriage Is Impossible', The Witherspoon Institute: Public Discourse on Ethics, Law and Common Good, 2, 3, 4 April 2012, http://www.thepublicdiscourse.com/2012/04/5069 (accessed 27 Aug. 2012).

Murphy, Bryan. 'The Trinity in Creation'. *The Master's Seminary Journal* 24/2 (2013): pp. 167–77.

Ortlund, Raymond C., Jr. *God's Unfaithful Wife: A Biblical Theology of Spiritual Adultery*, New Studies in Biblical Theology 2 (Downers Grove, IL: InterVarsity Press, 2003).

———. *Marriage and the Mystery of the Gospel* (Wheaton, IL: Crossway, 2016).

Pagels, Elaine. 'Exegesis of Genesis 1 in the Gospels of Thomas and John'. *Journal of Biblical Literature* 118/3 (1999): pp. 477–96.

Parker, Pierson. 'Bethany beyond Jordan'. *Journal of Biblical Literature* 74/4 (1955): pp. 257–61.

Patterson, Todd. 'Man-Woman Shaped Hole in the Heart of Creation'. (Paper presented at the Annual Meeting of the Evangelical Theological Society, Atlanta, GA, 18 November 2015.)

von Rad, Gerhard. *Genesis: A Commentary*. Old Testament Library (Philadelphia: Westminster John Knox, rev. edn, 1973).

Rogers, James. 'God's Image, Man's Crimes'. *First Things* (2017) https://www.firstthings.com/web-exclusives/2017/03/gods-image-mans-crimes (accessed 31 March 2017).

Sailhamer, John H. 'A Database Approach to the Analysis of Hebrew Narrative'. *MAARAV* 5/6 (1990): pp. 319–35.

———. *The Pentateuch as Narrative: A Biblical-Theological Commentary* (Grand Rapids: Zondervan, 1995).

Schroeder, H.J., trans. *The Canons and Decrees of the Council of Trent* (Rockford, IL: TAN, 1978).

Shenk, Richard. 'Is Marriage among the Sacraments? Were Luther and Calvin Wrong?' Pages 105–21 in *Reformation Faith: Exegesis and Theology in the Protestant Reformations* (ed. Michael Parsons; Eugene, OR: Wipf & Stock, 2014).

———. *The Virgin Birth of Christ: The Rich Meaning of a Biblical Truth* (Milton Keynes: Paternoster, 2016).

Stuart, Douglas. *Hosea – Jonah*, Word Biblical Commentary 31 (Waco, TX: Word, 1987).

Tertullian. 'Against Praxeas'. Pages 597–632 in *Latin Christianity: Its Founder, Tertullian*, 3, Ante-Nicene Fathers (ed. Philip Schaff; Grand Rapids: Christian Classics Ethereal Library, 2001).

———. 'An Exhortation to Charity'. Pages 37–84 in *Treatises on Marriage and Remarriage: To His Wife, An Exhortation to Chastity, Monogamy*, Ancient Christian Writers (Philadelphia: Westminster, 1956).

Thielman, Frank. *Ephesians*, Baker Exegetical Commentary on the New Testament (Grand Rapids: Baker Academic, 2010).

Trenham, Josiah B. *Marriage and Virginity According to St. John Chrysostom* (Platina, CA: St Herman of Alaska Monastery, 1st edn, 2013).

Van Til, Cornelius. *The Defense of the Faith* (ed. K. Scott Oliphant; Phillipsburg, NJ: Presbyterian & Reformed, 4th edn, 2008).

Vanhoozer, Kevin J. *First Theology: God, Scripture & Hermeneutics* (Downers Grove, IL: InterVarsity Press, 2002).

———. *Is There a Meaning in This Text? The Bible, The Reader and the Morality of Knowledge* (Grand Rapids: Zondervan, 1998).

Vines, Matthew, and Caleb Kaltenbach. 'Debating Bible Verses on Homosexuality', *The New York Times*, 8 June 2015 https://www.nytimes.com/interactive/2015/06/05/us/samesex-scriptures.html (accessed 27 April 2017).

Waltke, Bruce K. *Genesis: A Commentary* (Grand Rapids: Zondervan, 2001).

Ware, Kallistos. *The Orthodox Way* (Crestwood, NY: St Vladimir's Seminary, 1995).

Wenham, Gordon John. *Genesis 1–15*, Word Biblical Commentary 1 (Waco, TX: Word, 1987).

Westermann, Claus. *Genesis 1–11*, A Continental Commentary (Minneapolis: Fortress Press, 1st edn, 1994).

Witte, John, Jr. *From Sacrament to Contract: Marriage, Religion, and Law in the Western Tradition* (Louisville, KY: Westminster John Knox Press, 2nd edn, 2012).

————. 'The Reformation of Marriage Law in Martin Luther's Germany: Its Significance Then and Now'. *Journal of Law and Religion* 4/2 (1968): pp. 293–351.

Wright, Christopher J.H. *Deuteronomy* (Grand Rapids: Baker, 1994).

Wright, N.T. *John for Everyone, Part 1: Chapters 1–10* (Louisville, KY: Westminster John Knox Press, 2004).

————. *Paul for Everyone: The Prison Letters: Ephesians, Philippians, Colossians, and Philemon*, New Testament for Everyone (Louisville, KY: Westminster John Knox Press, 2nd edn, 2004).

————. *The Resurrection of the Son of God*, Christian Origins and the Question of God 3 (Minneapolis: Fortress Press, 2003).

Youngblood, Ronald. *The Book of Genesis: An Introductory Commentary* (Eugene, OR: Wipf & Stock, 2nd edn, 1991).

Notes

Preface

[1] Hos. 2:14, my paraphrase.

Introduction

[1] Betsy Cooper and others, 'Exodus: Why Americans Are Leaving Religion – and Why They're Unlikely to Come Back', *PRRI* (2016) http://www.prri.org/research/prri-rns-2016-religiously-unaffiliated-americans/ (accessed 20 Oct. 2016).

[2] This term, first used in my book *The Wonder of the Cross* (Eugene, OR: Cascade, 2013) identifies people, first as God's creation, his creatures. Second, we are his wilful-creatures, and so like God; distinct (on Augustine) from rocks (which have being) and animals (which have being and life), people also have understanding (and so, a will). Last, we are specifically human, rather than angelic. To simply say 'person' is sufficient in many contexts, but God is also Persons: three persons, One-and-Many, the Trinity. We are, uniquely, God's human wilful-creatures.

[3] Kevin J. Vanhoozer, *Is There a Meaning in This Text? The Bible, The Reader and the Morality of Knowledge* (Grand Rapids: Zondervan, 1998).

[4] This is something I explain more thoroughly in ch. 2 of *The Virgin Birth of Christ: The Rich Meaning of a Biblical Truth* (Milton Keynes: Paternoster, 2016).

[5] Speech is first God's, and words constitute God's communication and the representation of his meaning. God is the author who means things. Human speech is like God's analogously, including our use of words and the vibrations heard by our ears or images seen by our eyes.

[6] The language of Matt. 28:18–20 reflects the Garden-priestly language of 'guard and keep' by which God commanded Adam and later the priests. Jesus said in Matthew, 'teaching them to obey everything I have commanded you' (διδάσκοντες αὐτοὺς τηρεῖν πάντα ὅσα ἐνετειλάμην ὑμῖν). Here the word translated by the NIV as 'obey' (*tareo*) means, more literally, to guard or keep or obey. This is very like the command to Adam in the Garden, 'to work and keep' or to 'serve and guard' (for a comparison of the Garden command to that of the priests in the Torah, see G.K. Beale, *The Temple and the Church's Mission: A Biblical Theology of the Dwelling Place of God*, NSBT 17 [Downers Grove, IL: InterVarsity Press, 2004], p. 7). So, our doctrine (*didachalia*) flows from our theology. Theology is what God intends and means by his words. Doctrine is our commitment to obey what God has commanded. So then, doctrine is the drama of God, enacted by the church by the power of the Spirit.

[7] For completeness, let me observe that if we fail to discern God's locution (exegesis of his word) and so fail to make correct claims about his illocution (theology is discernment of his intent), then this failure is named heterodoxy or heresy. Heresy is to divide locution from illocution. But if we correctly discern God's locution and illocution, and so have good theology, we may still fail to display the glory of God's perlocution. If God's perlocution (the effect of God's word) is not displayed in us by his Spirit in keeping with his illocution (God's intent and our theology), we fail by hypocrisy. Hypocrisy is to divide locution and illocution from perlocution.

1. Genesis 2:18–25: Imaging the Trinity

[1] Karl Barth, *Church Dogmatics* (Peabody, MA: Hendrickson, 2nd edn, 2010), 3/4, p. 142.

[2] I am ignoring, for this book, Barth's use of the word 'saga'. Still it is worth offering his own definition, 'an intuitive and poetic picture of a pre-historical reality of history which is enacted once and for all within the confines of time and space' (Barth, *Church Dogmatics*, 3/1, p. 81). While not a few papers have been written on the significance of 'saga' for Barth, I will note here only that he intended the term to be more like history than myth and he used it to make a distinction against those who affirm the ahistorical nature of the biblical narrative such as Rudolf Bultmann.

³ Having cited Moses as the author of Genesis (and the Torah), I must acknowledge that there are authorial issues with which I will not engage. Nor need I do so, as nothing I will discuss here depends on authorship, only that there is an author. We have a text and that text means 'something'. This text has an author or authors who desired to express a particular meaning by the words in context, syntactically, literarily and by the words selected. If the text we have is the work of unknown redactors, the same claims can be made about them, and the text as they gave it to us. This also raises the issue of divine authorship. Rather than taking up a defence of hard or soft inerrancy, or issues of biblical authority, I will acknowledge that I am speaking to those who accept a kind of divine authorship of Scripture which entails God as the author 'in, with, and under' the human author(s) and/or redactor(s). As Jesus is at once wholly divine and wholly human, so is the text. So we also can speak of human authorial intention and divine authorial intention, but have no need to differentiate between them, if differentiation is even a coherent idea. I will refer to biblical authors by conventional attribution, such as Moses or John, or by the divine author, or by the generic 'author' or 'Evangelist'. I will acknowledge here my own affinity with an Augustinian understanding of textual authority and traditional authorship, yet I neither need to take time to make that case nor argue with one who disagrees. It is enough for this project to accept that the author of this Text, as it stands, intends a meaning. It is this I will investigate.

⁴ John Chrysostom, *St. John Chrysostom: Homilies on Genesis, 1–17,* 74, FC (ed. Robert C. Hill; Washington, DC: Catholic University of America Press, 1986), Homily 14.15; p. 189.

⁵ The beginning of Chrysostom's exposition of the Marriage Text occurs in the middle of Homily 14 which covers Genesis 2:15–20a. This textual division shows at least a difference in regard to the importance of perceiving 18–25 as a unit, or as a Marriage Text, or as a climax to Genesis 1–2.

⁶ Jerome, *The Homilies of Saint Jerome (Homilies 1–59 on the Psalms),* FC: A New Translation (trans. Marie Liguori Ewald; Washington, DC: Catholic University of America, 1966), 1:65.

⁷ Augustine, 'The Literal Meaning of Genesis', in *On Genesis: A Refutation of the Manichees, Unfinished Literal Commentary on Genesis* and *The Literal Meaning of Genesis,* 13, The Works of Saint Augustine: A Translation for the 21st Century, 1 (trans. Edmund Hill; Hyde Park, NY: New City Press, 2004), 6.1.1–2.

8 Augustine, 'The Literal Meaning of Genesis', 11.1.3.

9 Martin Luther, *Lectures on Genesis: Chapters 1–5*, Martin Luther's Works, 1, (ed. Jaroslav Pelikan; Saint Louis: Concordia, 1958), 1:132. However, in Part Two, when I explore the Gospel of John, I will return to this fruitful idea.

10 John Calvin, *Commentaries on the First Book of Moses Called Genesis* (trans. John King; Grand Rapids: Eerdmans, 1948), p. 128.

11 Kathryn Greene-McCreight notes that for modern exegetes who are interested in source criticism, knowing the sources is sufficient and 'the matter of its significance is usually left unaddressed' (Kathryn Greene-McCreight, *Ad Litteram: How Augustine, Calvin, and Barth Read the 'Plain Sense' of Genesis 1–3*, Issues in Systematic Theology 5 [ed. Paul D. Molnar; New York: Lang, 1999], p. 69).

12 Gerhard von Rad, *Genesis: A Commentary*, OTL (Philadelphia: Westminster John Knox Press, rev. edn, 1973), p. 25.

13 von Rad, *Genesis: A Commentary*, p. 82.

14 Augustine certainly did not read misogyny into Moses, for he wrote, 'Is there anyone who would exclude females from this [trinitarian] association [with man], seeing that together with us men, they are fellow heirs of grace?' (Augustine, *Trinity* [trans. Edmund Hill; Brooklyn: New City Press, 1991], 12.12). Von Rad does give an answer to Augustine's questions: There is. Von Rad would have us believe that Moses did!

15 von Rad, *Genesis: A Commentary*, p. 84.

16 In fact, writing about the first (Priestly) account he makes it clear that the intent is neither myth nor saga, nor even theological, but merely Priestly knowledge (von Rad, *Genesis: A Commentary*, p. 63).

17 Claus Westermann, *Genesis 1–11*, CC (Minneapolis: Fortress Press, 1st edn, 1994), p. 233.

18 Derek Kidner, *Genesis: An Introduction and Commentary* (London: Tyndale Press, 1968), p. 65.

19 John H. Sailhamer, *The Pentateuch as Narrative: A Biblical-Theological Commentary* (Grand Rapids: Zondervan, 1995), p. 35. This same literary device is used by the author of Genesis in the succeeding Fall narrative, specifically 3:14–19.

20 Sailhamer, *The Pentateuch as Narrative*, p. 35.

21 John H. Sailhamer, 'A Database Approach to the Analysis of Hebrew Narrative', *MAARAV*, 5/6 (1990): p. 328. All Hebrew grammars note that the *wayyiqtol* form of the verb indicates narrative continuity. That is, the Hebrew consonant *waw*, when used as a prefix to the Hebrew verb in the imperfect tense, indicates a continuation of a narrative movement

from one thought unit to the next. This conjunctive is the *wayyiqtol* form. Similarly, the lack of a *waw* indicates discontinuity. But Sailhamer noticed a more complex verbal disjunctive pattern: the use of a perfect tense verb (*qatal*), without a preformative *waw*, which does not fall in the initial position in the phrase – the usual Hebrew form. While the simple lack of a *waw* is a disjunctive *within* a narrative, this more complex pattern represents a distinctive pattern between narrative sections. He denotes this form of the phrase as the '0 + X + QATAL' form. It is worth noting that while this article focused on Genesis 1 and 2, the article was an argument for computer software that tagged not only words, but phrases, something that has since been provided by contemporary biblical research tools.

22 It must be noted that Sailhamer is aware that while this disjunctive pattern does not have *waw* in the first position, that is the case for 1:2 and 3:1. Still, the verb is the perfect form and it is not in the first position of the sentence. In his article, Sailhamer argues that this pattern can clarify our reading of Genesis.

23 There is another dominant pattern in Genesis indicated by the word 'generations' or *toledot* in Hebrew. As Sailhamer acknowledges, this postpositive (second position) *wayyiqtol* pattern does not replace the *toledot* pattern of the Genesis text. Instead it is another layer, another pattern, created by the author. Both patterns are used by the author to frame (communicate) distinct truths. I will address the *toledot* pattern in the next chapter.

24 Greene-McCreight, *Ad Litteram*, 199. All of these many citations are drawn from *Church Dogmatics*, 3/3, sec. 41.

25 This same 'pause' was noted by Victor Hamilton who says it 'prepare[s] the reader for something momentous' (Victor P. Hamilton, *The Book of Genesis 1–17*, NICOT [Grand Rapids: Eerdmans, 1990], p. 134).

26 Barth, *Church Dogmatics*, 3/1, p. 289. Emphasis added.

27 I recently read an unpublished paper by Todd Patterson, 'Man-Woman Shaped Hole in the Heart of Creation', which was presented at the Evangelical Theological Society in 2015. He argues well that Gen. 2 is wholly dependent upon Gen. 1, which together create a single whole. Further, he shows that the plot-structure (*muthos*) is driven toward the Marriage Text for a resolution: 'The theological thrust of the narrative is that creation has a hole in its heart that only man-woman can fill.' This comes close to making the Marriage Text a conclusion and climax.

28 Paul Evdokimov, *The Sacrament of Love: The Nuptial Mystery in the Light of the Orthodox Tradition* (trans. Anthony P. Gythiel and Victoria Steadman; Crestwood, NY: St Vladimir's Seminary, 1995), p. 115.

[29] Henri Blocher, *In the Beginning: The Opening Chapters of Genesis* (Downers Grove, IL: InterVarsity Press, 1984), p. 96.

[30] The Hebrew for 'therefore' in this text is: עַל־כֵּן.

[31] Day two stands out from the rest, an exception, with no such affirmation. Many suggestions have presented themselves, though an explanation is beyond the scope of this investigation. Even so, I can note that on day six, the intensification 'very good' may be understood as an affirmation covering all of God's creative work to this point, all of heaven and earth: 'and God saw everything that he had made, and behold, it was very good' (Gen. 1:31).

[32] Blocher, *In the Beginning*, p. 109. Specifically, Blocher and Barth observed the radical distinction between the provision for procreation of animals and people: 'It is impossible to differ from Barth when he observes, following the text, that "in the case of man the differentiation of sex is the only differentiation". No other distinction, racial, ethnic or social, belongs to his essence. Mankind is the only living creature lacking the formula "according to their kind" (which has a distributive sense); the reason is that he does not divide into different species like the feathered tribe or cattle' (p. 92).

[33] Blocher, *In the Beginning*, p. 97. Here he writes, 'Why, however, should there be the difference between the man and the woman, and not simply the distinction between one person and another? Sexuality is certainly not necessary to being-with . . . God does not institute an abstract otherness. He gives a neighbour and not merely an "other" . . . Genesis throws light on this privileged relationship.'

[34] A thorough exploration of this can be found in Jonathan Edwards, *The End for Which God Created the World* (Los Angeles: HardPress, 2013).

[35] For example, Wayne Grudem writes, 'People have sometimes thought that God created human beings because he was lonely and needed fellowship with other persons. If this were true, it would certainly mean that God is not completely independent of creation. It would mean that God would need to create persons in order to be completely happy or completely fulfilled in his personal existence' (Wayne A. Grudem, *Systematic Theology: An Introduction to Biblical Doctrine* [Grand Rapids: Zondervan, 1974], p. 161).

[36] Bruce K. Waltke, *Genesis: A Commentary* (Grand Rapids: Zondervan, 2001), p. 88. Blocher speaks also to this point: 'The oneness of the Lord is not loneliness, since he deliberates with himself, with his Spirit. This he wished to show in the course of his creation.' Christians agree: YHWH Elohim of this text is One, but he is not only One, or even primarily One.

[37] The translation bears at least one other option: 'YHWH is our God, YHWH alone' (Daniel Block, 'How Many Is God: An Investigation into the Meaning of Deuteronomy 6:4–5', *JETS* 47/2 [2004]: pp. 193–212). This is a translation that I affirm. Contextually, the issue that Moses is refuting is not that God is One-and-Many, but that God alone is worthy of our worship and no other (e.g. Deut. 6:13–14). And regardless of the translation of the Shema, the oneness (not in dispute) of God does not testify against God's 'manyness', his trinitarian nature. Indeed, this same verse was on the lips of Jesus Christ in Matt. 19, who himself claimed to be God.

[38] Cornelius Van Til, *The Defense of the Faith* (ed. K. Scott Oliphant; Phillipsburg, NJ: Presbyterian & Reformed, 4th edn, 2008), p. 46.

[39] 'Neither' parts nor whole is only an option if a person is prepared to reject the reality of the experience of creation by our senses, which not a few have done. While logically possible, this is excluded from this discussion.

[40] Van Til, *The Defense of the Faith*, p. 48.

[41] Justin Martyr, 'Dialogues with Trypho', in *The Apostolic Fathers with Justin Martyr and Irenaeus*, 1, ANF (ed. Philip Schaff; Grand Rapids: Christian Classics Ethereal Library, 2001), ch. 62.

[42] Augustine, 'The Literal Meaning of Genesis', 1.6 (p. 12).

[43] Augustine, 'The Literal Meaning of Genesis', 3.19 (p. 29). He makes this same point in 7.12 of *The Trinity*: 'That man is spoken of as "after our image", and so "our", that man might be an image of the Trinity.'

[44] Augustine, 'The Literal Meaning of Genesis', 3.19 (p. 29). He also writes, 'This Trinity is a triad in such a way as to be one God, is one God in such a way as to be a triad.' Saint Augustine, 'Unfinished Literal Commentary on Genesis', in *On Genesis: A Refutation of the Manichees, Unfinished Literal Commentary on Genesis, The Literal Meaning of Genesis*, 13, The Works of Saint Augustine: A Translation for the 21st Century, 1, (trans. Edmund Hill; Hyde Park, NY: New City Press, 2004), sec. 61.

[45] Peter Lombard, *The Sentences Book 1: The Mystery of the Trinity* (trans. Giulio Silano; Toronto: PIMS, 1st edn, 2007), 1.7.2.

[46] Calvin, *Commentaries on the First Book of Moses Called Genesis*, p. 92.

[47] Calvin, *Commentaries on the First Book of Moses Called Genesis*, p. 97.

[48] Barth, *Church Dogmatics*, 3/1, p. 116.

[49] Calvin, *Commentaries on the First Book of Moses Called Genesis*, pp. 70–72.

[50] Bryan Murphy, 'The Trinity in Creation', *The Master's Seminary Journal*, 24/2 (2013): p. 170. Murphy cites Ps. 7:10 and Deut. 7:10 as examples which would at least make us unwilling to see any strong evidence of 'many' in the simple use of the plural.

[51] Millard Erickson, *Christian Theology* (Grand Rapids: Baker Academic, 2nd edn, 2009), p. 354.

[52] John M. Frame, *The Doctrine of God* (Phillipsburg, NJ: Presbyterian & Reformed, 1st edn, 2002), p. 355. For example, in Hebrew the plural form of 'waters' (*mayim*) is used for water (in general), so also the plural form of 'heavens' (*shamayim*) for 'heaven'. This is not an issue in full agreement among scholars. The -*im* ending may also reflect a collection of parts into one thing (like many drops of water into one body of water).

[53] Calvin, *Commentaries on the First Book of Moses Called Genesis*, p. 73.

[54] Hamilton, *The Book of Genesis 1–17*, p. 133.

[55] U. Cassuto, *A Commentary on the Book of Genesis* (Jerusalem: Varda, 2012), p. 55. Cassuto himself rejects any idea that conflicts with the idea that God is the unique creator of the world, and notes that the phrasing in this text is not one of consultation and moreover the text is oddly missing the object. He does, however, settle on a plural of exhortation, as in 'Let us rise up!' and finds no indication of Many in God in this text.

[56] Hamilton, *The Book of Genesis 1–17*, p. 134.

[57] Hamilton, *The Book of Genesis 1–17*, p. 134.

[58] Lombard, *The Sentences Book 1*, 1.101.5 (citing St Hilary, *Trinity*, Book 4).

[59] Michael Horton, *We Believe: Recovering the Essentials of the Apostles' Creed* (Nashville: Nelson, 1998), p. 52.

[60] Blocher, *In the Beginning*, p. 97.

[61] Barth, *Church Dogmatics*, 3/1, p. 324.

[62] Walter Brueggemann, *Genesis* (Atlanta: John Knox Press, 1982), p. 47.

[63] See Part Two.

[64] Another issue concerns the challenge of attempting to understand the intention of the author in Genesis 2:19b which the ESV puts this way: 'And whatever the man called every living creature, that was its name.' It seems simple enough to understand. But there are phrases here in the Hebrew which stand in obscure relationship to each other: 'whatever the man named (to) it' and 'living creatures' and 'that (was) its name'. The question is this: who or what is Adam naming? While both of these issues are interesting, it turns out that neither of these is determinative in our search for an understanding to the questions I have posed. I affirm Cassuto's reading (and that of the NASB), 'and whatever name the man would give to each one of the living creatures that was its name.' See Cassuto, *A Commentary on the Book of Genesis*, pp. 126, 130–31. This serves the narrative well, but again the resolution, while worth noting, does not affect our understanding of the weight of the Marriage Text in the context of the two creation accounts.

[65] Kidner, *Genesis: An Introduction and Commentary*, p. 65.

[66] Cassuto, *A Commentary on the Book of Genesis*, p. 134.

[67] The Hebrew is הַצֵּלָע. Ronald Youngblood observed that this Hebrew word for rib also means 'life' in the closely related Sumerian language. *The Book of Genesis: An Introductory Commentary* (Eugene, OR: Wipf & Stock, 2nd edn, 1991), p. 40.

[68] Hamilton, *The Book of Genesis 1–17*, p. 179.

[69] All emphasis in biblical quotations throughout this work is mine.

[70] In the Hebrew Bible, this is Gen. 32:33.

[71] Luther, *Lectures on Genesis*, 1:139. Chrysostom also considered these words as the speech of Adam (Josiah B. Trenham, *Marriage and Virginity According to St. John Chrysostom* [Platina, CA: St Herman of Alaska Monastery, 1st edn, 2013], pp. 108–9).

[72] In Hebrew narrative, accents, vowel pointing, and the single letter *waw* used as a prefix, can establish a narrative flow (conjunction) with what went before. This verse and this particle stands disjunctively with what came before. The words used also seem to argue against this being the continued speech of Adam, as 'father' and 'mother' have no context for Adam, neither as terms nor in their meaning. However, it is still within possibility that he is the author.

[73] Rather than say 'Three-in-One' or 'Trinity' (true and correct terms for the mystery which is only revealed as biblical revelation advances), I chose a less precise term which can be sustained in this text. And though less precise, it is, perhaps, more foundational.

[74] Nothing about this account of marriage undermines singleness. I will compare marriage to a drama (in ch. 5, developed in the following chapters). As a drama, everyone need not marry for God to image himself in human marriage. Indeed, the whole cast of a dramatic presentation need not, even cannot, have the prominent role, yet the meaning of the drama is evoked as the whole cast performs their part.

[75] Augustine, *Trinity*, 12.8–9.

[76] The *Gospel of Thomas* is part of the Gnostic Nag Hammadi Library, discovered in Nag Hammadi, Egypt, in 1945. It is a non-canonical, late-date, collection of sayings of Jesus, self-attributed to Thomas by the text.

[77] Elaine Pagels, 'Exegesis of Genesis 1 in the Gospels of Thomas and John', *JBL* 118/3 (1999): pp. 482–3.

[78] John Chrysostom, *Saint Chrysostom: Homilies on Galatians, Ephesians, Philippians, Colossians, Thessalonians, Timothy, Titus, and Philemon*, 13, NPNF, 1 (ed. Robert C. Hill; Washington, DC: Catholic University of America Press, 1986), p. 318.

[79] As cited by Evdokimov (and many others) with no specific reference in the opus of Cyril (p. 117). I searched for this quote which 'everyone' cites, but could not locate it.

[80] Calvin, *Commentaries on the First Book of Moses Called Genesis*, p. 97.

[81] I will return to this later in this work.

[82] Kevin J. Vanhoozer, *First Theology: God, Scripture & Hermeneutics* (Downers Grove, IL: InterVarsity Press, 2002), p. 61.

2. Genesis 2:18–25: Anticipating God's Covenant-Faithfulness

[1] Hos. 2:14.

[2] Raymond C. Ortlund Jr, *God's Unfaithful Wife: A Biblical Theology of Spiritual Adultery*, NSBT 2 (Downers Grove, IL: InterVarsity Press, 2003), p. 55.

[3] The Greek is πλανάω which means to lead astray or to cause to wander. The Hebrew is פתה (*patah*). The identification of the Hebrew stem is critical here. The qal stem for *patah* means to deceive or be simple and deceivable. But the piel stem, the so-called intensive, which is found in Hos. 2:14 (2:16 in the Hebrew text), means to allure or even seduce. The only other use of *patah* in Hosea is in the qal stem, found in Hos. 7:11, 'Ephraim is a dove, *acting naively*, without heart' (author's translation). Exod. 22:15 is also the piel stem and means 'seduce'. However, Jer. 20:7 is also found in the piel stem and clearly means 'deceive' in context. Could that be the case here? Unlikely. The translation 'allure' is confirmed by the context and the parallel verb in the next phrase, 'speak tenderly', which fits neither with 'deceive' nor 'act naively', but only with 'allure'.

[4] Henri Blocher, *In the Beginning: The Opening Chapters of Genesis* (Downers Grove, IL: InterVarsity Press, 1984), p. 136.

[5] I am writing this from a (modified) covenantal position. Those reading this book with a scholarly bent will know that some scholars dispute whether or not God made an actual covenant with Adam, for in Genesis 1–3 we do not find explicit covenantal language. I am in basic agreement with Gentry and Wellum who defend this Adamic covenant in *Kingdom through Covenant* (Wheaton, IL: Crossway, 2012). Peter Gentry shows the exegetical relationship between the (accepted) covenant with Noah and the (disputed) covenant with Adam in ch. 6. Stephen Wellum makes the same argument theologically in ch. 16 (pp. 612–27).

[6] St. John Chrysostom *Homilies on Genesis 1–17*. Fathers of the Church 74 (ed. Robert C. Hill; Washington, DC: Catholic University of America Press, 1986) p. 203.

7   Augustine, 'The Literal Meaning of Genesis', 11.1.3. Here, like Chrysostom, he cites Gen. 2:25, 'naked but not ashamed', as an anticipation of the Fall. But for Augustine, the focus is more intensely on the sexual failures which would follow and 'would whip up the disorderly behavior of disobedient members in the bodies of disobedient human beings'.

8   I dealt with this more fully in the previous chapter where I cited both Blocher and Barth in this regard.

9   Thomas Aquinas, *Summa Theologica*, 1a.92.1, reply to objection 3, http://www.newadvent.org/summa/ (ed. Kevin Knight [2008]; accessed 24 Oct. 2014).

10 Martin Luther, *Lectures on Genesis: Chapters 1–5*, Martin Luther's Works, 1, (ed. Jaroslav Pelikan; Saint Louis: Concordia, 1958), 1:115.

11 The Hebrew here is כְּנֶגְדּוֹ. Augustine's translation, 'before him', emphasizes the relational aspect, face to face, which compares to the ESV translation, 'fit for him'.

12 Luther, *Lectures on Genesis*, 1:117.

13 A chiasm is a particular literary structure in which the author works into an idea step by step, strikes the key point in the middle, and then works out again, paralleling each of the initial points as he works back out. The displayed text above shows this kind of structure. Scenes 1–3 work into his point. Scene 4 is the key. Scenes 5–7 work his way out, paralleling the first three scenes. Wenham uses the term 'palistrophic' rather than 'chiastic'.

14 Gordon John Wenham, *Genesis 1–15*, WBC 1 (Waco, TX: Word, 1987), pp. 50–51. So also John H. Sailhamer, *The Pentateuch as Narrative: A Biblical-Theological Commentary* (Grand Rapids: Zondervan, 1995), p. 97.

15 Dietrich Bonhoeffer, *Creation and Fall: Two Biblical Studies* (ed. John W. de Gruchy, trans. John C. Fletcher; New York: Simon & Schuster, 1997), p. 63.

16 Bonhoeffer, *Creation and Fall*, p. 64.

17 Derek Kidner, *Genesis: An Introduction and Commentary* (London: Tyndale Press, 1968), p. 59.

18 Kidner, *Genesis: An Introduction and Commentary*, p. 66.

19 Sailhamer, *The Pentateuch as Narrative*, p. 97.

20 Sailhamer, *The Pentateuch as Narrative*, p. 97.

21 Sailhamer, *The Pentateuch as Narrative*, p. 97.

22 John H. Sailhamer, 'A Database Approach to the Analysis of Hebrew Narrative', *MAARAV* 5/6 (1990): p. 328.

23 *elleh toledot* ('these are [the] generations'): 2:4; 5:1 ('this is [the] book of [the] generations'): 6:9; 10:1; 11:10; 11:27; 25:12, 19; 36:1; [36:9;] 37:2.

24 Jason DeRouchie, 'The Blessing-Commission, the Promised Offspring, and the Toledot Structure of Genesis', *JETS* 56/2 (2013): p. 219.

25 DeRouchie, 'Toledot Structure of Genesis', p. 226.

26 *waw*, pronounced as 'vav'.

27 I am ignoring here, as outside the scope of this project, DeRouchie's other observation of narrative-genealogy and the structural distinction between segmented and linear genealogies – segmented genealogies are always a minor division, supporting a major section, and only found following a *toledot* introduced by a *waw*.

28 C. John Collins, *Genesis 1–4: A Linguistic, Literary, and Theological Commentary* (Phillipsburg, NJ: Presbyterian & Reformed, 2005), p. 137. To the list of unifying textual issues, Collins includes the location in Eden, the human characters, two special trees, and the command of 2:17 (p. 150).

29 עֲרוּמִּים , *aroom*, as it appears in the text is masculine and plural, modifying both Adam and Eve.

30 Wenham, *Genesis 1–15*, p. 72.

31 Victor P. Hamilton, *The Book of Genesis 1–17*, NICOT (Grand Rapids: Eerdmans, 1990), p. 181. Hamilton cites all other uses to be 'some form of humiliation'. As such nakedness is a description of the poor, a sign of shame, or a reference to a birth. I note that it is also quite specifically used as a sign of God's judgment, particularly in Isaiah and Ezekiel (and implied by the word 'shame' in Jeremiah).

32 G.K. Beale, *The Book of Revelation*, NIGTC (Grand Rapids: Eerdmans, 1999), p. 7. Similar citations of 'serve and guard' in the books of Moses in the Old Testament include: Num. 3:7–8; 8:25–26; 18:5–6; 1 Chr. 23:32; Ezek. 44:14.

33 We find a hint of this at the end of the Bible, at the end of Revelation. As Genesis 1–3 is the first Creation & Crisis (heavens and earth created, followed by the crisis of the Fall), so Revelation 19–22 is the third Creation & Crisis (the judgment of all people followed by the new heavens and the new earth) – the second Creation & Crisis being constituted by the incarnation (creation) and death (crisis) and resurrection (creation) of Christ. So in Rev. 21:27 we read of the new creation that 'nothing *unclean* will ever enter it, nor anyone who does what is detestable or false, but only those who are written in the Lamb's book of life.' This bookending comment calls the readers' attention to the unclean creature which did enter the first Garden. This will not happen again!

[34] She herself claimed this, and Paul affirmed it to Timothy in 1 Tim. 2:13–15. These verses describe the creation, fall, and redemption from the perspectives of both Adam and Eve as a teaching to us. For further explanation of this point – minor to this discussion – see Richard A. Shenk, *The Virgin Birth of Christ: The Rich Meaning of a Biblical Truth* (Milton Keynes: Paternoster, 2016), pp. 109–19.

[35] Here is Milton's argument in *Paradise Lost*. Adam, knowing the penalty, and believing God, saw that Eve had eaten the fruit. She would now die, leaving Adam again alone. Having discovered the great gift that Eve was to him, and unwilling again to be 'alone', he exchanged God for what God made: Eve. He ate the fruit to join her against God. Eve was deceived. Adam rebelled.

[36] The usual and (somewhat) comforting understanding of this text (Gen. 3:8) is God walking in the Garden in the cool of the day as his usual practice. This position is offered by Victor Hamilton (*The Book of Genesis 1–17*, p, 192). However, another understanding of the text is that this is the (first) day of the Lord on which the wind of judgment blows, thus Adam and Eve hid from him in their nakedness. The verb 'walk' in the Hebrew *hithpael* stem can mean to 'walk back and forth', or 'to pace'. And the breeze is called the 'wind of the day' which is like Isa. 27:8, 'he [God] removed them with his fierce breath in the day of the east wind'. Thus, this text in Genesis may read, 'they heard the sound of the LORD God, pacing in the Garden, the wind of judgment blowing, and the man and his wife hid themselves among the trees of the garden.' See Mark Futato, http://dailydoseofhebrew.com/read-hebrew/genesis-3/page/2/, Gen. 3:8.

[37] Gordon Wenham is an example of a scholar who takes this text in a complementarian way, that is, 3:16 is not a judgment that puts the woman under the man, and so in subordination, as a punishment for sin. The curse is rather a disruption of marriage so that roles and relationship are undermined. See *Genesis 1–15*, p. 81. But others connect 3:15 to 4:7 so that 'the proper remedy is to return to the creation pattern of man's leadership – loving, not dominating' (Collins, *Genesis 1–4*, p. 160). Also, Hamilton, *The Book of Genesis 1–17*, pp. 201–2.

[38] Claus Westermann is an example of a scholar who acknowledges the position that is taken by some in which the woman is subordinated to the man *because* of sin, so that the egalitarian relationship is to be desired. However, he cautions against knowing so much: 'one cannot reconstruct a state which preceded the present state'. Still, he does conclude, 'Despite this, the domination of the husband and the consequent subordination of

the wife is seen as something which is not normal (hence as punishment).'
See *Genesis 1–11*, CC (Minneapolis: Fortress Press, 1st edn, 1994), p. 262.

[39] We could also observe the Song of Moses (32:1–43, retrospective of Israel's desert history and anticipation of their exile) and the epilogue (32:44–52, anticipation of the death of Moses) as closing the prior section or, perhaps better, a double ending on the whole of the Pentateuch.

[40] I am indebted for this observation to my friend and teaching assistant, Brian Verrett, who is an excellent exegete and a man passionate for God.

[41] It is worth noting here that Tertullian observed the dereliction of marriage in Lamech, strategically positioned. He writes, 'Plurality of marriage began with a man accursed. Lamech was the first who, in espousing two women, made three in one flesh.' Tertullian, 'An Exhortation to Charity', in *Treatises on Marriage and Remarriage: To His Wife, An Exhortation to Chastity, Monogamy*, ACW (Philadelphia: Westminster, 1956), ch. 5 (p. 51).

3. Seeking God's Trinitarian Covenant-Faithfulness in the Old Testament

[1] Raymond C. Ortlund Jr, *Marriage and the Mystery of the Gospel* (Wheaton, IL: Crossway, 2016), p. 111.

[2] Paul Evdokimov, *The Sacrament of Love: The Nuptial Mystery in the Light of the Orthodox Tradition* (trans. Anthony P. Gythiel and Victoria Steadman; Crestwood, NY: St Vladimir's Seminary, 1995), p. 116. It is worth adding here that Evdokimov cites Homily 20, 'On Ephesians 5:22–33', yet having read through this text in two translations, I was not able to discover this quote or one similar. However, whether or not Chrysostom said it, these words are well applied to the text of Gen. 5.

[3] Ibid. p. 118.

[4] One early church Father, Methodius (260–312), in his writing on marriage in 'the Banquet', observed immediate corruption in marriage followed by progress: after the Fall there was polygamy with close family members, then only polygamy, then an eradication of polygamy and adultery, then monogamy became normative with 'continence', and then after Christ came an introduction of virginity. See Josiah B. Trenham, *Marriage and Virginity According to St. John Chrysostom* (Platina, CA: St Herman of Alaska Monastery, 1st edn, 2013), pp. 62–3.

[5] Christopher J.H. Wright, *Deuteronomy* (Grand Rapids: Baker, 1994), p. 86. He notices the tight parallel between these, not on the point of

adultery v. idolatry, but on the failure of desire: 'To break the tenth command is to break the first . . . When society has so profoundly and deliberately abandoned the first and tenth commandments, the moral vacuum that results from the loss of all those commandments in between follows.' Both parallels are seemingly intended by Moses.

6   Other examples of this same use are in Deut. 4:4; 11:22; 13:4,7; 30:20. Interestingly, Moses uses this same word in regard to our sin 'clinging' to us (Deut. 28:60).

7   A somewhat long note is required here for those who have been influenced by (or heard) the idea that monotheism (religious monogamy) was a late historical development in Israel, rather than the original standard, arising from polytheism (religious polygamy). William Dever is an outstanding advocate and exemplar proponent: 'The development of monotheism came very late in the monarchy, if not later still after ancient Israel's history was over. Yahwistic monotheism was the ideal of most of the orthodox, nationalist parties who wrote and edited the Hebrew Bible, but for the majority it had not been the reality throughout most of ancient Israel's history.' See *Did God Have A Wife? Archaeology and Folk Religion in Ancient Israel* (Grand Rapids: Eerdmans, 2005), p. 252. That is, Dever asserts that the monotheism of the Tanakh was a late revision, obscuring the reality of formalized poly-theism, though he acknowledges the late editors preserved, against their own preferences, the practical and repeated polytheism (idolatry/adul-tery) of the people and the leaders. Indeed it is known and agreed that Israel worshipped other gods, including Asherah. The issue is whether or not Israel's 'official cult' (the Law and the Prophets) originally taught that God had a consort and wife, Asherah. If so, such would undermine the idea of 'idolatry' as 'adultery' in the early text and make them to be a novel addition to the history of Israel. This makes a biblical theology of marriage impossible to ground in the Marriage Text and introduces discontinuity in any attempt to trace it through the Tanakh. While this is not the place to debate this position, it is the place for an observa-tion and a position. I affirm that the biblical text is edited in some degree and in some places – who would argue that Moses wrote the last chapter of the Torah or that the book of Jeremiah was not strangely (to us) edited by him or Baruch or by another? Further, the biblical text we have is the (marvellous) product of textual criticism in which each purported and fragmentary biblical text is weighed and compared by scholars, resulting in a robust OT Hebrew text. Yet, there is no critical evidence for another text which antedates the current manuscripts and

diverges from them in any significant way, let alone in so fundamental a way. Dever's proposal is not only an argument without a text, but it does appear to be a pretext, arguing from the commonly acknowledged (idol-atrous/adulterous) actions of Israel to an imagined and undiscovered text. The common understanding of sinful divergence is sufficient and reasonable cause (given human nature and our own experience) to successfully oppose the posited and imagined text which supports such behaviour. Dever has no foundation beyond the agreed behaviour of Israel. But notice also that such a proposal (an imagined text) cannot be disproved any more than a pink elephant. That is, because I can conceive of pink elephants, and though they diverge from all evidence and positive evidence of known species of elephants, such evidence and experience cannot, in themselves, disprove a pink elephant. It might be out there, undiscovered in the dark jungles. We can be grateful to Dever for his thorough investigation of the history of Israel's worship of Asherah and even for exposing their willingness to position Asherah as the wife of YHWH (just as she was also positioned previously as the wife of Baal). It is also quite possible that Asherah was the basis of a women's cult in Israel. No one disputes that such a women's cult to the Queen of Heaven is exposed in Jer. 44 (as written or edited; it is so preserved). Indeed this is quite late in Israel's history. Yet, this is not evidence for an earlier (and original?) text and official cult which supported 'idolatry' and spiritual polygamy.

8   These include: Jephthah (son of a prostitute, Judg. 11–12), Samson (failed marriage and then Delilah, Judg. 13–16), Micah (if he was the illegitimate son of Samson, Judg. 17–18), the Levite and his concubine (Judg. 19), and the rather strange affair of getting sons for Benjamin (Judg. 20–21).

9   Before you, dear reader, object to my introduction of 'love' (in the sense of passion and cherishing) in biblical marriages without prior warrant, I tell you here that I read warrant backwards from the Writings. Keep reading.

10 While not essential to the point here, it is worth noting that some would not include Samson in the (so-called) 'Hall of the Faithful'. In a private email, one of my students, Mark Dickson, has argued with some persuasiveness that Samson was not among the faithful who gained 'the things hoped for' (Heb. 11:1). The multitude of Israel who crossed the Red Sea by faith (Heb. 11:29) did not gain 'the things hoped for' (Heb. 3:16–19). Yet on balance, grouping Samson with David, and others in Heb. 11:32, and affirming the group as faithful, seems to

affirm Samson as also among the faithful. These men and women, despite their sin, were attested to be grounded in faith, the conviction of things hoped for but not yet seen.

[11] As I am using the Hebrew canonical structure here, I must note that Chronicles is from the Writings, not the Prophets, as are Samuel and Kings.

[12] Raymond C. Ortlund Jr, *Marriage and the Mystery of the Gospel* (Wheaton, IL: Crossway, 2016), p. 74.

[13] The word 'loose woman' in the ESV is from the same Hebrew root as I discussed earlier in this chapter, *znh*, meaning 'whoring' or 'unfaithfulness'.

[14] Raymond C. Ortlund Jr, *God's Unfaithful Wife: A Biblical Theology of Spiritual Adultery*, NSBT 2 (InterVarsity Press: Downers Grove, IL, 2003), p. 81.

[15] The actual historical-geographical reference to which the name Jezreel refers is not clear to contemporary readers, but that the name called the original readers' attention to God's discipline is clear from the text.

[16] In the first, the command is to 'take' and in the second to 'love'. An intensification. In the latter 'another man' is explicit but in the former the 'other man' is referenced by implication, 'whoredom'. In both, Hosea is the subject and actor, Gomer is the object, and God is the director of the drama.

[17] Some question whether or not this is the same woman, Gomer (e.g. Douglas Stuart, *Hosea – Jonah*, WBC 31 [Waco, TX: Word, 1987], p. 66). Yes, from this text alone, it is not clear. However, 2:14, as will be shown, is about God reclaiming Israel from her lovers and this human drama is played out in parallel. Gomer is most likely.

[18] Quotation taken from *Song of Songs* by Dennis F. Kinlaw. Copyright © 1991 by Dennis F. Kinlaw. Used by permission of Zondervan. www.zondervan.com (EBC 5 [Grand Rapids: Zondervan, 1991], p. 1207).

[19] Tremper Longman III, *Song of Songs*, NICOT (Grand Rapids: Eerdmans, 2001), p. 70.

[20] I am ignoring, for reasons I will not defend here, the oft-suggested reading of two lovers, a young shepherd and King Solomon.

[21] This translation is mine, rather than from ESV. It is quite literal, and 'woman of Solomon' is a not-unlikely translation of the Hebrew for 'Shulamite' – 'Solomon's woman'.

[22] References to unfaithful (*ma'al*) include: 1 Chr. 2:7; 5:25; 9:1; 10:13; 14:2; 22:5; 23:3,17,24,27; 29:3,25; 2 Chr. 1:1; 4:4; 5:8; 12:2; 16:12; 17:12; 20:19; 25:5; 26:8,16,18; 28:19,22; 29:6,19; 30:7; 31:16–17; 33:19; 34:4; 36:14.

4. Discovering God's Trinitarian Covenant-Faithfulness in the New Testament

[1] Abiola Mbamalu, 'Life in the Fourth Gospel and Its Resonances with Genesis 1–3', *In die Skriflig*, 48/1 (2014): p. 2.

[2] C.K. Barrett, *The Gospel According to St. John: An Introduction with Commentary and Notes on the Greek Text* (Philadelphia, Westminster Press, 2nd edn, 1978), p. 474. Also noted by Maarten J.J. Menken in 'Genesis in John's Gospel and 1 John', in *Genesis in the New Testament*, LNTS 466 (ed. Maarten J.J. Menken and Steve Moyise; London, T&T Clark, 2012), p. 91.

[3] N.T. Wright, *The Resurrection of the Son of God*, Christian Origins and the Question of God 3 (Minneapolis: Fortress Press, 2003), p. 440.

[4] Mbamalu, 'Life in the Fourth Gospel and Its Resonances with Genesis 1–3', pp. 3–5. This is especially apparent in John 3 when Jesus speaks of new birth with Nicodemus and follows this with a comparison of death and life with darkness and light; in John 4 when Jesus speaks of 'living water' with the Samaritan woman; in John 5 when Jesus declares that the religious leaders refuse to come to him to have life though Moses wrote of him; in John 6 where Jesus declares that he is the bread of life; in John 7 where Jesus testifies to rivers of living water from the Spirit; and the raising of Lazarus in which Jesus identifies himself as 'life'. These are merely a few examples.

[5] Menken, 'Genesis in John's Gospel and 1 John', p. 90.

[6] Rosa Hunt, 'Reading Genesis with the Church Fathers: Metaphors of Creation in John Chrysostom's Homilies on Genesis', *JEBS* 12/2 (2012): p. 26. Here she cites Chrysostom in *Homilies on Genesis*, 3.7.

[7] More about this can be found in Richard A. Shenk, *The Virgin Birth of Christ: The Rich Meaning of a Biblical Truth* (Milton Keynes: Paternoster, 2016).

[8] In the first Genesis creation account, 'Let there be' is followed by one or both of the twin affirmations: 'God made' (active) or 'the earth brought forth' (passive) and/or 'it was so'. The distinctions and differences of these affirmations for each day of the Genesis account are not the issue for this study in the light of the singularity of the incarnational creation declared in John 1:14.

[9] This observation is made by many, and the image of the Shekinah glory is anticipated by the Evangelist's unique verb selection: σκηνόω (erect a tent as dwelling/tabernacle). Leon Morris specifically notes many literary parallels between John 1:14–18 and Exodus 33:7–23 in which

the author establishes Jesus as the tabernacle/temple (Leon Morris, *The Gospel According to John*, NICNT [Grand Rapids: Eerdmans, rev. edn, 1995], p. 92).

[10] Many are the proposals for the relationship of Gen. 1 and 2. The differences and similarities are abundant, but they were selected by the author, and juxtaposed here for us. I am not examining the relationship here – however worthwhile that may be. Let me merely state what is true and necessary for this examination: Gen. 2 has an emphasis on preparing this place for Adam.

[11] D.A. Carson, *The Gospel According to John*, PNTC (Grand Rapids, MI: Eerdmans, 1990), pp. 146–7.

[12] Pierson Parker, 'Bethany beyond Jordan', *JBL* 74/4 (1955): pp. 257–61. In this paper he argues that the Bethany of John 1 is probably the Bethany of Mark 11, both of which are associated with fig trees, connecting this to the fig tree of John 1:48. In Hebrew, Bethany is: בית עניא (or in English usage, *beth-any*, 'house of figs').

[13] It is also worth noting that Nathanael is about to become a 'fitting helper' to Jesus and he is discovered under a *fig tree*. Whatever the idiomatic or literal intent of this phrase, this is the second occurrence of 'fig' in this chapter and the only specific fruit tree either in this chapter or in Gen. 1 – 3.

[14] Karl Barth, *Church Dogmatics* (Peabody, MA: Hendrickson, 2nd edn, 2010), 3/1, p. 321.

[15] The words here for the vegetation seem to be chosen by Moses to anticipate the kinds of plants to which God refers after sin and judgment in Gen. 3:18.

[16] Leon Morris, *The Apostolic Preaching of the Cross* (London: Tyndale Press, 3rd edn, 1965), pp. 130–41. Martin Hengel sees Isa. 53 and Exod.12 behind the identification ('The Old Testament in the Fourth Gospel', in *The Gospels and the Scriptures of Israel*, JSNTSup 104; SSEJC 3 [ed. Craig A. Evans and W. Richard Stegner; Sheffield: Sheffield Academic Press, 1994], p. 390).

[17] Some have strongly opposed this. Leon Morris for example (Morris, *The Apostolic Preaching of the Cross*, pp. 130–41). However, a biblical-theological perspective, rather than a purely exegetical approach, makes this quite likely as an antecedent.

[18] Andreas J. Köstenberger, *John*, BECNT (Grand Rapids: Baker Academic, 2004), pp. 89–90. On Köstenberger and others, there are seven signs in John which anticipate the declaration of his narrative intent in John 20:30–31 ('these [signs] are written so that you may believe that

Jesus is the Christ'). They are: water to wine (2:1–11), temple clearing (2:13–22), royal official's son (4:36–54); healing of lame man (5:1–15); feeding of multitude (6:1–15); healing of blind man (9:1–41); and the raising of Lazarus (11:1–44).

[19] N.T. Wright has also perceived a connection between John 2:1 and Gen. 1 in the gospel words, 'on the third day', in which these words sound a powerful echo (Wright, *The Resurrection of the Son of God*, p. 440).

[20] Carson, *The Gospel According to John*, p. 168. Also Köstenberger (*John*, p. 91).

[21] Carson, *The Gospel According to John*, p. 168.

[22] What kind of days did God intend in creation: 24-hour, epical, or analogical? This is hardly the place to investigate this well-worn, but unresolved, issue. It might be the place to note that if Gen. 2:18–25 is the conclusion of both creation accounts then perhaps the nature of the conclusion might itself assist in determining an answer. Still, it need only be said here that John's references are analogical to creation days. This is sufficient to make the connection with the first Genesis account.

[23] Carson, *The Gospel According to John*, pp. 172–3. Also noted by N.T. Wright in *John for Everyone, Part 1: Chapters 1–10* (Louisville, KY: Westminster John Knox Press, 2004), p. 22.

[24] This view is often referred to as the literary framework view. Without affirming this model as the chief intent of the author of the first creation account, I offer it rather as an observation of clear structure which has some intended meaning in the account. Distinct interpretive grids such as John Walton's 'function and functionaries' still observe a similar structure, if distinct in meaning.

[25] The position described above is that of Leon Morris (Morris, *The Gospel According to John*, pp. 158–9). His position is typical of many others. Calvin explicitly expresses the confusion of Jesus' refusal, followed by action, asserting that he was not willing to act at his mother's suggestion (but rather God's) and that his apparent slight in addressing her as woman rather than mother was a 'necessary warning' to us against elevating Mary above her God-given honour to excessive honour (John Calvin, *Commentary on the Gospel According to John, Chapters 1–11* [trans. William Pringle; Grand Rapids: Eerdmans, 1949], 1:83–5). So also Calvin, with Morris and others, agrees that Jesus speaks not of his death, but rather of his ministry.

[26] Wright, *John for Everyone, Part 1*, p. 22.

[27] The Greek here is τί ἐμοὶ καὶ σοί, γύναι. In Luke 8:28 and Mark 5:8 it is τί ἐμοὶ καὶ σοί. In Luke 4:24 it is ἔα, τί ἡμῖν καὶ σοί. All similar grammatically.

[28] The Greek construction here is not identical to John 2, but quite reminiscent: τί πρὸς σέ; σύ μοι ἀκολούθει (here I ignore a textual variant in 21:23, similar in wording, as redundant to this point).

[29] Menken, 'Genesis in John's Gospel and 1 John', p. 90. This pattern is echoed in Pharaoh's trust of Joseph in Gen. 41:55 when the lack is satisfied.

[30] Generally attributed to Anton Chekhov, the principle called 'Chekhov's Gun'.

[31] Notice that this was anticipated in John 1:14–18.

[32] I am grateful to my former graduate student Marcus Leman. He offered this observation when he heard these ideas presented in my paper at the 2015 Evangelical Theological Society in Atlanta. Marcus is currently a PhD candidate at Southern Baptist Theological Seminary and by the time this work is published I trust he will be Marcus Leman, PhD.

[33] Allan Chapple argues that John reports the first of two distinct such events which took place in Jesus' ministry. See Allan Chapple, 'Jesus' Intervention in the Temple: Once or Twice?', *JETS* 58/3 (2015): pp. 545–69. Chapple notes that in the modern era, this view has lost much support. So also, Andreas Köstenberger shows that a majority of scholars believe this to be John's narrative of a unique event from late in Jesus' ministry, but placed here for theological-thematic reasons, though Köstenberger favours a repeated event, a 'doublet', in which John records the first event and the synoptics the second (*John*, p. 111).

[34] Adam did not 'guard' the temple against the serpent – though he was commanded to do so. See the discussion of Gen. 2:15, 'cultivate and keep', in Part One.

[35] In fact, the temple was even yet under construction. The forty-six years represent the investment to date, as Carson indicates (Carson, *The Gospel According to John*, p. 20). It will not be finished until AD 63, just seven years before it is destroyed.

[36] Not essential to this proposal, but intriguing, is the proposal of Paul Kim who sees God's provision of a Covenant of Grace, prior to Gen. 3:15, in Gen. 1:28. He argues that God's grace is not a response to sin, but his first and grounding way of acting. He notes that Gregg Beale begins to perceive this when he affirms that Gen. 1:28 has not only a commandment, but a promise, a 'promise that God will provide the ability to humanity to carry it out', even tying 1:28 directly to Matt. 28:19–20, the Great Commission. But Kim goes further, depending on the work of Yong Ki Park. He sees in Gen. 1:28 a threefold covenant. If so, then 1:28 is not a 'cultural mandate', but a kingdom covenant of God which

is fulfilled, not in Adam, but in Christ and his work – revealing God's glory. If so, then 'then they believed scriptures' is not limited to Gen. 3:15 alone, as its singular antecedent, but also 1:28. (Paul Kim, 'Critical Reinterpretation of Genesis 1:28: A Neglected Key to Unlock the Structural Coherence of the Whole Bible' [unpublished paper given at the Evangelical Theological Society, 2015].)

[37] Matthew Godshall, 'Marriage and New Creation: The Re-Contextualization of Genesis 2:24 in Ephesians 5:31' (Evangelical Theological Society, Atlanta, GA, 2015).

[38] This is sometimes translated 'therefore', in keeping with the Hebrew in Gen. 2:24, but in the Greek Septuagint available to Paul and in the light of Paul's citation, it could be translated either way.

[39] One example of this position is Frank Thielman, who writes of Paul's use of Gen. 2:24 in Eph. 5:31, 'This probably means that the union of husband and wife in "one flesh" was originally intended to prefigure and to illustrate the union that Christ now has with the church,' and of Eph. 5:21, he paraphrases Paul, 'The mystery I am about to describe is especially mysterious, but I am going to say it anyway: when I refer to the well-known establishment of marriage in the book of Genesis, I am talking about Christ and the church.' (See *Ephesians*, BECNT [Grand Rapids: Baker Academic, 2010], pp. 389–90.) The distinction between my position and Thielman's is one of degree. I understand in Paul's declaration less of a 'mapping' and more an 'intertwining' of human marriage and the Christological telos of marriage. It is a 'glorious and mysterious confusion' of sign and referent. If that is the case, as I understand, then both sign and reference are real and significant to God, even if neither are ultimate. N.T. Wright makes this point in regard to this text: 'Contemplate the many-sided way in which the truth about God himself, and the truth about how we live out our most precious relationships, *intertwine* and create a God-given beauty the world never dreams of.' (N.T. Wright, *Paul for Everyone: The Prison Letters: Ephesians, Philippians, Colossians, and Philemon*, New Testament for Everyone [Louisville, KY: Westminster John Knox Press, 2nd edn, 2004], p. 68. emphasis mine.)

[40] If these terms, and the idea they refer to, are new, a further explanation can be gained by reading Kallistos Ware, *The Orthodox Way* (Crestwood, NY: St Vladimir's Seminary, 1995). See ch. 6, 'God as Prayer', in the 'Union with God' section.

[41] Oliver D. Crisp, *The Word Enfleshed: Exploring the Person and Work of Christ* (Grand Rapids: Baker Academic, 2016), p. 158.

[42] Here I am using G.K. Beale's taxonomy. See Beale, *The Book of Revelation*, NIGTC (Grand Rapids: Eerdmans, 1999), pp. 44–50.

[43] I want to acknowledge a significant divide among Christians here, which I am overlooking as not essential to the goals of this project: in what sense does the church 'replace' Israel, or in what sense does the church join the existing people of God? Yet, without arguing for a perspective, there is a wedding of God to his people. The bride is variously called Israel, the church, and the people of God. The distinction is worth discerning, but not here.

5. Historical Theology: Revealing Marriage as a Sacrament

[1] This chapter (and parts of chapter 7), though significantly edited for this publication, first appeared as 'Is Marriage among the Sacraments? Were Luther and Calvin Wrong?', in *Reformation Faith: Exegesis and Theology in the Protestant Reformations* (ed. Michael Parsons; Eugene, OR: Wipf & Stock, 2014). It is edited for use in this volume and used with permission.

[2] See Louis Berkhof, *Systematic Theology* (Grand Rapids: Eerdmans, 1941), p. 617. Also, Tertullian reveals its etymology as a military oath and insists on a disjuncture between the divine and military use, though even in so doing, he reveals the relationship ('Against Praxeas', in *Latin Christianity: Its Founder, Tertullian; ANF* 3 [ed. Philip Schaff; Grand Rapids: Christian Classics Ethereal Library, 2001], ch. 19).

[3] E.g., 'I see no coherence and consistency; no, not even in the very sacrament of his faith! For what end does baptism serve, according to him?' (*ANF* 3.1.28 http://www.ccel.org [accessed 27 Aug. 2012]). 'Happy is our sacrament of water, in that, by washing away the sins of our early blindness, we are set free and admitted into eternal life!' (*ANF* 3.1 http://www.ccel.org [accessed 27 Aug. 2012]). But it should be remembered that the meaning of *sacramentum* was not limited at that time to a specific set of religious practices, or even of religious practice.

[4] The Vulgate translated the NT Greek μυστήριον (*musterion*) as *sacramentum* eight times: Eph. 1:9; 3:3,9; 5:32; Col. 1:27; 1 Tim. 3:16; Rev. 1:20; 17:7. This was amended more precisely to *mysterium* in the *Nova Volgata* (1971).

[5] See Augustine, 'On the Catechizing of the Uninstructed', in *A Select Library of the Nicene and Post-Nicene Fathers of the Christian Church* (*NPNF*) (ed. and trans. Philip Schaff and Henry Wace; New York: Christian Literature, 1890), 3.26.50 http://www.ccel.org (accessed 27 Aug. 2012); Augustine,

Confessions, NPNF 3.17 http://www.ccel.org (accessed 27 Aug. 2012). Here and elsewhere this is a theme of his writing as he speaks primarily of creation and natural revelation, not 'sacraments', perhaps based on Rom. 1:20. Still, he may be thinking *sacrament*ally.

6   *NPNF*, series 1, vol. 7, 'John's Gospel', 80.3.344, emphasis added.

7   'If we are willing to explain clearly what we mean, it does not seem to make any difference whether we use the word sacrament or not . . . I will use both "ordinances" and "sacraments" interchangeably, and regard them as synonymous in meaning.' Wayne A. Grudem, *Systematic Theology: An Introduction to Biblical Doctrine* (Grand Rapids: Zondervan, 1974), p. 966. Berkhof, *Systematic Theology*, pp. 560, 631, also makes use of 'ordinance' and 'sacrament' as synonyms. As a Lutheran, he leans strongly to the use of 'sacrament'.

8   Grudem, *Systematic Theology*, p. 966.

9   Millard Erickson, *Christian Theology* (Grand Rapids: Baker, 1998), p. 1105. Interestingly, there is no explicit definition of the term 'ordinance' in his text.

10 This definition was referenced on the New Advent website at http://www.newadvent.org/cathen/13295a.htm (accessed 31 Aug. 2011).

11 This definition was referenced on the Vatican website: http://www.vatican.va/archive/ENG0015/__P35.HTM, paragraph 1131 (accessed 27 Aug. 2012).

12 H.J. Schroeder, trans., *The Canons and Decrees of the Council of Trent* (Rockford, IL: TAN, 1978), Session 7, 'Canons on the Sacraments in General', canons 1, 5, 6, 7. Though Trent made explicit both the number of the sacraments and the conferring of grace through the sacraments, this was not a new idea. Peter Lombard (1100–60) had proposed both in *Sentences* (4.1.2; 4.2.1). And the Council of Florence (1439) enumerated seven. Interestingly, while Trent hardened the division with the Lutherans in regard to grace in the sacraments, Trent also reversed the position of the RCC on indulgences. Though indulgences themselves were retained, the council 'absolutely abolished' the 'evil traffic' of indulgences, asserting that they are administered for piety, not gain, so relieving Luther's presenting concern (July 1562, Session 21, 'Decree Concerning Reform', ch. 9, and later in December 1563, Session 25, ch. 21).

13 In regard to the rejection of seven, he writes, 'The first thing for me to do is to deny that there are seven sacraments, and, for the present, to propound three: baptism, penance, and the Lord's Supper. All these

have been taken for us into miserable servitude by the Roman curia and the church has been robbed of all her liberty. If, however, I were to use the language of Scripture, I should say that there was only one sacrament [cf. 1 Tim. 3:16] but three sacramental signs of which I shall speak in detail in the proper place.' See Martin Luther, *Martin Luther: Selections from His Writings* (ed. John Dillenberger; Garden City, NY: Anchor, 1962, p. 256). Later, he rejected penance from the list (John Witte Jr, 'The Reformation of Marriage Law in Martin Luther's Germany: Its Significance Then and Now', *J.L. & Relig.* 4/2 [1968]: p. 312, n. 32). His rejection is based, as he anticipated even in *Captivity*, upon the lack of a *sign* in penance, unlike baptism and the Lord's Supper which have water and the elements, respectively (*Selections*, p. 357). Arguing against the book of James he writes, 'I should say that it was not lawful for an apostle to institute a sacrament by his own authority; that is, to give a divine promise with a sign annexed to it' (*Selections*, p. 351). He also writes, 'It follows that, strictly speaking, there are but two sacraments in the church of God: Baptism and the Lord's Supper, since we find in these alone a sign divinely instituted, and here alone the promise of the forgiveness of sins' (*Selections*, p. 357).

14 *Selections*, p. 326.

15 This understanding is reflected in Berkhof: 'The church is not a means of grace alongside of the Word and the sacraments, because her power in promoting the work of the grace of God consists only in the administration of these. She is not instrumental in communicating grace, except by means of the Word and of the sacraments. Moreover, faith, conversion, and prayer, are first of all fruits of the grace of God, though they may in turn become instrumental in strengthening the spiritual life. They are not objective ordinances, but subjective conditions for the possession and enjoyment of the blessings of the covenant' (*Systematic Theology*, p. 604).

16 Berkhof, *Systematic Theology*, p. 617.

17 *Institutes of the Christian Religion*, 4.19.34.

18 *Institutes of the Christian Religion*, 4.14.1.

19 Calvin writes, 'It is therefore certain that the Lord offers us mercy and the pledge of his grace both in his Sacred Word and in his sacraments. But it is understood only by those who take Word and sacraments with sure faith, just as Christ is offered and held forth by the Father to all unto salvation, yet not all acknowledge and receive him. In one place Augustine, meaning to convey this, said that the efficacy of the Word is brought to light in the sacrament, not because it is spoken, but because it

is believed' (*Institutes of the Christian Religion*, 4.14.7). But sacraments are not only by faith. In keeping with his illustration of a mirror, *sacraments* also confirm our faith (*Institutes of the Christian Religion*, 4.19.16).

[20] *Institutes of the Christian Religion*, 4.14.9.

[21] *Institutes of the Christian Religion*, 4.14.14.

[22] In Calvin's understanding, this in no way diminishes the import of sacraments. He writes, 'We might call them "the pillars of our faith." For as a building stands and rests upon its own foundation but is more surely established by columns placed underneath, so faith rests upon the Word of God as a foundation; but when the sacraments are added, it rests more firmly upon them as upon columns. Or we might call them mirrors in which we may contemplate the riches of God's grace, which he lavishes upon us' (*Institutes of the Christian Religion*, 4.14.6).

[23] *Institutes of the Christian Religion*, 4.19.14–17.

[24] Notice here that in my definition, in contrast to the New Advent website, I have substituted 'God' for 'Christ'. That is not without intention. I do so in order to have access to the Old and New Covenants, the commands of God to his people, not only the church. I do this with warrant: Christ is the Word of God. It does not stand, in the light of John 1, Hebrews 1, and the witness of the whole of the New Testament, to make a sharp distinction between the 'command of God' and the 'command of Christ'. While this might require more in the way of exegetical substantiation, I offer it here, explicitly, as my warrant for this amendment of the historical definition.

[25] *Systematic Theology*, p. 617.

[26] I acknowledge here the minority positions which retain confession (or penance) or add foot-washing. While worthy of exegetical discussion, this is outside the scope and interest of this chapter.

[27] Michael Parsons, *Reformation Marriage: The Husband and Wife Relationship in the Theology of Luther and Calvin* (Eugene, OR: Wipf & Stock, 2011), p. 146.

[28] *Selections*, p. 326.

[29] *Selections*, p. 326.

[30] *Institutes of the Christian Religion*, 4.19.35–36. These listed reasons all come from this section of the *Institutes*. In regard to Eph. 5, his position is explained by the inexact translation from Greek to Latin, but even more so by the application of *sacramentum* to marriage rather than to Christ and the church.

[31] *Institutes of the Christian Religion*, 4.19.34. In regard to Gregory, cited above by Calvin, the specific Gregory to whom he refers is unresolved. Gregory VII (c. 1025–85), to whom this reference is sometimes

attributed, reformed marriage and morals among the priests. Also, he was prior to Lombard, the generally agreed antecedent for both the number of sacraments and conferred grace in the sacraments. However, Gregory X (c. 1210–76) was given such an enumeration by Michael VIII Palaiologos (1223–82, the emperor of the Byzantine Empire) at the Council of Lyons (1274, an attempt to unify the Eastern and Western Church). This makes Gregory X a more likely candidate for Calvin's reference.

[32] This can be seen in Parsons, *Reformation Marriage*, ch. 5. See esp. p. 122 (n. 9) which gives a clear tabular representation of the distinctions between kingdoms.

[33] Witte, 'The Reformation of Marriage Law in Martin Luther's Germany', p. 311.

[34] John Witte Jr, *From Sacrament to Contract: Marriage, Religion, and Law in the Western Tradition* (Louisville, KY: Westminster John Knox Press, 1997), pp. 5–6.

[35] 'I am reluctant to do it because I am afraid if I once get really involved in the subject it will make a lot of work for me and for others. The shameful confusion wrought by the accursed papal law has occasioned so much distress, and the lax authority of both the spiritual and the temporal swords has given rise to so many dreadful abuses and false situations, that I would much prefer neither to look into the matter nor to hear of it. But timidity is no help in an emergency.' Referenced on http://pages.uoregon.edu/dluebke/Reformations441/Luthermarriage.htm. 'Introduction' (accessed 27 Aug. 2012).

[36] John Witte Jr, *From Sacrament to Contract: Marriage, Religion, and Law in the Western Tradition* (Louisville, KY: Westminster John Knox Press, 2nd edn, 2012), p. 111.

[37] Witte, *From Sacrament to Contract*, pp. 39–40.

[38] Stephanie Coontz, *Marriage, a History: How Love Conquered Marriage* (New York: Viking, repr. edn, 2005), pp. 5–6.

[39] For the sake of historical comparison over long periods of time, allow me to loosen the categories: government rather than state, and family and religious community rather than church. So, it can be said that historically, marriage has never been under the authority of the government, but instead only under the family or religious community.

[40] Stephanie Coontz, *Marriage, a History*, p. 81. See also p. 79.

[41] Coontz, *Marriage, a History*, p. 66.

[42] Stephanie Coontz, 'Taking Marriage Private,' *New York Times* Op Ed, 26 Nov. 2007, referenced at http://www.nytimes.com/2007/11/26/opinion/26coontz.html?_r=2 (accessed 1 Sept. 2012).

43 Coontz writes, 'The American colonies officially required marriages to be registered, but until the mid-19th century, state supreme courts routinely ruled that public cohabitation was sufficient evidence of a valid marriage' ('Taking Marriage Private').

44 What of Calvin's and Luther's concern about the historical exegesis of Eph. 5:32? They were correct in saying that the incidental use of the Latin *sacramentum* does not indicate that marriage is a sacrament. However, this particular discussion is not over a biblical term, but rather for the most helpful category and term. I would also set aside their concern that marriage as a sacrament is either too old or too new. Luther objected that it was too old (the Old Covenant) and Calvin that it was too new (since Gregory). These arguments are only a distraction and not in itself an argument.

45 *Selections*, p. 326.

46 Parsons, *Reformation Marriage*, p. 165. Here Parsons is giving Calvin's position, having already established Luther's in quite similar terms. Moreover, their common understanding leans heavily on Augustine's sense of the 'good of marriage': procreation, chastity, and the bond of union (p. 56).

47 It is worth adding here that since I have excluded the concept of sacraments actually 'conferring saving grace', in favour of 'mirroring grace', this also is a reason to understand why asymmetry is permitted. Marriage is about the drama enacted, rather than individual salvation. Sacraments must be seen by all, but do not have to be participated in by all.

48 *Institutes of the Christian Religion*, 4.19.3.

49 I want to say more about this whole-Bible chiasm – or outline of the Bible. I suspect it is a new and not wholly intuitive idea. In a book about marriage, I cannot go into much detail, nor can I 'prove' the chiasm here. Still, perhaps I can suggest reasonable foundations. The proposal of three creations, rather than two, or even one, is founded on identifying what is biblically considered a creation. The key indication of biblical creation is the presence of the Spirit who hovers in order to give birth. In the first creation, we see the Spirit hovering gestatively in Gen. 1:2. Then the second creation is indicated in Luke 1:35 when we see a similar gestative work of the Spirit in the incarnation. This is parallel to the work of the Spirit who descends to create the church in Acts 2:1–4, hovering over each of the 120, creating the church. Finally, the Spirit is seen in the third (new) creation when he cries out the invitation to the wedding feast in Rev. 22:17, 'Come!' There are more markers for creation, but

the Holy Spirit's anticipating presence is primary. For each of the creations there is also a paired crisis. These are marked by the presence of the serpent. The first creation moves to crisis with the serpent's introduction in Gen. 3:1. The second creation, incarnation, moves to the central crisis (the chiastic centre) with the raising of the serpent on the cross – an image given to us by Christ himself in John 3:14. The third creation is preceded, rather than followed, by the crisis, the chiastic reversal of order (see Table 5.2 if this is confusing). This occurs when the serpent is judged and removed in Rev. 20:7–10. The effect is that there is no serpent in the new creation (Rev. 21:7). It is not unimportant that here the serpent's absence is complete absence, indicated by 'no unclean thing'. Even naming is a grace of God no longer afforded. As with creation, there are more identifiers of crisis, but this will have to serve as a beginning for a foundation for this whole-Bible chiasm.

6. Pursuing the Doctrinal Drama Intended by the Spirit for the Church

[1] Shaunti Feldhahn, *The Good News about Marriage: Debunking Discouraging Myths about Marriage and Divorce* (Colorado Springs, CO: Multnomah, 2014).

[2] Feldhahn, *The Good News about Marriage*, pp. 130–32.

[3] Jacques Ellul, *To Will and to Do* (Cleveland, OH: Pilgrim, 1969), p. 16.

[4] If I had time, I would love to expound here Paul's argument from Romans, which parallels this concern of Ellul. While space does not permit, let me hint at Paul's direction. His famous theme in Rom. 1:16–17, citing Habakkuk, declares that 'the righteous shall live by faith'. To understand this (and following the context in Habakkuk) we must recall that Paul began Romans with this goal, 'to bring about the obedience of faith' (1:5) and concluded similarly, 'to bring about the obedience of faith' (16:26). Given this framework, his theme could be written in this way: 'conquered by God's righteousness, we are led to the faithful obedience in Christ'. This is not a call to 'ethics' or 'good works', but a life which is like Christ, with Christ, and for Christ – and so dramatically portrayed in obedience.

[5] Ellul, *To Will and to Do*, p. 224.

[6] Ellul, *To Will and to Do*, p. 265.

7 Communication in a private email, Dec. 2016.

8 James Rogers, 'God's Image, Man's Crimes', *First Things* (2017) https://www.firstthings.com/web-exclusives/2017/03/gods-image-mans-crimes (accessed 31 March 2017).

9 Josiah B. Trenham, *Marriage and Virginity According to St. John Chrysostom* (Platina, CA: St Herman of Alaska Monastery, 1st edn, 2013), p. 106.

10 Trenham, *Marriage and Virginity According to St. John Chrysostom*, p. 63. From Methodius, 'On the Banquet'.

11 Trenham, *Marriage and Virginity According to St. John Chrysostom*, p. 114. Here he speaks for Chrysostom, the early Fathers, and himself when he writes, 'the sexual necessities of fallen nature and the tremendous sexual impulses, appetites, and drives of post-Fall man simply did not exist to trouble Adam and Eve. Sexual intercourse did not exist in the Garden.'

12 In Matt. 22:30, 'For in the resurrection they neither marry nor are given in marriage, but are like the angels in heaven.' It is worth noting that this text tells us much less than we may think at first reading. The comparative, 'like', is problematic since we do not know from Scripture how it is with the angels in heaven.

13 Richard A. Shenk, *The Virgin Birth of Christ: The Rich Meaning of a Biblical Truth* (Milton Keynes: Paternoster, 2016), pp. 31–8. The danger of concupiscence weighed heavily on Augustine, and so it should; he even wondered if the stain of this sin could be passed to children by the sexual intimacy (or lusts!) of the parents.

14 John Calvin, *Calvin: Institutes of the Christian Religion* (ed. John T. McNeill, trans. Ford Lewis Battles; Philadelphia: Westminster Press, 1559 translation edn, 1960), sec. 2.8.18.

15 Calvin also writes that because 'God loves chastity and purity, we ought to guard against all uncleanness' (*Institutes of the Christian Religion*, 2.8.41).

16 Daniel R. Heimbach, *True Sexual Morality: Recovering Biblical Standards for a Culture in Crisis* (Wheaton, IL: Crossway, 2004), p. 135.

17 Here Paul uses the Marriage Text as a foundation to declare the 'couple' to be 'one flesh', married.

18 David Instone-Brewer, *Divorce and Remarriage in the Bible: The Social and Literary Context* (Grand Rapids: Eerdmans, 2002).

19 Deut. 24 also prohibits restoring a wife to her former husband, once divorced.

20 There is value, but no opportunity here, for deep consideration of 1 Pet. 2, where Peter declares that suffering for doing good is commendable before God. The context is slavery – or the work environment. He calls us to suffer, contentedly and toward God, when we suffer undeserved

physical suffering. This is a hard teaching: suffer abuse and trust God. This is a teaching that could conceivably get a pastor dismissed or a book burned. There is also a close connection between this text in 1 Pet. 2 (suffering unfairly at work) and 1 Pet. 3 (submitting fearlessly in marriage). And a connection is not merely proximity. In 1 Pet. 3, Peter calls women to submit to their husbands, refusing to give in to normal human fear. He says nothing here of physical abuse, though by referencing Sarah's fearlessness with Abraham, surely he has in mind her commendable trust in God when Abraham went off to sacrifice her son, Isaac (Gen. 22) and also the two times Abraham gave her away to a local dignitary, subject to his sexual desires (Gen. 12 and 20). God saved her in all three occasions from actual loss, but not from fear. Surely these are in the author's mind in 1 Pet. 3. How could this be taught to God's people in regard to the drama of marriage in our culture? Who would stand for it?

[21] Henri Blocher, *In the Beginning: The Opening Chapters of Genesis* (Downers Grove, IL: InterVarsity Press, 1984), p. 97.

[22] Some might know that there are three families of matter and that the electron does exist in three distinct mass domains with the same quantum numbers, but distinct masses, muon, and tau particles. But here too, the mass is as it is in creation; we cannot change it or predict it.

[23] Of course, some of the affirmations of homosexuality (and so LGBTQ marriage) come from within the confessing Christian church. I could respond here to Matthew Vine, but others have done a better job than I could do. A brief engagement on key biblical texts can be seen in the *New York Times* between Vines and Caleb Kaltenbach (lead pastor of Discovery Church in Simi Valley, CA): Matthew Vines and Caleb Kaltenbach, 'Debating Bible Verses on Homosexuality', *The New York Times* (2015) https://www.nytimes.com/interactive/2015/06/05/us/samesex-scriptures.html (accessed 27 Apr. 2017).

[24] Feldhahn, *The Good News about Marriage*, pp. 130–33.

7. If Marriage Is a Sacrament, What Does the Church Do?

[1] *NPNF*, series 1, vol. 3, 'On the Good of Marriage', sec. 17 (p. 406).

[2] I examined above the more moderate observations of Feldhahn. The Barna Group's most recent data shows that approximately one-third of all adults have been divorced, and while some groups do better, including

committed Christians and active Roman Catholics, the difference is not large. This polling data is from 2008 and was referenced on http://www .barna.org/family-kids-articles/42-new-marriage-and-divorce-statistics-released. Also, marriage rates and divorce rates have both declined over the last ten years (2000–10), with marriage declining faster; http://www.cdc .gov/nchs/nvss/marriage_divorce_tables.htm (accessed 27 Aug. 2012).

3   Coontz, 'Taking Marriage Private'.

4   Jennifer Roback Morse, 'Privatizing Marriage Is Impossible', The Witherspoon Institute: Public Discourse on Ethics, Law and Common Good, 2, 3, 4 April 2012, http://www.thepublicdiscourse .com/2012/04/5069 (accessed 27 Aug. 2012). She writes, 'As a libertarian myself, I have been quite disappointed that the "default" libertarian position on marriage has become little more than a sound-bite: "Let's get the state out of the marriage business." With all due respect, this position is unsound.'

5   Coontz also writes in 'Taking Marriage Private', 'Possession of a marriage license is no longer the chief determinant of which obligations a couple must keep, either to their children or to each other. But it still determines which obligations a couple can keep – who gets hospital visitation rights, family leave, health care and survivor's benefits. This may serve the purpose of some moralists. But it doesn't serve the public interest of helping individuals meet their care-giving commitments.' *New York Times*, 26 Nov 2007, https://www.nytimes.com/2007/11/26/opinion/ 26coontz.html (accessed 27 Aug. 2012).

6   As I write this, Minnesota is embattled over a marriage Amendment which seeks to define marriage in our State Constitution as uniquely between one man and one woman.

Conclusion: Marriage in Eschatology

1   Stanley N. Gundry and others, *Two Views on Homosexuality, the Bible, and the Church* (ed. Preston Sprinkle; Grand Rapids: Zondervan, 2016), p. 208.

2   As my physics text used to say on challenging problem: I leave this as an investigation for the student.

3   Of course, the possibility exists that these words continue the discourse of Adam. In that case, he gives the explanation of his own 'vows' in the previous declaration. This is problematic, however, for even if he spoke as

a prophet, then Adam would have been using terms for which he has no experience (with the word or concept): father and mother.

4 It is worth observing that in Hebrew the word for 'Woman' (אִשָּׁה, Ish-shah), while sounding like that for 'Man' (אִישׁ, Ish), probably comes from a different root. It is commonly observed that these two words are related more by sound than by etymology.

5 Canada is hardly an exception. Indeed, the United States is in the minority. Not only in Canada, but in most of Latin American and Europe, the state marriage is a separate function from the church wedding. However, the country known for its (so-named) separation of church and state blurs (at least in this regard) the distinction here between church and state. The observation calls for a brief pause to ask whether by the historical affirmation of a 'separation of church and state' we meant more than we now intend? This historic practice (and perhaps others) might make this a question worth investigating more thoroughly.

Scripture Index

Index of Names